DIVE YORKSHIRE

A **DIVER** GUIDE

by
ARTHUR GODFREY
and
PETER LASSEY

W0007615

UNDERWATER WORLD PUBLICATIONS LTD

© Copyright 1988
by Underwater World Publications Ltd
40 Grays Inn Road
London WC1X 8LR

(081) 943 4288

Cover photograph by Lawson Wood

Book designed and produced
by Alan Morgan

Maps by Suzanne Blyskal

Typeset in Helvetica by Graphic Studios (Southern) Ltd,
39 Beak Street, London W1
and printed by The Camelot Press,
Shirley Road, Southampton SO9 1WF

ISBN: 0 946020 17 5

In the same series:

The Diver Guide to South Cornwall by Richard Larn

The Diver Guide to Dorset by John & Vicki Hinchcliffe

The Diver Guide to West Scotland by Gordon Ridley

The Diver Guide to North-West Scotland by Gordon Ridley

The Diver Guide to Sussex by Kendall McDonald

The Diver Guide to South Devon by Kendall McDonald and Derek Cockbill

The Diver Guide to Wight and Hampshire by Martin Pritchard and Kendall McDonald

The Diver Guide to the North East by Dave Shaw and Barry Winfield

Contents

Maps showing the location of dive sites accompany each Area.

Advertisements are on pages 186, 187, 188

Preface

This book could not have been so comprehensive without the help of a great number of divers who operate off the Yorkshire coast. The ones who have given the most help are named below, with apologies to any we have accidentally omitted.

Gordon Wadsworth and Joyce Town, who have dived virtually the whole Yorkshire coast from their boat *Maisie Graham*, Steve Cooper, Rob Dawson, Gerard Leyden, Pete Fergus, Eddie Kirkpatrick, "Robbie" Robinson, Bill Gill for the Withernsea area; Terry Dealtry, Mike Radley, Billy Woolford, Nick Hegarty, Ian Stewart, Graham Hirst for Bridlington Area; Alan Davis, John Adams, Pete Hodgkins, Chris Baker for Filey area; Andy Jackson, Ian Robinson, Steve Parker, Peter Sellars for Scarborough area; John Stephenson, Kath Young, Brian Clarkson, Geoff Sutton for Whitby area; Ian Denney for Redcar area and Geoff Sutton for Staithes area.

Trawler skipper Fred Normandale and Colin Jenkinson for Decca readings of wrecks.

Thanks must also be given to George Scales of Scarborough for help with photographs and trawler information, and to the staff at Scarborough and Redcar Public libraries, and to Cleveland Leisure Services Officers.

We are grateful for sight of the records of the Royal Navy Hydrographic Section, and to those of the R.N.L.I.

Scarborough Sub-Aqua Club has been helpful in many ways, with its members offering information almost dive by dive.

How to use
this book

In this book the Yorkshire coast is divided from north to south into seven areas, starting at the River Tees and running down to the Humber. Each of the seven areas is dealt with separately and each area chapter is supported by information important to divers planning to dive in the area. This includes launch sites, information on shore diving where this is possible, parking places, contact telephone numbers for Coastguards and other emergency services, air supplies, weather information and accommodation contacts.

Because of the nature of the Yorkshire coast, servicing and repair centres for outboard motors are not available in every area, and visiting divers are advised to take account of this when planning a trip.

Chart and map numbers are included, as are contacts for charter vessels when these are available.

Depths are given in metres and distances in miles. Ship dimensions are in feet and tonnages are gross.

The contents page lists the seven areas into which the Yorkshire coast has been split for ease of reference. Each area has an introduction, describing things of interest and importance. Then follows the dive site descriptions, numbered from north to south. The site descriptions are numbered to follow the numbered area maps which precede each main chapter. In general, all the sites listed are of wrecks positively identified, except for those marked as Unknowns.

It is as well to remember that this is an exposed coast and prudent divers will approach their operations here with caution and good sense. There are still many rewarding discoveries to be made.

An Introduction to Yorkshire

The Yorkshire coast begins at the River Tees and runs for some 110 miles to the River Humber. Some years ago, bureaucrats decided that the northern bit would be called Cleveland, the middle bit North Yorkshire, and the southern bit North Humberside, and all kinds of organisations changed their paperwork to match. But those of us who know the 110 miles well, have tramped the cliffs, the rocks and the beaches and have sailed and swum over and under these waters know where God meant the boundaries to be. After all, it is well known that God was a Yorkshireman, and he wouldn't take kindly to having bits of His chosen county lopped off and given another name!

The Yorkshire coast is a place of great contrasts; it has the highest range of cliffs on the English coast, and long stretches of unbroken sands. There are jagged rocks running into dangerous offshore reefs, and shallow, sheltered sandy bays within a few miles of each other. There are huge industrial complexes bordering some parts of the coast, while other parts provide some of the most picturesque and dramatic scenery in the country. None of the towns on the Yorkshire coast are big by inland standards, and all of them are holiday resorts. There are three harbours, all of which were known as harbours of refuge in the days of sail. They are at Whitby, Scarborough and Bridlington. Between these places are a number of small fishing communities where boats are hauled up when not in use. At either end of the coast is a major estuary, with rivers leading up to large commercial ports, Teesport and Middlesbrough in the north, and Hull and Grimsby in the south. These places are not really relevant to the diver, but it is because of their positions that we have so many modern wrecks in this part of the world; many of the ships that were lost in wartime, especially in WW2, were making for or leaving these estuaries.

With the exception of the Borough of Scarborough area, the Yorkshire coast is quite sparsely populated, and some of its beaches are often deserted, even in the height of summer. East Yorkshire, between the Wolds and the sea, had the distinction of having the least number of cars per mile of road of any place in England in a recent survey.

Access by Road

The main routes leading to the Yorkshire coast are the A1 and A19 from the north and the A1 and M62 from the south. Divers coming from the north should leave the A19 at Middlesbrough, and take the A174, if they are heading for Redcar and Saltburn or Whitby.

Those making for Scarborough should stay on the A19 until Thirsk, then take the A170 to Scarborough. If towing a boat however, this route is best avoided because of the very steep climb at Sutton Bank. A better bet is to leave the A19 at York, and take the A64 to Scarborough.

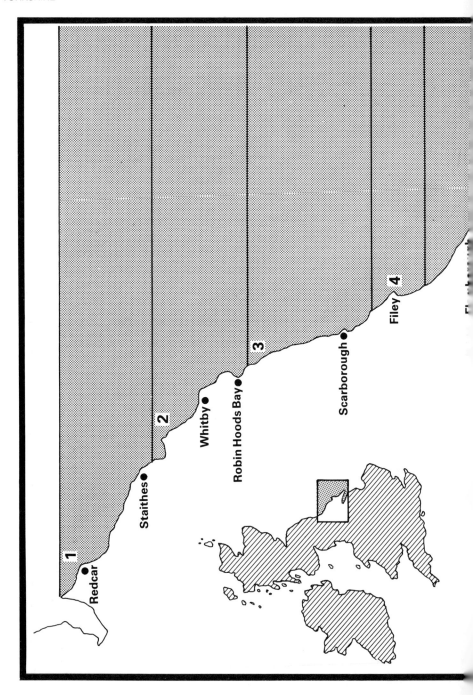

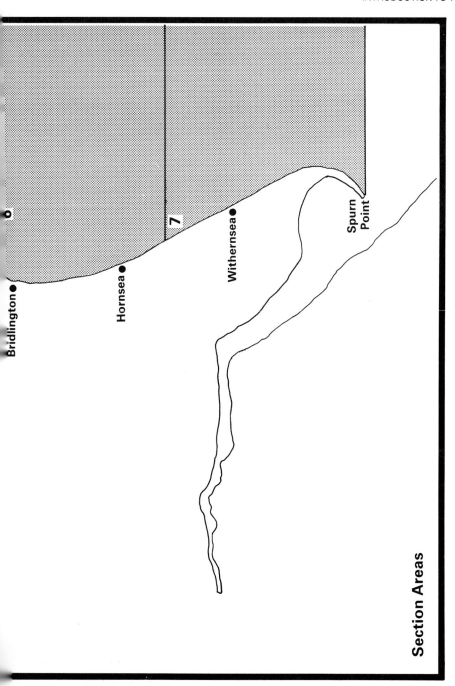

Bridlington ●

Hornsea ●

Withernsea ●

7

Spurn Point

Section Areas

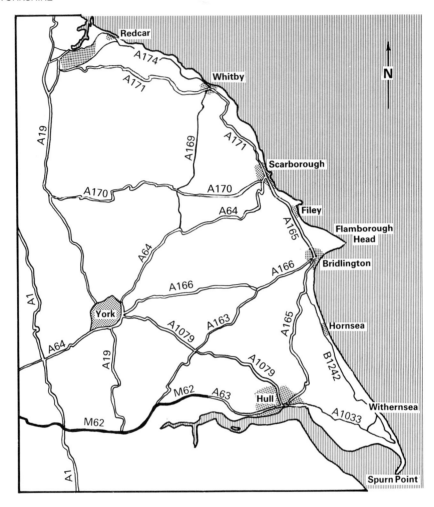

Approaching from the south or west by the M62 gives two main alternatives; either continue directly into Hull, and from there by the A1033 to Withernsea, or leave the M62 immediately after the Ouse bridge into Howden and along the A614 to Bridlington and Flamborough. Once at the coast, it is a simple matter to drive from one dive site to another, as there is just one coast road to follow. As with any holiday area, the roads do become very congested, and the only satisfactory answer to this is to beat the crowds by travelling early; it is a real joy to have the roads to oneself in the early hours of a summer's day here.

The AA always maintain a strong presence in the area during the holiday season and are very helpful in giving up-to-date route information.

Accommodation

Since the whole of the Yorkshire coast is a holiday area, there is plenty of accommodation of all kinds on the coast. There are numerous caravan sites on the cliff tops (which do nothing for the scenery, incidentally), and every town has an abundance of bed and breakfast type accommodation, at low prices by national standards. It is worth making the point that an increasing number of caravan site owners dislike taking bookings from large groups of young single-sex visitors, as they cater normally for family groups who are generally less noisy! For up-to-date information, ring the various tourist offices whose numbers appear in the area information sections.

Marine Life

The fishing ports of Yorkshire rely heavily on their catches of cod and codling, which abound in these waters, and are found on every wreck, sometimes in great numbers. There are pollack, coalfish, whiting, weavers, skate, ling, conger eels, dabs, plaice and blennies aplenty. Queenies, a type of small scallop, have been caught in quantity recently, and this is one of the best lobster fishing areas in Britain. (The others being Northumberland, Norfolk, Sussex, Hampshire and Cornwall.) Edible crabs are plentiful too, though we never see a crayfish here. There are huge mussel beds along the northern part of the Yorkshire coast, but these are not normally eaten by humans. In the summer, there are mackerel shoals, though these are less common than before. Haddock make up another major part of the local fishermen's haul, and periodically, these professionals come up with a sturgeon or a shark – usually a basking shark, though other types are not unknown. Codling, pouting and pollack are easily observed by those willing to forfeit the luxury of a noisy aqualung and glide silently among the kelp with a snorkel. Flat fish such as plaice, dabs and flounders are less easily spotted as they lie buried on the sandier bottoms. Sea urchins are much in evidence on rocky parts of the coast too, but commercial exploitation of these creatures some years back has meant that there are fewer now than there were thirty years ago.

S.M.S. Kolberg at Stettin in 1912. In 1914 she wsa one of a squadron of battle cruisers involved in the bombardment of Scarborough. The mines she laid created havoc on this stretch of coast. (Site 157)

Dive Planning

Since the prevailing wind in this country is westerly, an east coast should be diveable at any time, but this of course is not the case. It is a wise move for inland divers to telephone either local diving clubs or the coastguard before setting off on a diving trip. Scarborough Sub-Aqua Club bar is regularly filled with visiting divers during bad weather weekends because they failed to check before leaving home. (Or maybe they knew, but decided to come anyway!) The best time to dive here is after a prolonged period of gentle south-westerlies, and if this is followed by a period of very light easterly winds, then spectacular underwater visibility can occur; it has been known to exceed 20m on occasion, and sometimes for days at a time. A northerly blow can reduce this to pea-soup however, and it will take some days to become clear again. Tidal movements are another crucial factor, and on really big spring tides, the slack water period can be so brief that it is perhaps better to mow the lawn that weekend. These tides not only make diving difficult, but they whip up the sediment and reduce visibility as well.

It is sometimes possible to dive south of Flamborough Head in a northerly blow, when everywhere else is impossible, but if the wind is easterly and strong, then there is nowhere on the coast that the diver can find a lee.

Emergencies

For the kind of emergencies that divers are concerned about in this area, there is one answer: call the Coastguard. At sea, use channel 16 VHF, ashore telephone 0262-672317 if you are operating between Spurn Point and Port Mulgrave, or 091-2572691 if you are between Port Mulgrave and the Tees. Sadly, there have been one or two decompression accidents here in recent years, and a meeting was held at Scarborough Hospital in 1986 to discuss these. Organised by Scarborough Sub-Aqua Club and consultant Dr. Alf Wilde, this meeting was attended by RAF Search and Rescue personnel, local diving clubs and HM Coastguard, and the outcome was, basically, ring the Coastguard in the event of any problem, and he will put

The cruel sea battering the S.S. Charles *at Whitby Nab. (Site 64)*

Diving on Lord Ernle *at Bempton. (Site 182)*

the wheels in motion. It should be borne in mind that there is no decompression chamber available for amateur divers' use within many miles of Yorkshire.

In the event of a decompression accident, it is vital that another diver remains with the victim throughout, in case of unconsciousness. Full details of the victim's dive profiles for the previous days should be available to those responsible for the treatment, together with full details of the dive that apparently caused the trouble.

Divers and Fishermen

The local diving clubs are justly proud of their excellent relations with the fishing community, and are anxious to preserve the status quo. There are in fact a number of professional fishermen who are members of diving clubs, and are active in the sport. In the summer, it is not uncommon for fleets of lobster pots to stretch for tens of miles up and down the Yorkshire coast, some of them close inshore, and others in up to 50m of water. These pots are carefully monitored, and some fishermen regard divers as unwelcome intruders. Whenever possible, it is better to give them a wide berth, and never, never use them as a convenient anchorage for the club inflatable while the anchor is made ready! Bear in mind that a fleet of pots will have cost the owner a considerable amount of time as well as money, and he has enough problems with natural disasters to his gear, without the threat of human intervention as well. If you are new to the coast, you will be regarded as suspicious until you have proved yourself to be competent and safety conscious. This is not local hostility, just suspicion borne out of natural respect for the sea.

The whole area of this book comes under the North Eastern Sea Fisheries Committee, who monitor all British vessels operating up to three miles offshore. They have a patrol boat called *North Eastern Guardian,* skipper Dave Bevan, which is based at Whitby but will regularly be seen at Scarborough and Bridlington. There are three Fishery Officers aboard the boat, with powers to stop and search any vessel, including inflatable dive boats, to ensure that no undersize fish or crustacean has been taken. In addition, there are five shorebased fishery officers who can meet any boat as it returns to the shore, with the same powers. There are heavy penalties for illegal landings. Minimum sizes are listed below: in force from January 1, 1989.

cod	35cm
haddock	30cm
plaice	27cm
dab	23cm
saithe	35cm
hake	25cm
witch	28cm
lemon sole	25cm
sole	24cm
turbot	30cm
brill	30cm
megrim	25cm
whiting	27cm
lobster	85mm
	(measured from either eye socket to rear end of body shell)
crabs	115mm across the broadest part of the shell

It is also an offence to land, or have in your possession, any edible crab carrying any spawn, or any edible crab which has recently cast its shell, or to land or have only the tails or claws of a lobster, or the claws of a crab. These statutory provisions were designed for the guidance of professional fishermen, but it must be borne in mind that they apply equally to divers. Fishery Officer Dave Bevan also reminded us that it is an offence to fish *for gain* from an unregistered boat, so if you are lucky enough to catch the odd lobster, eat it yourself!

Restrictions

Divers in Bridlington Bay should be aware of a bombing and gunnery range, Cowden Range, which is just south of Hornsea, and covers a semicircle some seven miles diameter. The range is used five days a week, between 0900 and 1700 normally, and a red flag is flown on shore at either end of the range when bombing is in progress. There are also seven buoys, rusty yellow in colour, which mark the perimeter.

The actual targets consist of a barge and a ring of buoys, some 2000 and 500 yards offshore respectively. Needless to say, this area is to be avoided

The magnificent Cap Palos, *completed in 1919, lost on tow, having survived a year stranded on rocks at Robin Hood's Bay. She broke in two and the bow section has never been located. (Area 3)*

during bombing practice! If in doubt, the Station Officer welcomes telephone enquiries at 0964-527275.

Shipwrecks

There can be no doubt that far and away the most exciting diving to most divers, is that which is done on wrecks, and the Yorkshire coast has more than its fair share of these, for a number of reasons. Since before written records began, coal from the north-east coalfields has been shipped from that area to London and beyond, and the coal trade was said to employ "more shipping than all the carrying trade of England" in the eighteenth century. During the World Wars, large numbers of steam colliers plied the east coast, and hundreds of them fell victims to the U-boats here. Large numbers of ships made for the major ports of the Tees and the Humber, which rivers enclose the Yorkshire coast, and consequently these places were favourite targets for enemy attacks by U-boats, mines, surface raiders, and later, aircraft. To go back even further however, in the early days of steamships, the Yorkshire coast seemed to draw them into its rugged cliffs like moths round a candle, and it will be seen that scores of them came to grief as a result of bad weather, bad visibility, bad compasses or bad navigation. Many other early steamers foundered at sea in bad weather off the headlands and even in the bays of the Yorkshire coast.

The number of sailing ships that have been wrecked off and on the Yorkshire coast runs into many thousands, but it will be seen that those listed in this book can be counted on the fingers of one hand, for in truth, there is rarely anything to be seen of them, and it would be misleading to include them as dive sites.

Positions

Positions in this book have been given in the traditional way of latitude and longitude using degrees, minutes and seconds, which is the way that the Hydrographic Department of the Royal Navy works. Divers using Decca type navigators must remember to convert the seconds to decimals; this is a simple matter best done on the chart scale rather than as a mathematical calculation. In some cases we have given bearings and distances from charted objects, and in other cases we have given radar rangefinder positions. This is one method favoured by the local diving boats, but we realise that few visiting boats will carry radar. It has to be said right away that sometimes the position obtained by radar cannot be made to tally exactly with that obtained by a Decca navigator, *on the same boat at the same time,* but this is inherent in the way that the instruments work, and the way charts are produced. It has also been noticed that the Decca-type navigator position changes very slightly from year to year, even when using the same instrument on the same boat while anchored into the same wreck. These anomalies in practice mean that even with the best equipment, the best divers can still experience difficulty in locating wrecks that they have found many times before. But nobody said that wreck diving was easy!

Identification

In recent years, local divers have adopted a method of identifying wrecks by checking out the details of the engines and boilers, and comparing these with known details as found in Lloyd's Registers. Often, it is impossible to find easy identification like the ship's bell, embossed nameplates, or makers' plates and it is then that the second line of attack can be used. Ships can have – in this area – anything between one and four boilers, each of which can have between one and four furnaces of one of three different types. Thus it will be seen that there are hundreds of possible combinations, and if finding the "right" one does not positively identify the wreck, it at least eliminates many others.

One item from the vast variety of artefacts which reward the efforts of divers. This brass valve cover came from wreckage at Horse Rocks, Gristhorpe.

A further aid to identification is obtained by checking out what type of steam engine the ship had, and by measuring the diameter of the cylinders. These vary so much that, together with the boiler details, these can virtually positively identify any wreck. The snag is that sometimes Lloyd's Register omits the boiler details from its pages!

Wherever possible, we have given the details of engines and boilers of wrecks in this book in order to make the detective work a little easier.

Below is a key to the abbreviations with an example:

C   – compound engine
T   – triple expansion engine
SB – single boiler (furnaces at one end only)
DB – double boiler (furnaces at both ends)
PF – plain furnaces (smooth surface inside the furnace)
CF – corrugated furnace (as in corrugated iron inside the furnace)
RF – ribbed furnace (similar to corrugated but more angular)

Thus 2SB 4CF, T 3cy 15″ 26″ 47″ – 36″ would indicate two single boilers, each having two corrugated furnaces; a triple expansion engine whose three cylinders measure 15″ 26″ and 47″ with a crank stroke of 36″.

The Hornsund *is a good dive at low water neap tides, and this gun from her is mounted at Scarborough Lighthouse. (Site 129)*

17

Area 1: River Tees to Runswick Bay

This area is bounded by a line running approximately east-north-east from South Gare, Tees Bay, to the north and a parallel line from Runswick Bay to the south and includes diving access points at Redcar, Saltburn, Skinningrove, Staithes and Runswick.

Diving conditions in the proximity of the Tees are for obvious reasons often poor. Teeside is a densely industrialised area with much river traffic, dredging operations and associated port operations which combine to preclude diving in the immediate area of the estuary.

Shore Diving Sites

REDCAR ROCKS

Within a couple of miles of the river mouth, the sand, mud and silt of the estuary give way to the broad beaches of Redcar, a popular holiday resort, and it is here that the reefs of the Redcar Rocks provide a handy start to an exploration of the Yorkshire Coast. These rocky finger-like scars point from the low water mark nearly a mile out to sea, and it is among these kelp lined reefs that several ships lay scattered, and which were, in the days of sail, the background to many legendary heroic lifeboat rescues.

A visit to the local Zetland lifeboat museum on the promenade is well worth a visit for this incredible craft is still in existence today, over a hundred years old, and the forerunner of our modern lifeboats. A wealth of history is perfectly preserved in this modest setting.

Of those steamers that have missed the entrance to the Tees – and there have been several – some were fortunate to avoid the clutches of the reefs or the shifting sands, but others remained to be cut up where they lay above the low water mark, convenient scrap for local foundries. Those trapped by the East, Salt and West Scars were less accessible to salvage and have remained pounded by the destructive forces of the sea.

To navigate the areas of the reefs it is advisable to observe the approaches at low water and to obtain local guidance. From a position on the promenade overlooking the scars and not far from the launching slip opposite the lifeboat house, the best information can be obtained from Ian Denney, proprietor of the local diving shop, who has a thorough knowledge of the area.

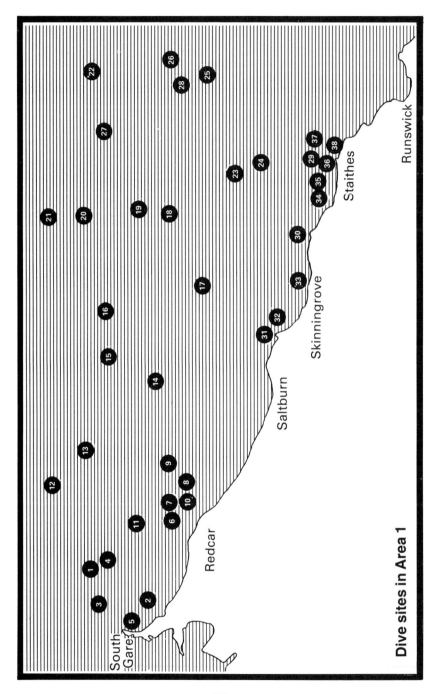

Dive sites in Area 1

Skinningrove Pier, with parked cobles.

SALTBURN

Moving south along the coast takes us through the sand dunes of Marske-by-the-Sea, and not until sand gives way to rock at Saltburn-by-Sea do we find our next site.

Saltburn is a small coastal town of 20 000 population which marks the commencement of the high ground of the North Yorkshire Moors.

To the south of the town rises the jutting mass of Huntcliff, at the foot of which is a rocky scar known as Saltburn Scar. Shore diving is possible here in calm conditions, but the extent of the rock scar round to Cattersty Cliff is some 2 miles and warrants a boat if extensive exploration is planned. The old smugglers' inn "The Ship", forms a convenient landmark for the slipway at Old Saltburn. Local coastguards warn of heavy shore swells which can arise, making beaching and launching hazardous in certain conditions.

SKINNINGROVE

Skinningrove is over the top of Huntcliff, the former site of intensive mining operations, where there is much of interest for the industrial archaeologist. The scene is of some desolation, due to the abandonment of the industry, but is slowly being transformed back to respectability. Diving is possible under Hummersea Cliffs and the ragged slipway provides an adequate launch site for boat support. The pier is somewhat derelict but can be used for small craft.

STAITHES

The quaint fishing village of Staithes is one of the most picturesque along the coast, and is famous for its traditional fishing "cobles" which have now sadly declined in number.

Shore access is possible both at Cowbar Nab to the north, over the breakwater, and to Penny Steel to the south. The drawback is the poor access, as Staithes suffers from severe congestion due to tourist pressure and vehicular access in summer is prohibited.

RUNSWICK BAY

The approach to Runswick by road is very steep, as is the slipway. A four-wheel drive vehicle is recommended. There are large car parks at the slipway but these fill rapidly in the season.

Boat Diving Sites

The majority of sites along this coast are largely inaccessible without a boat of some kind. The offshore wrecks need the wonders of new technology to locate them, and even small inflatables now have the capacity to take the sonar and navigational aids required.

WRECKS AT SOUTH GARE

Any busy estuary can be notoriously difficult to navigate and the narrow navigation channel into the Tees is no exception particularly in exposed northerly gales and in fog. There have been numerous wrecks here and most have been dispersed because of danger to navigation, but some remains can be seen in conditions of good visibility. Launch from Redcar lifeboat slip and choose the conditions carefully to get the best visibility.

Staithes and Cowbar Nab from the air.

1 Afridi. Described at the time of loss as a British ex-destroyer of 872 tons, this wreck has been surveyed by divers and is well dispersed in positionn 1.76 miles .076 degrees from South Gare Light, in a depth of 18m.

Approximate position 54 39 34N 01 05 26.5W. Dimensions were 250ft long by 25ft beam.

2 Guildford. This 1871 ton collier was built in 1953 by the Burntisland Ship Building Company for the South East Gas Board, London. She was 265ft long with a beam of 39ft and was powered by an 8 cylinder oil engine. The *Guildford* was abandoned after collision on March 10 1954, and sank in position 54 38 31N 01 06 13W. She appears as "foul" on the 10m depth contour. Admiralty Chart No 134; no diving information on her is available. Near the same location the Royal Navy collier *Lemnos,* 1530 tons was lost on December 16 1915.

3 La Basiase. or (La Bastaise). A French patrol vessel lost at the mouth of the Tees on June 22 1940. Position given as 54 39 36N 01 07 04W. Charting details indicate that the depth here is 13m.

4 Harraton. On April 19 1896, the steamship *Harraton* sank on the approaches to Teesmouth after a collision with the *Engineer* of London. Position is estimated as 54 39 15.50N 01 05 12W, 1.78 miles 282 degrees from South Gare Light. The condition of the wreck is likely to be poor owing to dispersal operations.

5 Harvest. This British steamship, of 1338 tons, sank at South Gare after a collision with the s.s.*Regent,* on September 12 1889. The *Harvest* was outward bound with a cargo of pig iron at the time.

At the same site are the wrecks of the steam trawler *Victory* which was wrecked on November 11 1897, together with the tug *Ida Duncan,* of 139 tons lost on 31 January 1917. A little to the east can be found the remains of the *Stirling* which sank on January 29 1920.

REDCAR ROCKS

Launching from the public slip opposite the lifeboat house, at low water, East Scar rocks are pointing off to the east, while the West Scar rocks are to the north-west. The outer most band form the Salt Scar rocks.

Launch from the lifeboat slipway. Hazards – High Stone Rocks just off the beach are just one metre below chart datum.

6 Fairplay II. Built in Hamburg in 1921, this 282 ton steam tug was originally named Fairplay XIV. She came into ownership of the Fairplay Towage and Shipping Company of London in the late 1930's and was requisitioned by the Admiralty in 1939. *Fairplay II* was wrecked on Salt Scar Rocks, Redcar on March 2 1940 in position 54 37 37N 01 03 00W. The remains of the vessel now lie in a gully on the end of the Scar and is of course well broken up. Dimensions 119ft x 24ft. Wreck bears 43 degrees magnetic from the lifeboat slip.

7 Montauban. On January 9 1940, the French collier *Montauban* ran ashore on the Salt Scar rocks at Redcar, and broke up in a gale afterwards, in position 54 37 45N 01 02 27W. The 4191ton *Montauban* was on route to Marseilles from the Tyne with coal, and was built by the Forth Ship

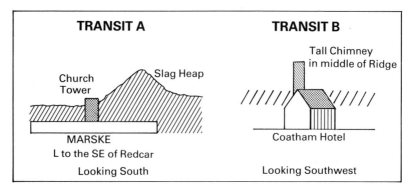

Marks for the Montauban. (Site 7)

Building and Engineering Company in 1920. Owned by the Compagnie Delmas Freres et Vieljeux her dimensions were 364.4 x 52.8 x 24.3 feet and her triple expansion engines, by Armstrong Whitworth of Newcastle, were of 347 horsepower. The wreck is well dispersed at the north-east point of the Salt Scars in 4-5m at low tide. The engines and prop shaft are still there to find, but be wary of diving outside slack water in strong spring tides. Best dived within 2 hours of low water. Wreck bears 55 degrees magnetic, three quarters of a mile from the lifeboat slip.

8 Dimitris. This 5250 ton Greek steamer, ex *Michel L Embiricos*, ex *War Malayan,* ran onto the East Scar rocks, Redcar, at 9.30pm on December 13 1953 and subsequently became a total loss. *Dimitris* had been a regular visitor to the Tees under her previous name and was carrying iron ore from Boma, North Africa to Middlesbrough. Redcar lifeboat, *City of Leeds,* and inshore fishing boats successfully rescued the crew of 36, despite a heavy swell. The wreck has been considerably dispersed and partly salvaged but substantial amounts of wreckage remain, the boiler being visible at low water. Divers hoping to dive this and the nearby *Montauban* are recommended to have a chat with Ian Denney of Denney's Dive Centre, overlooking the site. He has considerable local knowledge of the area and is happy to advise on launching sites, local regulations and conditions.

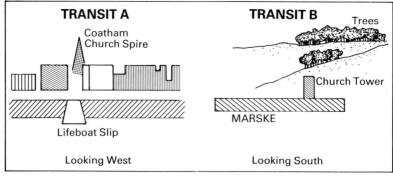

Marks for Dimitris: (Site 8)

French collier Montauban *ashore at Redcar Rocks. (Site 7)*

Position for the Dimitris is 54 37 15N 01 01 40W. She was dispersed in 1954. Her dimensions were 412ft long with a beam of 52ft. Engines T.3cy 3SB 9CF.

9 Teesdale. This 2470 ton steamer foundered 3 miles north of Saltburn on August 2, 1917 despite surviving a torpedo attack in the English Channel earlier in June, after which she was beached. She was bound for the Tees for repair and it is possible that the damage she sustained was responsible for her subsequent sinking. Dimensions of the ship were 310ft long by 44.2ft beam, built in 1904 by Ropner & Son and owned by the same company. Engines; T.3cy.

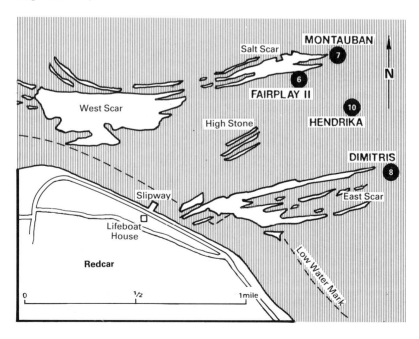

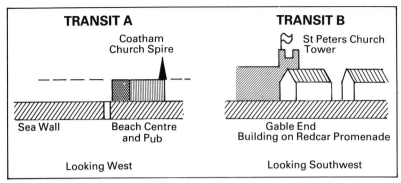

TRANSIT A	TRANSIT B

Marks for Hendrika. (Site 10)

10 Hendrika. This 810 ton coaster capsized after running aground south of the Salt Scar Rocks, Redcar on May 4 1973, whilst on route from Aberdeen with grain. An attempt at salvage failed and the wreck was dispersed with explosives, but parts are still recognisable. Lying in just seven metres of water the wreck makes a good training dive. Position 54 37 34N 01 02 54W.

11 Ernrix. On June 22 1939, the 692 ton coaster sprang a leak off Staithes, while on route from Hull to Thornaby-on-Tees with wheat. An attempt by the *Kings Cross* to tow the vessel in the heavy sea and strong northerly breeze was unsuccessful and the ship sank before reaching the Tees. The motor lifeboat *Louisa Polden* of Staithes was launched at 11.30pm in response to a report by Staithes coastguard that distress rockets were seen from a three-masted vessel, and all ten crew were swiftly rescued after leaping the perilous gap between the stricken vessel and the lifeboat. *Ernrix* was built in 1921 for Humber Steam Coasters of Hull. Her dimensions were 175ft x 29ft x 11ft.

Reported position of the Ernrix is 54 38 38N 01 03 26W in 18m where she was dispersed in 1960.

12 Kilkris. Sunk in position 54 41 00N 00 59 00W. The Greek registered *Kilkris* was torpedoed during WW1 carrying 6800 tons of iron ore. The dimensions of the ship were 365ft long and 50ft beam.

13 Talisman. The 153 ton *Talisman* was captured by submarine only 7 miles east-south-east of Hartlepool and blown up by means of a bomb placed on board. There is an uncharted obstruction at this point in position 54 39 58N 01 00 47W.

14 John Miles. She was the victim of a mine some 11 miles south-east of Hartlepool on February 26 1917. The 687 ton vessel sank quickly and with the consequent loss of her 10 crew including the master. Owned by the Stephenson Clarke Company the *John Miles* was built by S.P. Austin and Company in 1908, and was 164ft x 30ft x 12ft.

15 Corsham. Nine crew were lost when the Cory collier *Corsham* was torpedoed in ballast 6 miles east-south-east of the Tees entrance on March 8 1918. This 2760 ton vessel was built by S.P. Austin and was defensively armed. Dimensions 312ft x 45ft x 21ft. Position given as 54 39 30N 00 56 30W.

John Miles, *a mine victim in 1917. (Site 14)*

16 Unknown. This is an obstruction on fishermens' charts and could be the resting place of the trawler, *Recepto,* sunk by mine on February 17 1917. The position for this obstruction is 54 38 00N 00 53 61W.

17 Ruthin Castle. An Admiralty commissioned trawler of 275 tons, she was mined off Skinningrove on April 21, 1917. Estimated position is given as 54 37 00N 00 53 00W. There are charted fishermen's "fasteners" (obstructions) near here at: 54 36 35N 00 52 28W: 54 36 39N 00 52 10W: 54 36 44N 00 51 58W: 54 36 47N 00 51 45W.

18 Moorwood. The 2056 ton *Moorwood* was torpedoed by enemy aircraft off the Tees on June 11 1940. Estimated location is 54 38 00N 00 50 00W.

SALTBURN AND SKINNINGROVE, OFFSHORE

19 Unknown. Near the *Moorwood* is a known "fastener" at 54 38 47N 00 50 03W.

20 Presto. The 971 ton *Presto* was lost off Teesmouth on March 15 1942. Hydrographic information suggests a position of 54 40 25N 00 50 28W, a charted fishermen's "fastener". Because of the approximate position for this wreck no diving details are available. Other sources of information give the position of loss of the *Presto* as Roker Point, Sunderland, some 20 miles north of this location, so this could be another mystery wreck!

21 Unknown. Near the *Presto* location is another unexplored obstruction at 54 41 14N 00 49 52W.

22 Disperser. This salvage steamer became a victim when on February 8 1934 she foundered off Runswick Bay while under tow for Ramsgate. Runswick lifeboat was launched in heavy seas and by the time she had reached the *Disperser,* seven of the eight crew had reached the safety of the towing vessel, but the eighth being injured, was unable to escape the sinking ship. Second coxswain Robert Patton boarded the *Disperser* and while assisting the injured man on board the lifeboat, was himself crushed between the two vessels when he fell into the sea. Local rumour has it that the *Disperser* went down with her salvage gear, including those much coveted copper hard-hat helmets! Owned by W H Loveridge of Hartlepool, the 139 ton *Disperser* had been built by J & G Rennie in Greenwich in 1871 as H.M. Gunboat *Bonetta*. Engines: Compound 16 and 15. The reported position of loss was 54 40 00N 00 4415W.

23 Lochiel. The hired trawler *Lochiel* was believed mined while on duty on July 24 1918. She was one of many fishing vessels commissioned by the Admiralty for war service such as escort or mine-sweeping. Approximate position 54 36 00N 00 48 00W.

24 Hartley. This 1150 ton steamer was torpedoed without warning just 2 miles north-east of Skinningrove on January 26 1918. Armed for defence, the *Hartley* had escaped a previous attack by an enemy seaplane which had attempted to torpedo her on June 9 1917. Approximate position is 54 35 30N 00 47 30W.

25 Pandora. The loss of the 203 ton Beaumaris steamer *Pandora* 4 miles off Staithes on October 1951, tells of one of the most unhappy of all local seafaring tales. A sixty mile-per-hour gale prevented the local lifeboats at Whitby, Runswick and Redcar from responding to the distress signals from the *Pandora*, sinking rapidly with her cargo of stone. Teesmouth lifeboat was launched but was unable to render assistance, and just as helpless as the nearby 2866 ton collier *Gripfast,* herself seeking shelter and in imminent danger of being blown ashore. The *Pandora* sank at 7.44am just over an hour after her first distress call taking her six crew with her. The ensuing controversy over the alleged failure to launch the lifeboats led to much recrimination and to the resignations of some crew. Great bitterness arose among the community, and the entire Whitby lifeboat crew resigned despite support from the RNLI. It became impossible to man the Runswick boat and the station was closed. The approximate position is 54 36 40N 00 46 20W. The position reported by Lloyds was 45 degrees 4 miles from Staithes. A known obstruction at this location is at 54 36 58N 00 42 03W.

26 Anboto Mendi. This 2114 ton Spanish steamship was torpedoed off Redcar on May 10 1918 in position 54 38 04N 00 41 30W steaming from the Tyne to Rouen. One reported position is indicated as 9 miles 135.5 degrees from South Gare Light, but another source gives a position of 54 37 50N 00 43 00W. Details of the ship were: Builder Compania Euskalduna of Bilbao 1907. Engines T.3cy 21.5, 34 and 57 -39. 2SB 6CF. Dimensions of the ship were 275ft long by 41ft beam.

27 Unknown. There is an uncharted fastener or obstruction recorded by fishermen lying in 54 39 31N 00 46 43W. No diving information has been obtained and this must be worth investigating. Could be an alternative site for the *Dispenser*. (Site 22)

28 Audax. Three lives were lost when the 975 ton 3-masted armed schooner *Audax* ex *Haardraade,* was torpedoed in a position reported as 6½ miles east by north from North Cheek, Robin Hoods Bay on September 6 1918. A known "fastener" exists at position 54 37 27N 00 44 11W. Built in 1903 in Norway the ship was 210ft long by 35ft beam. Engines; 16.5, 26.5, & 43-40, 1SB, 3CF.

S.S. Deptford, *first stranded at Whitby Rock, sank at Soulby, Staithes in 1862. (Site 29)*

29 Deptford. The early Shields steamer *Deptford* was unfortunate to become stranded on Whitby Rock. Successfully refloated, she then sank off Boulby, Staithes on March 13, 1862. There is a very old wreck off Staithes which could be the *Deptford.* Lying in 40m of water it is known locally as the "Navigator". The wreck rises to 3m off the sea bed and the bows are reported intact. The machinery details suggest that it could indeed be the *Deptford.* Engines 2 cylinder compound, 2 boilers with 2 plain furnaces.

30 Waldridge. On January 31 1895 two men were lost when the steamship *Waldridge* went ashore north of Port Mulgrave. On December 30 of the same year the *Beaver* was lost of Staithes.

31 Clarence. One man was drowned when the tug *Clarence* foundered at the foot of Huntcliff on November 18, 1893, during the great gale of that year, when many ships were lost along the coast.

32 Elemore. This Sunderland steamer was lost with all hands off Huntcliff on October 28 1880.

33 Casamance. 5817 ton Free French vessel built in 1921 by Atel. et Chateliers de la Loire, St Nazaire and was 391ft long with a beam of 56ft.
  She was powered by three steam turbines, directly geared to one screw shaft, and was registered at Le Havre. Early in the 1940's she was wrecked

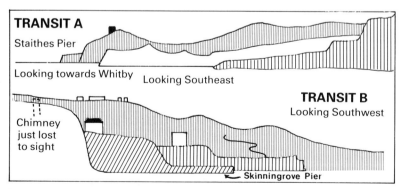

Marks for Casamance. (Site 33)

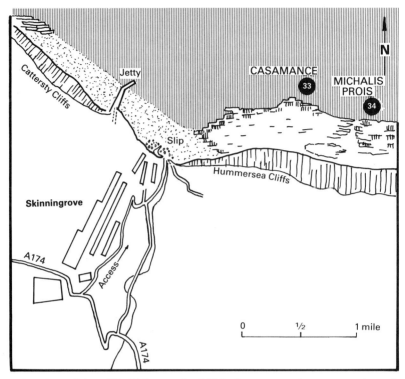

at the foot of the cliffs 500m south of Skinningrove, and some wreckage is still there today. Her bows point in toward the cliff, in very shallow water; at low water there is only about one and a half metres over one of the boilers and the kelp growing on it breaks the surface on spring tides. The wreck is well dispersed and is owned by a Redcar man who has carried out a considerable amount of salvage here. However, it is still possible to see how the ship lays.

WRECKS ASHORE AT STAITHES

34 Michalis Prois. Built by the Sunderland Ship Building Company in 1900, this 4167 ton steamer carried the names *Saint George* and *Labor* before becoming *Michalis Prois* when she was sold to the Greek Prois Bros. and re-registered at Chios. She was 365ft long and had a beam of 48ft. On May 28 1929 *Michalis Prois* ran ashore during fog about one and one half miles north of Staithes while on route from the Tyne with coal. She struck at high water and was badly holed, and the 29 crew were taken off by local fishing cobles and landed at Staithes. The young captain remained on board in a vain attempt to save his ship, but she was doomed and became wrecked at the foot of the 600ft cliffs, a little north of Redcliff Point.

There is a huge amount of wreckage spread over hundreds of square metres, well dispersed and little showing over 2m in water of 9m. Further

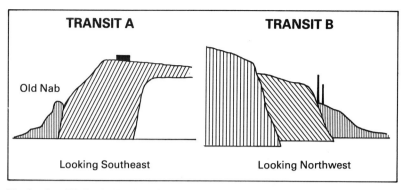

Marks for Michalis Prois. (Site 34)

details: Position 54 34 25N 00 50 54W. By Radar 1.66 miles from Huntcliff and 0.1 miles from nearest land. *Michalis Prois* had engines by the North Eastern Marine Engineering Company, T.3cy, 26,42, and 69-45. 3SB 9PF.

35 Skipjack. On the evening of November 16 1909, this 1120 ton collier struck on Cowbar Steel, in a heavy snowstorm during a north-west gale. The *Skipjack* was built by Witherington and Everett, and owned by the J.G. Hill Steamship Co. She was bound for Portland with 1500 tons of coal from Blyth. Dimensions of ship: 222ft × 33ft beam. T.3cy 18,24 & 48-33 by North Eastern Marine Engineering Company. 1SB 3DF.

The year 1909 had been an eventful one for shipwrecks here for in February a small iron vessel of 317 tons, the *Elise* had been smashed to pieces on the shore and had been the scene of both dramatic rescue and tragic loss of life.

The doomed Michalis Prois *off Staithes. (Site 31)*

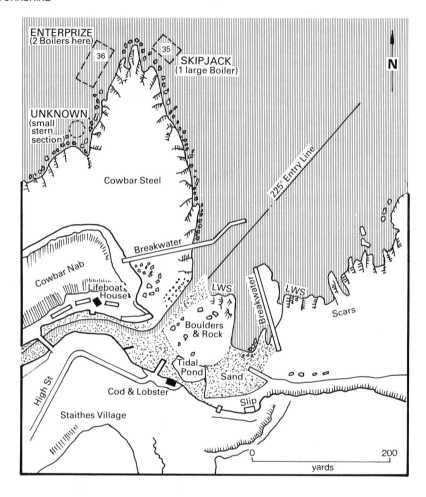

36 Enterprize. At 11 o'clock on a foggy Saturday night, June 15 1907, the 1227 ton steamer *Enterprize* of Cardiff, laden with coal from Wallsend and bound for Rotterdam, struck Cowbar Steel and began to fill. A local coble took off the captain's wife and daughter, and the Staithes lifeboat *James Gowland* took off the fifteen crew, the captain refusing to leave until it became obvious that the ship was doomed.

By Sunday morning soundings confirmed that there were seven feet of water in the engine room and Captain Round, a well-known local salvor was engaged to recover the steam winches and deck machinery, which he landed at the Scotch Head, Whitby on the following Thursday.

37 Beaver. This 155 ton collier was wrecked in thick fog at Cowbar Steel, Staithes on December 30, 1895. All ten crew were saved by the lifeboat.

Enterprize *after striking Cowbar Steel. (Site 36)*

38 Bebside. Scant records from an early edition of the lifeboat journal tell us of the wreck of the Newcastle steamer *Bebside,* 605 ton at Cowbar Steel, Staithes on March 15 1876 during a north-westerly gale. A total of eighteen were saved by the combined efforts of the lifeboat and a local fishing coble. It is likely that some of the wreckage littering this area is from the *Bebside.*

Bebside was one of the earliest steamships, built in 1864 by Richardsons of Newcastle. Her dimensions were 185ft × 28ft × 16ft, compound engines 36 and 28.

Area Information and Services

Admiralty Charts. River Tees to Flamborough Head Chart No 1200 or Tees to Scarbrough No 134.

Ordnance Survey. Landranger series L93 and L94.

Local Weather. Marinecall Area 3 North East Tel 0898-500 453.

Shipping Forecast. Tyne.

Coastguard. Tyne-Tees 091-257 2691 Redcar (Sector Office) 0642-483811 Staithes (Auxiliary) 0947-840539 Whitby (afternoons and weekends) 0947-602107.

Weather Bulletins from HM Coastguard on VHF marine radio. Begin at 0340 hours then 4 hourly. Gale and small craft warnings issued on receipt from the Meteorological Office, repeated at 2 hourly intervals.

BS-AC. Tees Branch No 43 Meetings Thursdays, South Gare club house. Tel 0642-484335 Area Coach – Steve Paige 0642-486201.

Tourist Information. Redcar Tourist Office 0642-471921.

Camping/Caravan Sites. Runswick Bay Caravan/Camp Site 0947-840997.

Air Supplies Denney's Dive Centre. The Promenade, Redcar Tel 0642-483507.

Outboard Repairs and Service. As above.

AA 24 hour service. Middlesbrough 0642-246832.

Accommodation. Contact Local Tourist Office 0642-471921.

Launching. Redcar – The Royal Slipway opposite the Royal pub. No slipway charges. Trailer park on beach. Saltburn – launching site available but not recommended as surf conditions can easily arise. Skinningrove – From the A174 take the road to Skinningrove and follow it to the sea where there is a small public slipway. Runswick Bay – Enquire at the local lifeboat house 0947-840965.

Area 2:
Whitby: Kettleness to Robin Hood's Bay

This area runs southward from Runswick Bay to Robin Hoods Bay, a distance of some 12 miles. The high cliffs along this stretch of the coast are only broken by the sandy bays of Runswick, Sandsend and Upgang north of Whitby, and diving any distance from these immediate access points onto the rocky sea-bed has to be by boat. Diving conditions in shallow water along the shore vary considerably with the sea conditions and the slightest onshore swell produces poor visibility conditions. In calm conditions following a flush of clean easterly borne water visibility can become impressive.

The first access point is at Runswick Bay where there is a handy slipway with public car parking adjacent. From the sandy beaches of Runswick there is an area three miles to the south past Kettleness and Keldhowe Steel, halfway to Whitby. To the north it is just a mile back to the derelict harbour of Port Mulgrave. There is rocky shore along most of this stretch and the diving is good if the water is clear. Diving conditions in the vicinity of Whitby harbour are also dependent on the flood water from the River Esk and so after heavy rain expect to find coloured river water hampering inshore sites. Away from the immediate mouth of the Esk and clear of the

Kettleness Point, from the wreck of Vanland. *(Site 41)*

35

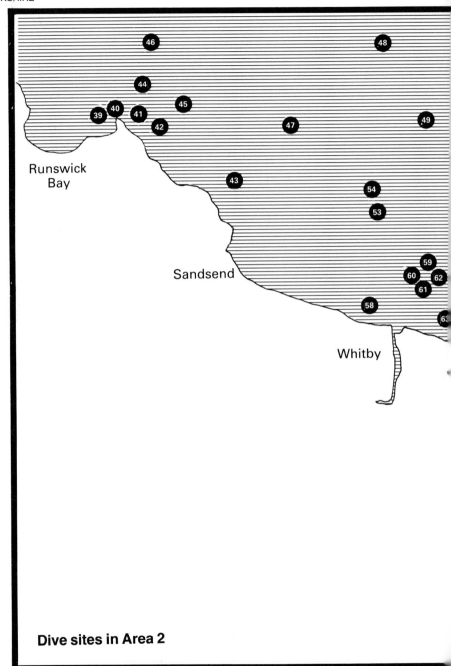

Runswick
Bay

Sandsend

Whitby

Dive sites in Area 2

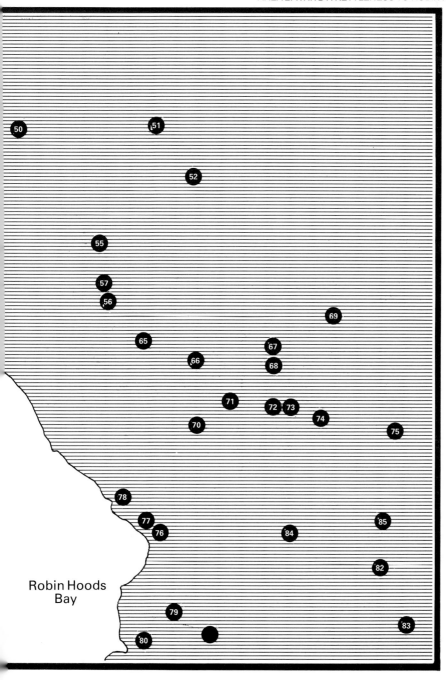

Robin Hoods
Bay

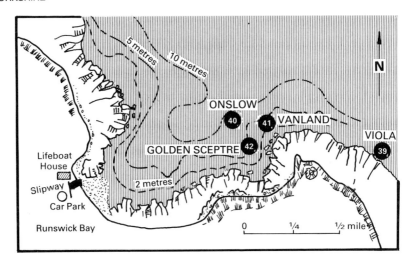

sandy beaches visibility improves markedly, although the sea bed contours here dip steeply into deep water.

One of the first points of call for any Whitby bound diver must be the famous wreck of the hospital ship *Rohilla,* just minutes from the harbour mouth of Saltwick. Whitby is an impressive port, steeped in centuries of shipping and whaling history, and the birthplace of that most famous of all navigators Captain James Cook, whose statue stands solemnly overlooking the harbour mouth from the high vantage point of Whitby's West Cliff. It *is* west cliff, because Whitby harbour mouth faces due north, a point to remember when assessing weather conditions. It is true to say that standing on the end of the piers there is nothing between Whitby and the North Pole, some 2500 miles due north!

Up the coast again from Whitby to North Cheek, the north point of Robin Hoods Bay, we see more rocky shoreline and again this stretch is accessible only by boat.

KETTLENESS

There are several wrecks ashore at Kettleness Point to the south of Runswick.

39 Viola. The 1204 ton steamer *Viola* went ashore half a mile south of Kettleness point on Saturday, September 19 1903 during thick fog. Bound for Middlesbrough with 2600 tonnes of iron ore from Cartegena, Spain, the *Viola* had been attempting to give Whitby a wide berth when disaster struck. Seventeen crew were successfully rescued by Runswick lifeboat, and later the captain and remaining crew were taken off when the weather worsened. The vessel broke in two some two weeks later. At the subsequent enquiry the master was suspended for three months for "neglect in the use of the lead."

Details of ship: Built at Willington Quay, 1879. Owners, Montauk Steam Ship Co.

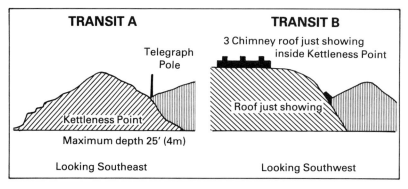

Marks for Vanland. (Site 41)

40 Onslow. This London registered collier of 2722 tons, ran ashore at Kettleness Point on August 12 1911, during dense fog. She was en route from Sunderland to Pireaus. *Onslow* soon took water and despite frantic salvage attempts during which much cargo was jettisoned, two days later the ship broke in half. Some months earlier a smaller vessel the SS *Pearl* of Goole, a small collier, had suffered a similar fate nearby.

Details of the *Onslow:* Built 1899 by Barclay Curle. Dimensions 312ft by 45ft beam. T.3cy.

Details of the *Pearl:* Built 1898 by Wood Skinner, 677 tons. Engines by North Eastern Marine Engineering Company.

Position 54 32 10N 00 43 30W.

41 Vanland. On July 24 1917 SS *Vanland* of Gothenburg, 1285 gross tons, was shelled in Runswick Bay by a German submarine. In an attempt to evade the pursuing attack, the *Vanland* struck Kettleness Point, and almost at the same time, a torpedo from the U-boat struck the vessel, causing a huge explosion which killed six men. As the Runswick Lifeboat sped to the scene of the wreck, the U-boat was seen to surface just outside the Bay, but no further attack came, and the lifeboat successfully rescued 18 survivors. No more torpedoes were needed, for *Vanland* was doomed; she burned for a week and smouldered for a few days more, her cargo of greaseproof paper, boxwood and undipped matches keeping the fire going. Eventually she keeled over, burnt out and sank.

She lies in about 4m of water just inside Kettleness Point, and her wreckage is spread over a large area, with nothing sticking up more than a few metres. Divers from a nearby diving club are reported to have found the bell from *Vanland,* in 10m and subsequently returned it to the vessel's former owners.

Built by the Campbeltown Shipbuilding Company in 1893, the ship was owned by Angf. Aktieb Suithied Weifdling of Gothenburg.

Dimensions: 227ft long by 32.7ft beam. Engines; T.3cy 17.5, 27.5, 44.5.

42 Golden Sceptre. On Monday night January 16 1912, during hazy weather, the Hull steam trawler *Golden Sceptre* ran ashore on Kettleness Steel. Heavy seas were breaking over the wreck when the Runswick lifeboat, the *Hester Rothschild* took off the 11 crew and 5 passengers.

Lucy ashore at Keldhowe Point . . .

The trawler lay broadside on against a rock ledge and soon sustained considerable damage in the heaving sea, becoming a total loss less than one hundred yards from the wreck of the *Onslow*.

43 Lucy. On Christmas Day, 1930 the Swedish steamer *Lucy* of Helsingborg, ex *Magdeburg* 1451 gross tons, ran ashore at Keldhowe Point (Kelder Steel) some 4 miles north of Whitby during hazy weather. The *Lucy* with her cargo of pitch, was on route from Grangemouth to the French port of Bordeaux, when she went ashore in a SSW breeze in moderate seas. She soon began to fill and the Whitby motor lifeboat was quickly on the scene. As the weather worsened her crew of 18 were swiftly brought to safety.

. . . and all that remains today.

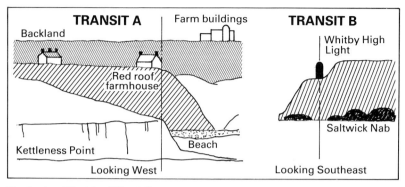

Marks for Giralda. (Site 44)

44 Giralda. On August 28 1918 the 1100 ton *Giralda* of Leith was torpedoed by *UC-70* 5 miles north-north-west of Whitby and sank with the loss of six crew. Runswick Bay lifeboat was able to save the lives of 13 others. Reports at the time state that the *Giralda* was beached at Kettleness, but the charted position at 54 32 30N 00 42 20W places the wreck at just over half-a-mile off Kettleness Point.

Details of the ship were: built by Osbourne of Sunderland 1887. Engines by T Clark and Sons of Sunderland 2cy, 28 and 53. 1SB 3PF. Dimensions of the ship were 225ft long by 33ft beam.

45 Athos. Built by Nylands Vaerksted in 1913, the 1708 ton Norwegian *Athos* was torpedoed in ballast and sunk by German submarine off Runswick Bay on January 26 1918.

Dimensions of the ship were 265ft long by 40ft beam. Engines; TCY, 19, 31 and 51-33.

An approximate position is 54 32 15N 00 41 30W.

46 African Transport. This armed steamship was lost to torpedo attack on June 25 1918. She is a relatively large wreck, being 4482 tons gross and carrying 6684 tons of coal at the time of loss. The estimated position of the wreck is some 3 miles north of Whitby although other sources indicate her

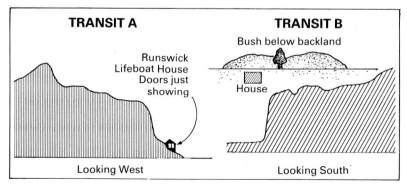

Marks for Athos. (Site 45)

as being 4 miles north of Whitby and 2 miles off shore. Charted position is given as 54 33 00N 00 42 00W. She was built by the Northumberland Ship Building Company in 1913, and had 320 nhp triple expansion engines measuring 25, 40 and 68 inches. Her dimensions were 385ft x 52ft x 27ft draught, and she was armed for defence. It has been reported that the gun has been removed, restored and mounted on a memorial plinth on Whitby West Cliff.

OFFSHORE WRECKS OF SANDSEND

There are several wrecks north of Whitby in the 30m band.

47 Venetia. The 3595 ton Glasgow steamer *Venitia* was torpedoed and sunk by German submarine on December 9 1917, some 3 miles north-north-west of Whitby Rock. *Venetia* carried a defence gun. The Whitby No 2 lifeboat rescued eight crew.

Details of the ship were: Builder: Short Bros. of Sunderland, 1898. Engines: T. Richardson Hartlepool. 3cy 24, 39 and 66-45. Port of Registry: Glasgow. Dimensions 353ft by 45ft beam.

There is an uncharted obstruction at 54 32 00N 00 39 00W which could be the *Venetia*. Also nearby is another uncharted obstruction at 54 32 00N 00 40 00W.

48 Ellida. This 1124 ton Norwegian steamship was torpedoed and sunk by German submarine off Runswick Bay on April 19 1917. Details of the ship were: Built Bergen 1901 Dimensions, 229ft long by 35ft beam. Engines 3cy 16, 25 and 43.

Approximate position for this wreck is 54 33 00N 00 37 00W.

49 Lampada. The 2220 ton armed collier *Lampada* ex *Snilesworth* was torpedoed and sunk by German submarine 3 miles north of Whitby on December 8 1917. Details of the ship were: Built by Short Bros. of Sunderland in 1889. Engines by J Dickenson of Sunderland 3cy 21, 35, and 58-42. 2SB, 6RF (ribbed furnaces). Dimensions of the ship were 281ft long by 40ft beam.

50 Afrique. This 2457 ton French steamship, built in 1911 by Ateliers et Chantiers de France, was torpedoed and sunk by German submarine on June 12 1918. Details of the ship were: Dimensions; 295ft long by 41ft beam. Engines: TCY 21, 33 and 56. 2SB 6CF. An approximate position is 54 32 00N 00 34 00W.

51 Guiana. A commissioned Admiralty tug of 166 tons, the *Guiana* sank after a collision on January 29 1918 in an approximate position of 54 32 00N 00 31 00W.

52 Brentwood. The Cory collier *Brentwood,* 1192 gross tons, was lost to a mine on January 12 1917 some 4 miles east-north-east of Whitby. One of the first casualties of the year, the loss of the *Brentwood* heralded the start of a particularly callous period in the escalating submarine war in this locality, as the loss of the *Hurstwood, Corsican Prince* and the *Saint Ninian* were to demonstrate. Contemporary reports claim that the master and one

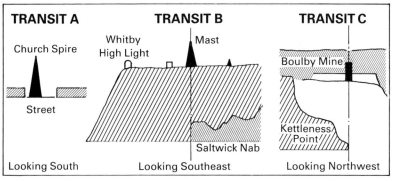

TRANSIT A — Looking South
TRANSIT B — Looking Southeast
TRANSIT C — Looking Northwest

Marks for Possible Spero. (Site 53)

crew member were taken prisoner in this incident.

Built by S P Austin and Co of Sunderland in 1904, the dimensions of the ship were 224ft long by 36ft beam. Engines TCY, 20,33 and 54 by Clark of Sunderland, 1SB, 4PF.

Sister ship to the *Brentwood,* the SS *Hurstwood,* lost four of her crew to submarine attack on Monday February 5 1917. When some 6 miles northeast of Whitby, her second mate saw a periscope just 150-200 yards away on the port side. The torpedo hit near the engine room, blowing a 3ft hole above and below the waterline. The *Hurstwood* sank with 4 of her 15 crew.

53 Spero. The Runswick Bay lifeboat, assisted by Whitby lifeboat rescued the crew of the SS *Spero* of Newcastle in the early hours of January 13 1923. The location is unknown. This wreck has become confused with that of the *Sparrow* reputed to have been lost off Whitby piers and positioned at 54 30 48N 00 37 01W, in 34m and known as the "Steeple-i'-Street" wreck. No information from Lloyds Register has been found relating to the *Sparrow.*

54 Unknown. An unknown wreck not far from the *Sparrow* is at 54 31 12N 00 37 12W. This may even be the same wreck with positions from different sources. Diving at slack water is 2 hours after predicted time.

55 Hercules. The 1295 ton Norwegian collier *Hercules* was torpedoed and sunk by German submarine 3 miles east-north-east of Whitby on December 30 1917.

Details of the ship were: Built Bergens Mek Vaerks. 1909. Engines 3CY 18.5, 30 and 50-33. Dimensions of the ship were 235ft long by 34ft beam.

56 Garthwaite. The armed steamship *Garthwaite*, of 5690 gross tons, was reported as torpedoed and sunk by German submarine on December 13 1917, 4 miles east of Whitby in position 54 29 45N 00 27 10W. There are two alternative positions for this wreck at 54 29 45N 00 32 00W and 54 29 45N 00 26 53W, and it could also be that of the *Crimdon.* (Site 57)

Details of the ship were: Built by W Dobson and Co., Newcastle in 1917. Registered London. Dimensions were 400ft long by 52ft beam by 33ft depth. Engines 3CY by NEME, 26, 43 and 72-48. 3SB 9CF.

57 Crimdon. This Swedish collier, of 1710 gross tons, was torpedoed and sunk by German submarine on July 27 1918 while carrying a cargo of 2050 tons of coal.

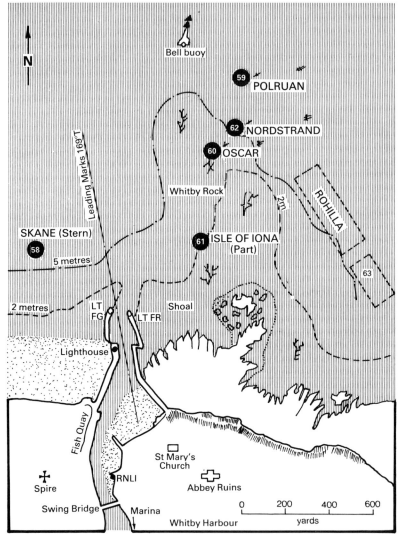

Dimensions of the ship were 262ft long by 34.7ft beam. Built by William Gray in Hartlepool in 1878. Compound engines by Richardsons of Hartlepool. 2SB. An approximate position is 54 30 00N 00 32 00W.

WHITBY ROCK

Many fine vessels have failed to negotiate Whitby harbour entrance or have foundered in the shoals of Whitby Rock, a mat of rocky scar reaching nearly a mile out to sea from Whitby Piers.

58 Skane. The Swedish cargo vessel *Skane* was on route from Stockholm to Calais with a cargo of timber when she ran onto Whitby Rock on the evening of November 30 1915, in fine weather. A party of intrepid fishermen put off in cobles to attempt to refloat the hapless vessel but were unsuccessful, as the *Skane* had been holed and the engine room flooded.

The next day a tug was able to tow her off but had to beach her in a sinking condition. During the same afternoon the wind backed to south-east and the sea became very rough. Whitby lifeboat was launched to rescue the 20 people still on board, including two women, and brought safely to shore those not desiring to remain aboard. The remaining eight salvage crew elected to stay to try to save the *Skane* but as the weather grew worse, were forced to send distress signals, bringing the lifeboat to their assistance once again.

The doomed vessel was to prove a continual hazard to the salvagers, in its exposed position, and two days before Christmas, seven salvagemen had to be rescued in dangerous seas by the local lifeboat, which was reported to have filled several times during the drama.

An approximate position is 54 29 36.6N 00 37 16.2W, but is unlikely that much of the vessel remains.

59 Polruan. Built in 1907 by W Gray & Co. at Hartlepool, this 3692 ton steamer carried the names *Polnay* and *Pollacsek* before becoming *Polruan*. She was requisitioned by the Admiralty, and put to work as a collier under the management of Hall Bros, Cairns Noble & Co. during WW1. The ship was 331ft long with a beam of 48ft and a depth of 22ft. On October 25 1916 she foundered off Whitby, and the Board of Trade Inquiry decided that this was as a result of striking Whitby Rock, though they did not deny that the vessel may also have struck a mine close by – as the captain maintained. Either way, the master was censured and ordered to pay £50 costs. The wreck is owned by Whitby divers, and is in position 54 30 17N 00 36 00W, in 27-30m of water. There is a fierce tide rip on this wreck and it is only possible to dive it at slack water, which occurs some 2 hours after high or low water ashore.

Polruan had T3cy engines by Central Marine Engineering Works, Hartlepool, 24" 40" 65" – 42", 2SB 6RF.

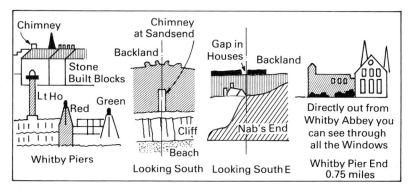

Marks for Polruan. (Site 59)

60 Oscar. Owned by the London and Edinburgh Steam Ship Company, the 824 ton *Oscar* of Leith became a total wreck on Whitby Rocks on March 5, 1878. The Whitby lifeboat successfully rescued the 22 crew in a heavy easterly swell. The *Oscar* was on route to Cadiz with a mixed cargo of coal, fireclay and fire bricks when she struck the rocks at 6½ knots in heavy seas and thick fog. She broke in two within a few days, and had to be dispersed as a danger to navigation. At the subsequent enquiry the master was found to be in "neglect in the use of the lead."

61 Isle of Iona. On the morning of December 7 1906 signal rockets were seen off the East Pier, Whitby. It soon became apparent that a vessel was aground about five hundred yards from the piers, and rescue services were quickly alerted. The vessel was in fact the *Isle of Iona,* 1139 tons, a fully laden Newcastle collier bound for Rochester, and she had first struck Upgang Rocks in hazy weather, to the west of the harbour, before finally grounding. Both Whitby rowing lifeboats, the No 1 *John Fielden,* and the No 2, *Robert and Mary Ellis,* were soon on the scene among heavy breakers crashing over the wreck and onto the beach. A classic rescue followed and all 17 crew except the captain, who remained aboard, were brought to safety.

The weather later moderated and the captain left the now mortally wounded vessel. Later, local small boats were to salvage around 600 tonnes of the vessel's cargo, the local slipways becoming grimy with coal grit, before the ship yielded to the elements and began to break up.

A wreck reported in this vicinity and heavily dispersed is located at 54 29 46N 00 37 04W, in 7-8m of water.

Details of ship: Builder T and W Smith, North Shields, 1889.

62 Nordstrand. On March 18 1918 the SS *Nordstrand,* 1939 tons ran aground on Whitby Rock just three quarters of a mile north east of Whitby piers. Carrying coal from the Tyne to Rouen, 23 crew were saved by the gallant crew of the Whitby No 2 lifeboat, before the vessel became a total loss. The position indicated for this wreck is 54 30 12N 00 36 00W.

Details of ship: Builder Richardson Duck and Co. 1891. Dimensions 270ft long by 36.6ft beam. T.3cy.

63 Rohilla. The loss of the hospital ship *Rohilla* is probably the most famous of the Yorkshire shipwrecks and of singular significance in the annals of lifeboat history. She was a commissioned liner owned by the British India Steam Navigation Company and on service as a hospital ship to recover wounded servicemen from France. *Rohilla* was lost in the early hours of Friday, October 30 1914, when in a severe south-east gale, and navigating under war-time restrictions of muffled navigation lights and buoys, she smashed onto a jagged reef just a mile south of Whitby Harbour and broke her back some 400 yards offshore.

The series of lifeboat rescues which followed can scarcely be imagined. One can vividly envisage the scenes from the High Cliff at Whitby, when, in those days of limited communications and motive power, the Upgang lifeboat was manhandled and, with grim determination and sheer dogged effort, lowered almost vertically down the cliffs at this point, only to be prevented from attempting rescue by the ferocity of the mounting storm.

Rescue from the shore was impossible because the crashing surf beat back the efforts of the local lifeboats, one of which was smashed beyond

Hospital ship Rohilla *in her glory . . .*

. . . a rocket attempt . . .

. . . and the remains of Whitby lifeboat with her wreckage. (Site 63)

repair. However, heroic efforts in the early hours had saved the lives of 35 people.

It was now the turn of the Tynemouth lifeboat, *Henry Vernon,* having battled through the storm, to lay the now famous pool of oil over the stormy waters round the stern of the *Rohilla.* In less than fifteen minutes over 40 were rescued from the breached vessel. The *Henry Vernon,* with over fifty survivors onboard, struggled through mountainous seas into the haven of Whitby harbour. Of those who had risked the surf only a handful reached shore and of the 229 crew, doctors and nurses originally on board the *Rohilla,* only 145 survived.

The wreck lies in a line from the Bell Buoy to Saltwick Nab, with the bows pointing to the shore. The inshore end is in about 6m of water, while the seaward end is about 15m deep. There are four complete boilers, with two pairs more or less in situ, and a further boiler is split open. A donkey boiler is upended close by. The shaft can be seen clearly. The forward end of the wreck is mixed up with wreckage from the wreck of *S.S. Charles.*(Site 64)

The area is divable almost any time, it is rare to have much tidal movement here.

Ben Dean, Sid Weatherill and Moia Porteus salvaged two spare prop blades, each weighing 2½ tons, 7ft long by 4ft wide. The blades were in a mud-hole 55ft deep. The ship's two propellors were removed "many years ago" together with all the valuable scrap. Her wheel is a treasured item in the lifeboat museum.

A visit to Whitby Lifeboat Museum is a must for those who wish to relive the drama of this era of heroic rescue by man-power in the early days of the engined rescue craft. The museum, with its vast collection of memorabilia, is located in the old lifeboat house at the harbour mouth and captures the essential character of Whitby, this ancient seaport nestling in the mouth of the Esk valley.

64 Unknown. There is a reported wreck in 54 29 17N 00 35 17W located during aerial surveys. It is likely to be that of the *Charles,* a Belgian steamer which was lost at Saltwick Nab, Whitby in February 1940, the wreckage of which is among some of the *Rohilla* debris.

Two crew members of Whitby lifeboat died during attempts to rescue the crew, and became the first lifeboatmen to die in WW2.

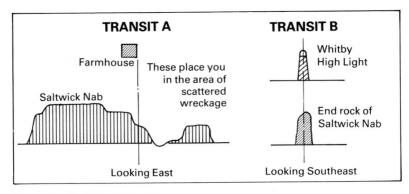

Marks for Rohilla. (Site 63)

OFFSHORE WRECKS

Many of the offshore wrecks in the vicinity of Whitby may well be out of reach of most divers as the sea-bed here shelves off steeply into the 40-50 metre mark within a couple of miles of the shore. There is however, for advanced groups, a wealth of wrecks to find, identify and explore.

65 Polanna. The 2345 tone British collier *Polanna,* was torpedoed and sunk by German submarine on August 6 1917, en route from the Tyne to Dunkirk. Diving reports pinpoint a position east of Whitby in 54 29 15N 00 31 15W, the wreck lying in at least 42m, with the midships section upright. The *Polanna* was built in 1893 as the *Antonia I,* renamed *Anna Woermann* in 1898. She had survived a previous torpedoing in the Cameroon River in September 1914.

Dimensions of ship: 282ft long by 38ft beam. Engines T.3cy 21, 34 & 56-39.

66 Modemi. The 1481 ton *Modemi* was torpedoed and sunk by German submarine off Whitby High Light on November 11 1917. Details of the ship were: Builders Antwerp Engineering Co in 1912. Engines 3cy 19 31 and 51. Dimensions of the ship: 243ft long by 38ft beam. Located in 1978 during a sea-bed sonar survey is a wreck which could easily be the *Modemi.* The position has also been reported as 54 29 10N 00 30 00W, which has also been given as a position for the *Martina.*

67 Corsican Prince. The steamer *Corsican Prince,* 2276 gross tons, was torpedoed 3 miles east of Whitby on February 7 1917, and a gallant bid to rescue survivors resulted in the loss of the 3026 tonne *Saint Ninian.* This Glasgow registered ship stopped to pick up the crew of the stricken vessel, and the rescue party in the ship's lifeboats were horrified to see the periscope of the submarine only 200 yards away. Their shouts and signals were unable to alert the *Saint Ninian* and a torpedo discharged at point blank range caused a massive explosion between the engine room and No 3 hold. The ship sank almost instantaneously. Half the crew of 28 were lost, including the master, and those rescued were found clinging to the upturned keel of a lifeboat.

From the *Corsican Prince,* all but one were saved by the selfless and heroic actions of the crew of *Saint Ninian,* whose brave efforts were in the finest tradition of the Merchant Service. *Corsican Prince* was built by Short Bros of Sunderland in 1900. Engines were 3cy, 23, 38 and 62-42 by North Eastern Marine Engineering Co. Dimensions of the ship were 316ft long by 42ft beam. 2SB 6CF.

68 Saint Ninian. Built by McKay and Company in 1894, this 3026 ton Glasgow steamer lost 16 of her crew, including the captain, during the heroic rescue of survivors of the *Corsican Prince.*

Details of the *Saint Ninian* were: Builder, Henderson and Co Glasgow 1894. Engines 3cy 24, 38 and 62-42. 2SB 6PF. Dimensions: 320ft long by 42ft beam. Engines: TCY.

There are wrecks in this area recorded by sonar surveys, one at 54 29 00N 00 28 25W rising 8m in a charted depth of 36m, and the other at 54 29 12N 00 28 20W.

69 Martina. This 335 ton West German motor vessel, sank on August 24 1972 when she took on a heavy list and sank in 48m of water while carrying a cargo of maize from Rotterdam to Hartlepool. She was 137ft long by 23ft beam. No diving information is available. Surveys suggest the wreck is in two pieces in positions 54 29 18N 00 26 33W and 54 29 10N 00 26 56W, but these are more likely to be two separate wrecks.

70 Harrow. The 1778 ton Cory collier *Harrow,* was torpedoed and sunk by German submarine on September 9 1917, 4 miles south-east of Whitby. Built by S P Austin of Sunderland in 1900. Engines by W Allen of Sunderland TCY 20, 33 and 54. 2SB 6CF. Dimensions of the ship were 268ft long by 38ft beam.

A recent hydrographic survey indicates an obstruction here at 54 28 12N 00 30 06W standing 7m high in 35m.

71 London. The 1706 ton *London,* was torpedoed and sunk by German submarine 4 miles east-by-south of Whitby on June 23 1918. Details of the ship were: Builders, Gourlay Bros Dundee in 1892. Engines 3cy 30, 47 and 77. 2DB 12 RF. Dimensions of the ship were 280ft long by 37ft beam. A sonar contact likely to be a wreck in this vicinity is at 54 28 33N 00 29 05W lying in 35m and rising 12m by soundings.

72 Unknown. Sonar surveys suggest a wreck in position 54 28 30N 00 28 18W rising 7m above the sea bed in 40m of water.

73 Moorlands. Carrying 5800 tons of iron ore at the time of her loss, the 3602 ton Whitby registered *Moorlands* was lost to torpedo attack by German submarine *UB88* on June 24 1918. Local divers have reported a large wreck with a cargo of iron ore and bows level with the sea bed, standing some 12m high at the midships and stern and laid to port. The position given by divers is 54 28 24N 00 28 00W in 52m of water. An alternative location is 54 28 26N 00 27 54W, a position reported from a sea bed sonar survey.

Built by Doxford and Sons, Sunderland, 1910. Owners: Eskside Steam Shipping Co. Engines 3cy 25, 40 and 67-45. 2SB 6CF. Dimensions were 357ft long by 50ft beam.

74 Lowtyne. The 3281 ton *Lowtyne,* ex *Slingsby,* was torpedoed and sunk by German submarine on June 10 1918. Built by Ropner and Son in Stockton-on-Teees in 1892 for the Lowland Shipping Company, the ship was 322ft long by 41.5ft beam. Engines: TCY 23.5, 39 and 64-42. 2SB 6CF. There is an unidentified survey contact at 54 28 18N 00 27 12W lying in 30m of water, which may be the *Lowtyne.*

75 Lanthorn. The 2299 ton collier *Lanthorn,* ex *Magnus Mail,* was scuttled after being captured by *UB41,* 3 miles east of Whitby on May 22 1917.

Built in 1889 for the Gas, Light and Coke Company, and subsequently managed by Stephenson Clarke, *Lanthorn* was one of the last clipper stemmed tramp steamers to be built. This should provide a valuable clue to identification. A wreck which could be the *Lanthorn* is in 54 28 10N 00 25 36W.

76 Knud. This Danish steamship of 1190 tons, ran ashore on the rocky scar at North Cheek, Robin Hood's Bay, on January 2 1900, in the early hours of the morning. The Robin Hoods Bay lifeboat took off the crew of thirteen. The vessel, in ballast on route from Ghent to the Tees, did not survive the heavy seas pounding the rocky shore. The wreckage littering this area is well dispersed owing to the exposed nature of the ground.

Dimensions of ship: 231ft long by 30ft beam. Engines C.2cy 30 and 60-36. 2SB 4PF. Built 1871. Registered Copenhagen.

77 Dunmail. On March 29 1911 the 966 ton schooner-rigged steamer *Dunmail*, went ashore at Ness point, North Cheek, Robin Hood's Bay, smashing off the rudder and sternpost on impact. The Robin Hood's Bay lifeboat the *Mary Ann Lockwood* stood by the *Dunmail* and took off the crew of fifteen as the vessel began to fill on the incoming tide. The *Dunmail* had run ashore at low water, and was soon a total loss.

Details of ship: Built 1884 by S P Austin and Co. Owned by Sharp Steamship Co of Newcastle. Dimensions 216ft long by 31ft beam. Engines C.2cy 27 and 53-33. 1SB 3PF.

78 Heatherfield. On January 26 1936, this 500 ton coaster, making her first journey on this coast, ran ashore at Ness Point, North Cheek, Robin Hoods Bay about 200 yards from the foot of the cliffs.

Usually working the west coast routes between Liverpool, Ireland and France, she was this time carrying 450 tons of scrap iron to the Thames. In a foggy haze and at low tide, the rescue of the captain and crew was carried out in classic style by the shore based Rocket Life Saving Brigades, famous for the breeches buoy rescue technique. The local brigade were on station within an hour and the second rocket fell across the vessel, fouling the ship's steam whistle, causing it to blow violently. One by one, the crew were dragged to safety by breeches buoy, although five had already risked their lives in the boiling surf and had scrambled over the rocks to safety. The captain was last to leave, and was given a rousing cheer as he was hauled to the cliff, complete with pet canary in a cage!

The *Heatherfield* was badly holed and remained fast on the rocks, the salvage of her scrap iron cargo being worked by the *Harvest Queen,* a small salvage vessel, herself becoming a victim of the scar on September 2 1936.

Details of Heatherfield: Built in Lytham, 1924. 142ft overall.

Heatherfield, *a coaster, on the rocks at Ness Point. (Site 78)*

79 Britannia. She was lost in Robin Hood's Bay on April 3 1920 and was the last vessel to be attended by the Robin Hoods Bay lifeboat before the station closed.

Britannia was on her way to the Tyne from Immingham, in ballast, when she struck rocks in Robin Hoods Bay. The 620 ton vessel was backed off but sank in deep water due to a large hole in her bottom, leaving just her masts sticking out of the water.

The position reported during dispersal operations was 1.5 miles east-south-east of Robin Hood's Bay coastguard station in position 54 25 54N 00 30 35W in only 8m of water. No recent diving history exists to confirm this wreck, and it may well be buried now.

Details of the ship: Builder S H Morton of Leith, 1885. Engines C.2cy 30 and 52. Dimensions 210ft long by 28ft beam.

80 Paris. The 1509 ton Danish collier *Paris,* carrying a cargo of timber, was beached in Robin Hood's Bay after a collision on February 15 1941 and became a total loss. Today all that remains are her large boilers, the rest of the wreck being scattered among the kelp-matted rocks in just 5-10m of water. The wreck is easy to find being 100m or so from the low water mark directly off Boggle Hole, and over the first of the kelp lines which appear at low water springs. This makes a good expedition and training site and is accessible from Boggle Hole as a shore dive. Details of vessel: Built Copenhagen 1927 by Burmeister and Wain. Dimensions 250ft long by 39ft beam. Ordnance Survey map ref: 042N 959E pinpoints the wreck.

The collier Paris, *now widely scattered. (Site 80)*

81 Paul, ex Ballochbuie. For a long time divers thought this to be the wreck of the *Lady Helen* but recent discovery of that wreck off Hayburn Wyke now suggests that the wreck in position 54 25 44N 00 29 04W is the Belgian registered *Paul.* The vessel is now broken up, in two pieces, in 30m, position 1.48 miles from North Cheek and 1.22 miles from South Cheek.

Built by Hall Russell of Aberdeen in 1880, dimensions of the ship were 190ft long by 31ft beam. Engines, compound 2 cylinder, 23.5 by 46-30. Boiler: 1SB 3PF.

82 Highgate. The Cory collier *Highgate* stands perfectly upright in 48m in Robin Hood's Bay and has been positively identified by divers from the Scarborough Sub-Aqua Club who have pieced together evidence from a number of dives to name the wreck. The ship is in one piece and in an excellent dive. Among the finds have been items of crockery bearing the Cory house flag. Beam measurements, together with engine and boiler details, confirm the wreck's identity. This 1780 ton vessel was torpedoed and sunk by German submarine on December 6 1917.

Details of the ship were: Built 1899 by S P Austin and Sons of Sunderland. Engines T.3cy 20.5, 33 and 54-39 by A Clark, Sunderland. Boilers: 2SB 6PF.

The position of the wreck is 54 26 19N 00 26 31W.

83 Melanie. The 2996 ton *Melanie* was torpedoed and sunk by *UC-40* on June 16 1918, 2 miles east of South Cheek Robin Hood's Bay, carrying 4300 tons of coal.

Sonar surveys have located a wreck in position 54 25 45N 00 225 27W or 02 25 03W (1986).

Diver reports indicate a large wreck corresponding to the details of the *Melanie,* on an even keel but well broken up, the engine and boilers being the highest part of the wreck at 40m. Another wreck is close to this one and the two positions given could be two different wrecks. Details of the ship were: Builder William Gray of Hartlepool, 1903. Engines by Central Marine Engine Works, Hartlepool. T.3cy 24, 38 and 64. Boilers: 2SB 6CF. Dimensions of the ship were 325ft long by 47ft beam.

84 Kathleen Lily. The 521 ton wooden screw schooner *Kathleen Lily,* had an assortment of owners and name changes after she was built in 1872. She met her fate by mine just 2 miles east of North Cheek, Robin Hood's Bay on March 29 1917. Her reported position at the time of loss was ". . . Whitby Light bearing 299, North Cheek, Robin Hood's Bay bearing 254. . ."

Details of the ship 163ft long by 27ft beam. Built by W Haggesund, Sundswall. Engines; T.3cy, 12, 18, 37-27 NB fitted 1908. Previous names: ex *Eidsvaag,* ex *Alban,* ex *Adelaer,* ex *Bjorn,* ex *Jemtland* and ex *Brage.* No definite position is available.

85 Quaggy ex Glenpark. This 993 ton steamer was lost to a mine 3 miles east of North Cheek, Robin Hood's Bay, on April 11 1917, and was armed for defence. Details of the ship: Builder J Brown, Greenock, 1094. Engines: T.3cy 16, 26 and 44. Boiler: 1SB 3CF. Dimensions of the ship were 222ft long by 32ft beam.

UNCHARTED WRECKS

There are many uncharted wrecks in the area and no doubt some of these will turn up as diving activities uncover more clues. Here are two early steamships whose loss was only briefly recorded at the time.

Countess of Strathmore. Little is known about this early collier, 527 tons gross, built in Newcastle in 1895 and which foundered off Whitby on July 14 of the same year.

Lost in similar circumstances on September 15 1865, was the *Earl Percy* of 605 tons by collision off Whitby. Another Tyne built boat she was engined by Hawthorn of Newcastle with compound engines of 28 and 56-36. Dimensions of ship: 236ft long by 28ft beam.

U-BOATS SUNK

UB107 She was a new boat, sent to the north east coast for training and had spent two unsuccessful cruises to this area. On July 26 1918, *UB107* set out on its last journey, for the next day observers on board a motor launch off Scarborough spotted her. Three trawlers and the destroyer *Vanessa* set out to hunt the marauder and when the submarine broke surface in heavy weather, the patrol trawler *Calvia,* and the *Vanessa,* attacked with depth charges and succeeded in raising air bubbles and oil from the submarine. Next morning a headless body was found and it was concluded that the *UB107* had been disposed of.

In 1974 divers found the wreck of a submarine at Flamborough Head, lying in 26m of water and apparently lying across the stern of a merchant ship wreck. (Site 215) One of the propellers of the submarine bore the stamping "UB107", and so the sinking off Scarborough remains somewhat of an enigma.

UB30 On August 13 1918 275 ton *UB30* fell victim to the armed patrol trawler *John Gillman* while attacking shipping off Whitby and was sunk by a combination of depth charging and shelling. *UB30* had torpedoed the steamer *Madame Renee* off Scarborough only three days previously.

UC70 On August 28 1918, the 420 ton *UC70* was spotted by a patrolling sea plane off Whitby following up a sighting of an oil slick in the area of the sinking of the *UB30*. Very lights were dropped along the track of the submarine as it submerged and a 520lb bomb was dropped into the sea, inflicting damage on the craft. The destroyer *Ouse* following up the flare track, completed the attack with a pattern of 10 depth charges set at 50ft. Divers later found the wreck of the UC70. She had left Zeebrugge seven days earlier for Whitby and had probably accounted for the *Giralda* at Runswick on the day of the attack.

Area Information and Services

Admiralty Charts. River Tees to Flamborough Head Chart No 1200 or Tees to Scarborough No 134.
Ordnance Survey. Landranger series L94 or Outdoor Leisure map No D27.

Local Weather. Marinecall Area 3 North East Tel 0898-500 453.

Shipping Forecast. Tyne.

Coastguard. Tyne-Tees 091-257 2691. Whitby (afternoons and weekends) 0947-602107.

Weather Bulletins from HM Coastguard on VHF marine radio. Begin at 0340 hours then 4 hourly. Gale and small craft warnings issued on receipt from the Meteorological Office, repeated at 2 hourly intervals.

BS-AC. Whitby branch No 1108. Meetings Buck Inn. Wednesdays 8.00pm. Contact: Tel 0947-600912.

Tourist Information. Whitby Information Centre 0947-602674 or 0947-602124. Whitby Museum, Pannet Park, (contains Whitby shipping and whaling history) 0947-602908.

Chandlers and Service. Coates Marine, Esk Terrace 0947-604486. Whitby Marine, 14 St Annes Staith 0947-600361.

AA 24 hour service. Middlesbrough 0642-246832.

Accommodation. Contact Whitby Information Centre 0947-602674.

Camping/Caravan Sites. Runswick Bay Caravan/Camp Site 0947-840997.

Launching

Runswick Bay. Slipway at the foot of the approach road next to the Lifeboat Station. Enquire at the local lifeboat house 0947-840965. Car park is council pay and display but is handy next to the slip.

Whitby. The Whitby Marina is a highly recommended launch site. The marina is a recent development at Whitby and its facilities and services are excellent with adjacent car-parking, shops and chandlery nearby. Advice on river pilotage is easily gained and understood and the short three quarters of a mile run to and from the harbour entrance is straightforward. Contact the Marina Supervisor on 0947-600165. Boat launching fees are well publicised and a prior call to the marina is recommended, especially if you want to make early morning launching arrangements. Facilities here are second to none along the coast.

For diving between Keldhowe (3½ miles) and Robin Hood's Bay (6 miles) this is also the best launch facility.

Area 3: Robin Hood's Bay to Scarborough

This area extends from the centre of Robin Hood's Bay to the largest of the three ports along the coast, at Scarborough. Because of the nature of the terrain in this area, diving will almost invariably require the use of boat support. This stretch of the coast is arguably the most scenic, being unspoiled by industrialisation, and forming the eastern boundary of the National Park. Diving both onshore and offshore is good, although most of the wreck sites are in deep water, towards the limit of safe diving depths in the 40-50m zone. Robin Hood's Bay is a picturesque former fishing village which has given way to tourism yet has remained largely unspoiled. Heavily congested in summer, traffic is prohibited in the only main street, winding down the steep bank to the slipway. Steep access points for shore diving at Boggle Hole and Stoupe Beck have eroded to the extent that boat launching is impossible for anything but the lightest of craft.

Ravenscar, just beyond the South Cheek, is accessible by boat, being at the south of this majestic bay, and diving under the high cliffs here is highly recommended.

Further south to Beast Cliff and Hayburn Wyke, we find similar scenery and one or two wrecks to dive although in shallower water, but again no

Robin Hood's Bay, looking towards North Cheek.

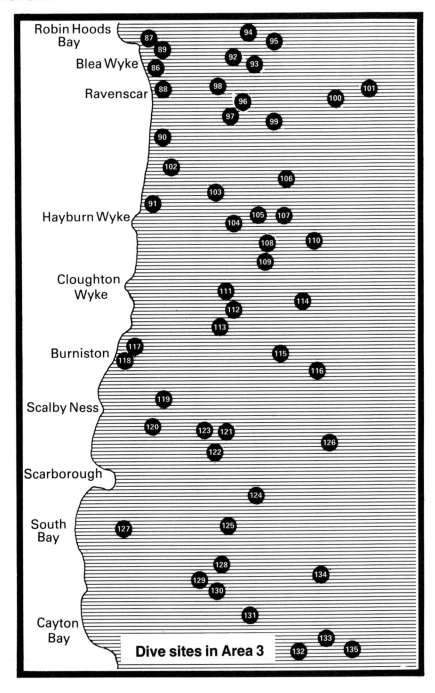

Dive sites in Area 3

shore access except for those prepared for an overland trek from Hayburn Wyke. Not recommended.

The next points of access are Cloughton Wyke and Burniston Bay, just north of Scarborough, where limited cliff top parking is available, for shore dives.

Shore Diving Sites

BOGGLE HOLE, ROBIN HOOD'S BAY

A small car park and a steep road, make this a difficult access point and there is a fair trek across flat rocky scar at low water, before the more interesting kelp lined reefs are found. Over one of these can be found the remains of the SS *Paris*. (Site 80)

BURNISTON BAY

Burniston is probably one of the easiest shore access points, and from the cliff-top car park which holds about a dozen cars, there is a short walk down a sloping path to the rocky bay below. To the north lies the wreck of the *San Antonio* and to the south at Cromer Point or "Cowlham" as it is locally known, that of the *Cognac*.

CLOUGHTON WYKE

Cloughton Wyke is accessible from the shore but involves a short climb down a steep path. Diving in the centre of the bay is not particularly exciting as it is fairly shallow and lacking in features, but to the north, kelp and boulder fields harbour a wealth of marine flora and fauna.

At the south, Hundale Scar runs out to sea and there are some interesting gullies at this point.

SCARBOROUGH NORTH BAY

The tunnel running under Scarborough's Marine Drive is a handy access point for beginners and for training parties. Access is very convenient, with no more than a 50m distance to the water, and straight into rock and kelp.

One word of warning! The causeway under the drive, through the tunnel is sloping, permanently wet and covered in slippery moss, so take care!

SCARBOROUGH SOUTH BAY

The shore access to Ramsdale Scar in Scarborough South Bay, is across the public holiday beach, which is incredibly busy in the height of the season. Avoid the northerly side of the scar as this is dangerously close to the harbour, and keep right away from any salmon nets if these are along the scar. As an old anchorage, the area is littered with the usual bits and pieces, including anchors, but old musket balls and other older relics have been brought up from time to time. Off the Spa is a further outcrop of rock in this otherwise sandy bay.

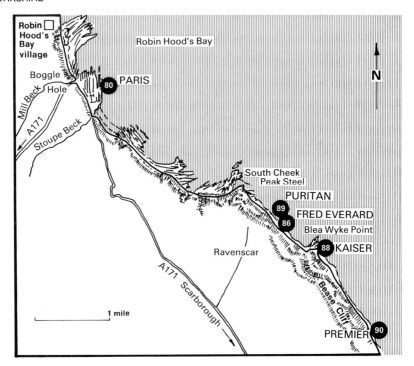

CAYTON BAY

Cayton Bay is accessible from a cliff top car park with a rather long haul to the beach. The Calf Allen Rocks in the centre of the bay are an interesting dive at low water.

Boat dives

RAVENSCAR

Boat diving sites accessible from Robin Hood's Bay include the shore wrecks at Ravenscar.

86 Fred Everard. The 1542 ton motor vessel *Fred Everard* came ashore in a blizzard in the early hours of Saturday November 27 1965, under the high cliffs of Ravenscar. Eighteen hours after leaving Lervic in Norway her deck cargo of pulp became wet and shifted causing a 30 degree list to starboard. She was driven, unmanageable, onto the rocks, breaking her back soon afterwards. Almost at the same time a Dutch cargo boat, the *Wega* went aground but refloated herself shortly afterwards. Whitby lifeboat successfully rescued the crew of 14, some of whom had taken to the ship's liferaft, and the vessel became almost totally submerged at high tide under the pounding of heavy breakers.

The Fred Everard, *ashore under the cliffs of Ravenscar. (Site 86)*

After some comical attempts at salvage – one scheme involving an attempt to drive a road round the foot of the cliffs from Robin Hoods Bay, and yet another to drag the vessel piece by piece up the 300ft high cliff by tracked vehicle, the wreck has been left to the elements and now lies scattered on the seabed, her bow just visible at low water and disguised by kelp. Inflatables beware! Diving depth is only 8m and is a superb site for training or club diving.

The *Fred Everard* was built by the Grangemouth Dockyard Co in 1958. Dimensions of the ship were 241ft long by 38ft beam.

The electronic navigator position for this wreck is 54 24 17N 00 28 76W. (Note the use of decimals of a minute and not seconds!) IT IS DANGEROUS TO APPROACH THIS WRECK FOR THE FIRST TIME OTHER THAN AT LOW WATER.

87 Zanetta. The cargo steamer *Zanetta* of 1334 tons, dragged her anchor during a heavy north easterly gale and drove ashore at South Cheek Robin Hood's Bay on November 13 1901. She was in ballast at the time on route from the Tyne to London.

Built by the Palmers Company in 1878, the *Zanetta* was owned by J Fenwick and Co of Newcastle and measured 242ft by 33ft by 20ft. C 2cy.

88 Kaiser. The 816 ton steamer *Kaiser,* a regular trader between Hartlepool and Hamburg, ran ashore at Blea Wyke, South of Ravenscar on July 25 1904, alongside a rocky scar and the crew had no difficulty in ferrying the passengers to safety. She was a regular trader between Hartlepool, Hamburg and Gothenburg, and owned by the West Hartlepool Steam

They say there was a rich jam harvest from the fruit cargo of the Kaiser. *(Site 88)*

Navigation Company, was carrying a mixed cargo including ironmongery, pianos, strawberries and fruit. She went ashore in a thick fog at her full speed of 11 knots after hearing the sound of her own fog signal echoing off nearby cliffs. There remains a rumour that, following the washing ashore of her fruit cargo, the aroma from jam-pans hung heavily in the air around Robin Hood's Bay!

To dive the scattered remains of the *Kaiser* approach Blea Wyke scar from the seaward at low water spring tide and dive 30m to the southward side. You will find the wreck in 5-8m of water and encounter the long propeller shaft lying parallel to the scar. To the seaward side of the wreckage you will find some of the tallest kelp to be found in the area among the maze of rocky gullies.

Details of the ship: Built 1880 by William Gray of Hartlepool. Engines by Richardson, Hartlepool.

An ordnance survey map co-ordinate thought to be very accurate is O.S. 015N 992E.

89 Puritan. On May 4 1903, a ship's siren was heard in Robin Hood's Bay early in the morning. There was a dense fog hanging over the area and the *Puritan,* laden with fish from an Icelandic trip, ran onto the rocks just north of Blea Wyke Point (pronounced locally "Blue-wick").

The impact pierced her sides and knocked off the blades of her propeller and she settled quickly to become a total loss. The crew of twelve took to the boats and were later picked up by a Scarborough trawler on its way to harbour.

The significant clue to the identity of this wreck is the propeller and this can still be seen today as by a strange coincidence the shattered *Fred*

The Grimsby trawler Premier *wrecked south of Ravenscar in 1923. (Site 90)*

Everard wreck (Site 86) partially covers it. To find the *Puritan* swim due north from the *Fred Everard's* collapsed stern. It is a mere ten metres away.

90 Premier. The Grimsby steam trawler *Premier* was wrecked south of Ravenscar at 8.15am on February 10 1923. Attempts to salvage the trawler failed and she was pounded to pieces in heavy seas. Robin Hood's Bay lifeboat saved the nine crew from the vessel. Amazingly some scant remains of the trawler remain, and the ship's boiler breaks surface just 100m south of the "Water Splash", a narrow but distinct waterfall below Beast Cliff.

91 Ella Sayer. The 1093 ton iron schooner, *Ella Sayer* ran ashore at Hayburn Wyke, north of Scarborough, just after midnight on August 31 1897. From the depositions of the crew the vessel was carrying a cargo of 2100 tons of pit props from Kotka, Finland, to Hull, when due to navigational error, the ship drove hard at 8 knots onto the rocky shore to the north of Hayburn Wyke. The master had underestimated the progress of the vessel, the patent log giving an erroneous reading and, after several alterations to avoid fishing vessels in the area, the ship wandered into a dangerous westerly course. The crew had been unable to see Whitby Light, and because of haze and rain showers, the stranding was sudden and unexpected. In those days ships were expected to keep strict records of the use of the log and the sounding lead and employ look-outs forward. Investigations following strandings came down heavily on any short comings in navigational procedures. Attempts to salvage her failed, and the scattered remains lie festooned in a rich carpet of fine purple weed.

Built by Doxford and Sons in 1883 for the Fisher Renwick Company of Newcastle, the *Ella Sayer* was 238ft by 37ft by 16.7ft and was powered by compound engines. The position of the wreck is under the highest point of the cliffs at 53 22 25N 00 27 00W in 5-8m.

Offshore sites

Moving offshore and into the wrecks off South Cheek one is immediately aware of the close proximity of wrecks in this area – and new ones are found here almost every year. However, the sea bed can be very deceptive and large sand peaks have convinced several divers of "finding" a wreck on their echo sounder, and subsequently wasting a dive!

Many of the wrecks here are victims of WW1 submarine ambushes on the vulnerable merchant convoy traffic which passed through a buoyed channel swept clear of mines. This was a favourite haunt of the U-boat commanders.

The sea bed dips steeply from the shore at Ravenscar and within half a mile from shore is over 30m, so the wreck diving is for advanced groups only. These are hard boat dives, from Whitby or Scarborough.

IN SEARCH OF THE UNKNOWN

Many of the wrecks in this area have defied attempts to identify them, and similarly, there are records of vessels lost in the vicinity which have never been found. Where possible we have suggested or linked unknown wrecks with charted or reported sea bed obstructions, and for this reason have included as much mechanical detail of wrecks as possible, in order to assist the growing band of wreck detectives. For example, boiler details are of great use in narrowing down a wreck's identity if the furnace details can be obtained, and a string line across the beam or diameters of cylinder heads can assist.

92 Aigburth. The new steamship *Aigburth* was torpedoed by a German submarine and reported sunk on December 5 1917, just 2 miles off South Cheek, Robin Hood's Bay. The wrecks in this location are very close together and identification is difficult so the dimensions and details are an obvious guide to divers wishing to identify this wreck. The ship was built by John Fullerton & Co of Paisley in 1917 and was of the engines-aft type of steamer of 824 tons gross, 195ft by 31ft by 12ft and having triple expansion engines T.3cy 15.25, 41-30 by Ross and Duncan Glasgow. Boiler: 1SB 3PF. Armed for defence.

93 Suntrap. The 1353 ton collier *Suntrap*, ex *Sherwood* was on route with coal from Newcastle to London when torpedoed and sunk by German submarine on November 19 1917. Diver reports indicate that the wreck is in position 54 25 18N 00 25 45W, lying on its starboard side and collapsed on the seabed in a general depth of 45m and standing up just 3m. Dimensions of the ship were 230ft long by 36ft beam, engines by North Eastern Marine Engineering Company, T.3cy 19, 31 and 51-36. Boiler: 1SB 4CF. Built in 1904 by Sunderland Shipbuilding Co.

An interesting tale of the *Suntrap* relates its value in those bygone times.

She was bought by France Fenwick, on the builder's stocks for just £16,850 and sold twelve years later in 1916 to the Gas, Light and Coke Company for £50,000, when she was renamed.

94 Sparrow. The *Sparrow* ex *Josephine I,* was a 266 ton steam trawler commissioned by the Admiralty for war service and built in 1908 by the Goole Shipbuilding Company. Dimensions of the ship were 130ft long by 23ft beam. Reports of a dive on a small armed trawler in Robin Hood's Bay, in 48m, have been received but the position could not be verified.

95 Oakwell. The Stockton registered 248 ton *Oakwell* was an aft engined coaster 125ft long and 22ft beam, and reported mined on March 23 1917 when off Robin Hood's Bay.

Details of the ship were: Builder Craig Taylor, Stockton 1887. Engines: 2 cylinder compound, 18 x 36-24 and boilers 1SB 2PF. The wreck has been positively identified by its bell, but the diivers reporting the find failed to record the position!

96 Naparima. The well-decked steamer *Naparima,* registered in Sweden, 1685 gross tons, was built in 1890 by the Edwards Ship Building Company of Newcastle and lost to torpedo attack on May 10 1918 off Blea Wyke, Ravenscar. Local fishermen bravely risked their lives to rescue the crew, putting off in cobles to guide the ship's boat containing 19 crew to safety in the darkness.

Details of the ship: Builder, Edwards and Co of Newcastle. Dimensions: 260ft long by 36ft beam. Engines North Eastern Marine Engineering Company: T.3cy, 20, 32.5 and 53-36. Boilers: 2SB 6PF.

97 Herdis. The British collier *Herdis*, 1157 tons, and carrying 1600 tons of coal, was torpedoed and sunk by *UB-40* on June 29 1918, when almost abreast of Scarborough. 20 minutes later, the *Florentia*, travelling in the same convoy, suffered the same fate. Diving surveys indicate that this may be the wreck in position 54 24 18N 00 25 42W, laid on its starboard side, although the position at the time of loss was thought to be 54 24 30N 00 25 00W.

Details of the ship: Builder: Trondheim Mek Verksted, 1911. Engines T.3cy 16, 25.5 and 44-30 inches. Registered in Hull. Dimensions 228ft long by 35ft beam.

98 Florentia. Another collier, the 3688 ton *Florentia,* armed for defence, was torpedoed and sunk by German submarine *UB-88* on June 29 1918, while carrying 5800 tons of coal, just 2 miles off Robin Hood's Bay. Diving reports indicate a wreck of similar dimensions in 54 24 30N 00 26 27W but the identity is not confirmed.

Built by the Tyne Iron Shipbuilding Company in 1912, the ship was 348ft long by 50ft beam and featured longitudinal framing. Engines: T.3cy, 24, 40, 66-45 by Dickenson of Glasgow, Boilers: 2SB 4PF.

99 Gimle. The 1131 ton Norwegian collier *Gimle,* was sunk in position 54 24 30N 00 24 31W off Ravenscar. The vessel has been identified from embossing on the ship's wheel, and is intact on the seabed at 48m standing 6m high. Dimensions of the ship: 229ft long by 36ft beam and she was built by Laxevaags Maskin and Jernskibs in 1904.

100 Castleford. The British steamer *Castleford* ex *Chateway*, 1741 gross tons, was torpedoed and sunk by German submarine *UC-40* on March 14 1918, and sank in three minutes off Robin Hood's Bay. Position reports conflict and a recent diver report gives a probable location at 54 25 37N 00 23 00W where there is an upturned wreck in 48m, collapsed at the stern and holed on the starboard side.

Dimensions of the ship were 255ft long by 37ft beam. Built by Short Bros of Sunderland in 1897. Engines by Allen and Co Sunderland T.3cy 19, 31 and 51-36. Boiler: 1SB 4PF.

101 Lerwick. The cruiser stern of the 5626 ton *Lerwick* and its massive size indicate that this is the wreck lying on its starboard side in location 54 26 00N 00 22 28W, off Robin Hood's Bay. The *Lerwick* was bombed and sunk on January 13 1942 during WW2. Built in 1938 by J L Thompson she was 409ft long by 58ft beam. Engines by Clark of Sunderland. T.3cy 22, 37.5, 63-45, boilers 3SB 9CF (superheated).

Unknown. Unknown wrecks abound in the maritime graveyard at Robin Hood's Bay. A favourite ambush point for WW1 U-Boats was from under the dark, high cliffs of Ravenscar which formed an ideal blind. Local legends describe U-Boats lurking in the shallows and visible from the high cliff and of errant torpedoes ending up on the beach!
    Position 54 26 00N 00 21 56W describes yet another sonar survey contact, but beware the seabed "sand waves" in this area which give alarming peaks on an echo sounder and have caused to our knowledge, at least one "Desert Dive".

HAYBURN WYKE TO SCARBOROUGH

Off Hayburn Wyke and towards Scarborough, are a string of wrecks between 30 and 50m available and accessible by boat from Scarborough.

102 Wallsend. The 2697 ton *Wallsend,* was torpedoed and sank in just 20 minutes after attack by *UB-104* on August 14 1918, when just half a mile off the coast south of Ravenscar. The ship was carrying 3850 tons of coal. Today the Wallsend lies in 27m of water, bows upside down, with the stern on its port side, and its gun lying off the stern on the sea bed. Being under the high cliffs at this point the *Wallsend* makes a good site in conditions of strong offshore winds when diving further off is impossible. The exact position is 54 22 55N 00 26 37W.
    Details of the ship: Builder Wood Skinner and Co Newcastle, 1917. Engines North Eastern Marine Engineering Company T.3cy 22.5, 37 and 61-42. Boilers: 2SB 8CF. Armed for defence. Dimensions of the ship: 321ft long by 43ft beam.

103 Lady Helen. The 811 ton collier *Lady Helen* was built by S P Austin in 1904 for the Marquis of Londonderry's Seaham Colliery operation. She was a fine vessel regularly using the east coast swept channel and was torpedoed and sunk by German submarine on October 27 1917, when in ballast, just over 1 mile from shore at Hayburn Wyke. She is upright on the seabed with damage to her port quarter, in 40m in position 54 22 49N 00 24 55W.
    Details of the ship: Engines T.3cy by North Eastern Marine Engineering Company 17, 28 and 46-30. Boiler: 1SB 3CF. Dimensions of the ship: 200ft long by 30ft beam.

104 Glow. The armed 1141 ton collier *Glow, ex Monkwood,* was torpedoed and sunk off South Cheek, Robin Hood's Bay by submarine on July 22 1917 when on passage from the Tyne to London in position 54 22 27N 00 23 48W, but we have no confirmation of this from divers. Dimensions of the ship were 265ft long by 40ft beam.

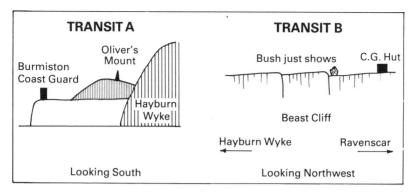

TRANSIT A

Oliver's Mount

Burmiston Coast Guard

Hayburn Wyke

Looking South

TRANSIT B

Bush just shows C.G. Hut

Beast Cliff

Hayburn Wyke   Ravenscar

Looking Northwest

Marks for Wallsend. (Site 102)

105 Constantia. The 772 ton *Constantia* lies in 42m 2 miles off Hayburn Wyke and is intact and on an even keel, rising to at least a depth of 38m. The Russian registered vessel was torpedoed and sunk by *UB-21* on May 8 1918 while carrying 717 tons of coal. The exact position of the wreck is 54 22 50N 00 23 26W.

Dimensions of the ship: 185ft long by 29ft beam. Builders: W. Rosenlew, Bjornborge, Finland 1890. Engines T.3cy 16, 26 and 43.

106 Glamorganbrook. The 805 ton steamer *Glamorganbrook* ex *Empire Worthtown*, sank in the early hours of October 11 1946 after springing a leak in her No 2 hold. Just refitted, this old veteran of the Dunkirk evacuations, developed a slight list to port shortly after leaving Blyth on route to the Isle of Wight with coal, and later when she radioed ". . .making water fast and proceeding full speed Robin Hood's Bay. . ." rescue services were alerted. Later the vessel reported that she was ". . .becoming unmanageable and heading for Scarborough. . ."

Local lifeboats were launched immediately and it was several hours before the survivors were found in the ship's lifeboat. *Glamorganbrook* had sunk just 30 minutes after the last distress call, and with the tragic loss of her captain, Eric Baker, who had given up his lifebelt to his wife, before giving orders to abandon ship.

The crew had only time to launch one boat and this was swept away from the ship with just two men aboard, the rest having to jump into the icy cold sea. The captain, a non-swimmer, was seen floating for a short while but disappeared before he could be rescued. The *Glamorganbrook* turned over within seven minutes and sank beneath the waves.

The *Glamorganbrook* had an interesting history, having been sunk at Dunkirk during war evacuations, salvaged by the German forces and after the war, taken over by the then Ministry of War Transport, along with 90 other captured ships, all renamed with the "Empire . . ." prefix. The ships were later offered for sale as prizes of war, and the *Worthtown* went to Messrs Comber Longstaff of London and later to the Williamstown Shipping Company.

Details of the vessel were dimensions 199ft long by 31ft beam. Triple expansion engine.

107 Southborough. The steel schooner *Southborough*, ex *Anerley*, 3709 tons gross, was carrying 5000 tons of iron ore when torpedoed and sunk by German submarine *UB-110* 4 to 5 miles from Ravenscar on July 16 1918. The probable location from recent diving information is 54 23 45N 00 23 12W, the wreck is upside down and iron ore spilled out onto the seabed in 46m.

Details of the ship: Builder: Sunderland Shipbuilding Co 1910. Port of Registration, Sydney, New South Wales. Engines: North Eastern Marine Engineering Company T.3cy 24.5, 40 and 66-45. Boilers: 2SB 6CF. Dimensions of the ship: 346ft long by 51ft beam.

108 SNA II. The 2294 ton French collier *SNA II*, ex *M E Harper* was reported lost in position 54 22 00N 00 22 30W when torpedoed and sunk by a submarine on June 6 1917. The exact location of the *SNA II* is not known but there are one or two wrecks close together here, one in position 54 22 16N 00 22 30W and the other, to the north in position 54 22 27N 00 22 42W. Diving depth is 46m to the sea bed but the wrecks stand over 4m high. One could be that of the *Novillo* (Site 109).

Details of the ship: Built by Great Lakes Engineering Works, Michigan, 1911. Engines: T.3cy 21, 34.5 and 57-42. Boilers: 2SB 4CF. Registered Le Havre. Owners: Societe Nationale D'Affretements, France. Dimensions of the *SNA II*: 247ft long by 33ft beam.

109 Novillo ex Amasis, a Danish collier of 2336 tons gross, was built by Hawthorn Leslie and Company in 1895, and torpedoed and sunk by German submarine off Hayburn Wyke on October 22 1917 while on route from the Tyne to Blaye.

Dimensions of the ship: 312ft long by 40ft beam and an approximate position is 54 23 00N 00 23 45W. Engines: T.3cy 22.5, 38 and 62.5-52. Boilers:2SB 6CF.

110 Balfron. A wreck suspected to be the *Balfron*, 362 tons gross, sunk by bombing on July 4 1914, lies in 42m at position 54 23 07N 00 21 12W. The ship caught fire as a result of the bombing and this would explain the absence of a deck on a wreck dived at this location.

Dimensions of the aft-engined *Balfron*: 141ft long by 24ft beam, built by Scott and Sons, Bowling. Engines were 2 Cylinder 16 and 24-24 by Fishers of Paisley, boiler 1SB 2PF.

111 Springhill. The 1507 ton *Springhill* was reported as mined off Cloughton Wyke on August 24 1917. Positively identified from boiler details, the *Springhill* lies collapsed on her port side in position 54 21 18N 00 23 10W, on a rocky seabed. The general depth of water is 38m here and the wreck stands some 4m high but is quite jumbled up.

Details of the ship: Builder: J C Crown, Sunderland 1904. Engines: North Eastern Marine Engineering Company T.3cy 19, 31 and 51. Boilers: 2SB 4PF. Dimensions: 253ft long by 36ft beam.

112 Sumus. The 223 ton *Sumus* is known locally as the "Slag Wreck", because of the presence of this cargo in and around the wreck. She was previously thought to have foundered off Gristhorpe where the bodies of four of her nine crew were found. Her position is 54 21 06N 00 22 35W, broken up, bows collapsed on the seabed and standing only 2.5m high on a rocky bottom in 40m, her cargo of 250 tons of rough slag scattered

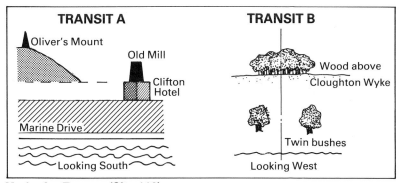

Marks for Taurus. (Site 113)

around. This old wreck, built in 1871, was owned by Hogg and Henderson of Middlesbrough. A local dive boat recently recovered the wrought iron anchor from this wreck and has found it still usable after nearly a century under the sea!

113 Taurus. This Norwegian steamer, 1238 tons, was torpedoed and sunk by *UB-80* on September 8 1918 in position 54 20 66N 00 22 75W just under 3.5 miles from Scarborough Castle.

Details of the ship: Builder: Campbeltown Shipbuilding Company 1902. Engines: Hutson and Sons, Glasgow. T.3cy 18, 27.5 and 45-33. Boiler: 1SB. Dimensions of the ship: 230ft long by 33ft beam and she lies in 36m, on an even keel.

114 Victoria. The 1620 ton Glasgow registered *Victoria,* was torpedoed and sunk by German submarine on April 29 1917, when 5 miles north-east of Scarborough.

Details of the ship: Built by Alexander Stephen of Glasgow in 1887. Engines: T.3cy 18, 29 and 46-39. 1DB 4CF. Dimensions of the ship: 260ft long by 37ft beam. There is a wreck in 46m of water at position 54 21 85N 00 20 64W which has a double ended boiler, and this may be the *Victoria.* The wreck is well broken up and stands on a rocky sea bed.

115 Elfrida. The 2624 ton collier *Elfrida* was mined 2 miles east-north-east of Scarborough on January 7 1915. Built by Wood Skinner in 1907, the ship

Elfrida, *mined off Scarborough in 1915. (Site 115)*

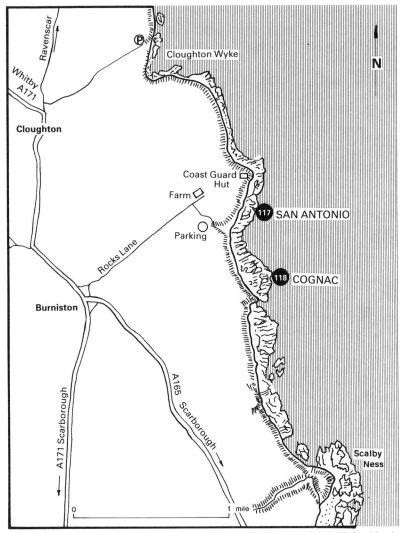

was 313ft long by 45ft beam. Engines: T.3cy 23, 37.5 and 61.5-39, by North Eastern Marine Engineering Company. Boilers: 2SB 6CF. The vessel has not been positively located but there is an unidentified wreck of this size in position 54 20 88N 00 20 51W.

116 Rikard Nordraak. The 1123 ton Norwegian collier *Rikard Nordraak* was taking coal from Sunderland to Rouen when torpedoed and sunk by German submarine on May 2 1917. The wreck now lies on an even keel in 48m, position 54 21 10N 00 19 17W, just under four-and-a-half miles from Scarborough Castle.

Dimensions of the ship were 231ft long by 34ft beam.

German submarine victim, Rikard Nordraak. *(Site 116)*

In between the offshore sites are two shore dives worthy of mention

117 San Antonio. The *San Antonio,* 1167 tons stranded in the centre of Burniston Bay just north of Scarborough on December 10 1900. The wreck is barely visible amongst the rocks and kelp below the low water mark but can be found and is a useful site for beginners in calm clear conditions. Access to the bay involves a half mile trek and the *San Antonio* is 150m towards the coastguard lookout from the bottom of the cliff steps.

118 Cognac. An alternative shore site, but a longer trek across rocks, is the wreck of the French barge *Cognac* at the south point of Burniston Bay. The *Cognac* went ashore in WW1 and parts of the dispersed wreck are still recognisable today in spite of the constant battering of the sea in this exposed position.

The wreck is just inside the Bay in Ordnance survey position O.S. 929N 031E.

SCARBOROUGH CASTLE TO CAYTON BAY

Wrecks in this patch vary in depth from 30 to 50m. The *Bur,* (Site 130) 3 miles south of Scarborough and 2 miles off Cayton Bay is highly recommended as a first dive in the area.

119 Phare. The armed British collier *Phare,* ex *Grovelea,* ex *Lady Furness,* of 1282 tons gross was a Stephenson Clarke collier, torpedoed and sunk by German submarine on October 31 1917, with the loss of 14 lives. No positive location has been established for this wreck but an approximate position is given 54 19 00N 00 23 00W. Hydrographic reports at the time of loss give the position between 2.5 and 3 miles north of Scarborough, between and inside "can buoy 'C' and can buoy 'S'". These were the swept channel markers in position during the war, and anyone who has a wartime chart of the area could put it to good use!

Details of the ship: Builders Blyth Ship Building Co, 1906. Engines: T.3cy 19, 31 and 51. Boiler: 1SB 4CF. Dimensions of the ship: 234ft long by 34ft beam and there should be a defence gun to help identification.

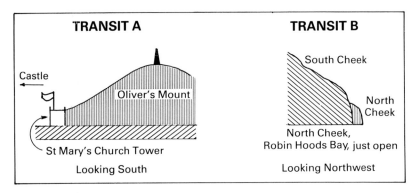

TRANSIT A	TRANSIT B

TRANSIT A

Castle ←

Oliver's Mount

St Mary's Church Tower

Looking South

TRANSIT B

South Cheek

North Cheek

North Cheek,
Robin Hoods Bay, just open

Looking Northwest

Marks for Madame Renée. (Site 120)

120 Madame Renee. The small aft-engined steamer, *Madame Renee*, ex *Thordis*, of 509 tons gross, was torpedoed and sunk by German submarine *UB-30* on August 10 1918, and settled on the seabed in the North Bay, Scarborough in 24m. While rumoured to have been carrying 500 tons of high grade copper pyrites, other sources point to a cargo of iron ore. The wreck lies partly buried on an even sandy bottom and is easy to navigate round. A good transit to the north is provided by North Cheek, Robin Hood's Bay, which just shows from behind the higher cliffs to the south. The position of the wreck is 54 18 33N 00 22 54W. Details of the ship: Builder Porsgrund Mek Verksted. Engines: C.2cy. Boiler: 1SB 2CF. Dimensions of the ship: 160ft long by 27ft beam by 11ft depth.

121 Sir Francis. The 1991 ton *Sir Francis* was a Cory collier sunk by torpedo on June 7 1917 and reported as lost 2 miles north-east of Scarborough.

The wreck has never been positively identified but may be one of several armed, unidentified wrecks in this area.

Built by S P Austin of Sunderland in 1910 her dimensions were 280ft by 40ft by 18ft. Engines: T.3cy 21, 34 and 56-39. Boilers: 2SB 6PF.

122 Sixty Six. This small steamer of 214 tons was well-known along the east coast. Built in Middlesbrough by Backhouse and Dixon in 1871, she was the sixty-sixth vessel to be launched at the yard and was so-named. The ship was owned by Cochrane and Company, Ormesby Ironworks, Middlesbrough when she was torpedoed 3 miles east of Scarborough on June 29 1918.

Sixty Six was regularly used for cargoes of Cochrane pipes to Amsterdam or Rotterdam, and would often call in to the Thames to pick up foundry sand on her return journey. In 1908 she grounded in the Tees entrance and stranded at Flamborough Head in 1916.

The ship was an aft engined single deck vessel of 214ft x 20ft and there is a wreck in this vicinity of similar size but very badly silted in a mud scour and hardly worth a dive. A reported position at the time of loss is in the area 54 18 00N 00 19 00W.

Details of the ship were: Engines: Compound 17.5 and 32 inches by Blair of Stockton. Boiler: 1SB 2PF. Armed for defence.

123 Elterwater. Mined 3 miles Cast of Scarborough, on December 16 1914 the 1228 ton collier *Elterwater,* laden with coal from the Tyne sank within three minutes, giving the crew no time to launch the boats. Twelve of the eighteen crew were picked up by the steamer *City of Newcastle* which was abreast of the *Elterwater* at the time, but the remaining six were lost.

Built by the Blyth Shipbuilding Company in 1907 the ship was 235ft long by 33.5ft beam. Engines: T.3cy 19, 31 and 51-36. By North Eastern Marine Engineering Company. Boiler: 1SB 4CF. No definite position has been recorded for this wreck.

124 Laconia. This 195 ton steam trawler *Laconia* sank 3 miles east-north-east of Scarborough Castle following a collision with the SS *Loch Lomond* on May 17 1911. It is believed to lie in position 54 20 52N 00 20 18W but this has not been confirmed.

125 Victo. (Stern) The *Victo* was a Norwegian merchant vessel bombed and broken in two by a German aircraft on the evening of November 8 1941.

The stern of the wreck, known locally as the "Wheel Wreck", is a favourite among local divers, lying just over two miles from Scarborough Castle in 30m of water. The *Victo* has been identified from various observations, mainly the existence of heavy copper degaussing cable, fitted to ships of WW2 as a counter-measure against magnetic mines.

The stern of the 3655 ton ship is impressive and still relatively intact with her stern gun pointing aft from the top of her poop deck, the wreck lying on her starboard side. An energetic swim along the starboard rail and across to midships along the propeller shaft, locates the massive bridge deck and engines and it is here that the vessel is abruptly severed. A magnificent sight in summer is the dense array of plumose anemones, festooning the inside of the bridge structure.

Position for the stern of the *Victo* is 54 16 22N 00 19 03W exact.

126 Victo (Bow). The bows of the *Victo* are well separated from the stern and were discovered by local divers well after the location of the stern lying in deep water in position 54 19 58N 00 17 47W exact.

Details of the ship: Builder R Thompson and Sons, Sunderland 1906. Registration: Oslo Engines T.3cy 25, 41 and 67-45. Original dimensions of the ship: 347ft long by 51ft beam.

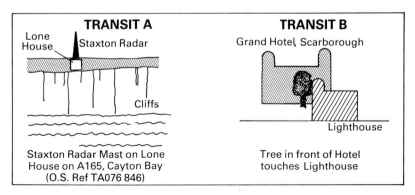

TRANSIT A	TRANSIT B
Lone House — Staxton Radar	Grand Hotel, Scarborough
Cliffs	Lighthouse
Staxton Radar Mast on Lone House on A165, Cayton Bay (O.S. Ref TA076 846)	Tree in front of Hotel touches Lighthouse

Marks for Victo. (Site 126)

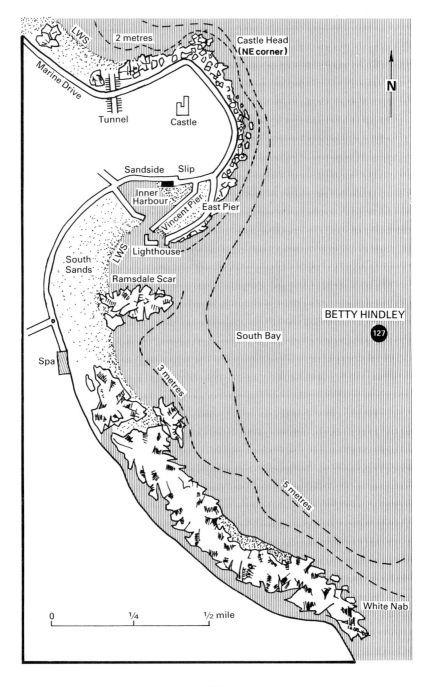

The Betty Hindley, *caught by a mine after WW2 in 1947. (Site 127)*

127 Betty Hindley. The 1771 ton Stephenson Clarke collier *Betty Hindley* was the second ship of the name to be lost as a result of WW2 activities. The first fell victim to the notorious Haisborough Sands off Norfolk while in convoy in 1941, and although the second vessel of the name survived the war, she became victim of an unswept mine in the early hours of October 7 1947, when just three miles off Scarborough. The townsfolk were rudely awakened by the shock of the explosion and local fishing boats raced to the scene in an attempt to tow the badly damaged vessel ashore. The collier did not survive and grounded in 12m, breaking her back in the process.

The wreck became well-known for its position, three-quarters of a mile from Scarborough lighthouse, the ship's masts being clearly visible. It was not until 1956 that Trinity House dispersed the vessel and removed the wreck buoy.

The wreck is now badly silted and slowly sinking into the sandy bottom. Dispersal operations left the wreck in two small parts, the bow section and the aft engine room, still an interesting training dive in conditions of clear visibility on neap tides.

The position of the wreck is 54 16 32N 00 21 58W. Difficult to locate in sandy scour.

128 Lady Ann. Owned by Lambton and Hetton Collieries, and built by S P Austin in 1882, the *Lady Ann,* of Sunderland, was one of the first victims of unrestricted submarine warfare, when merchant ships were attacked without prior warning. This led to defensive armament being fitted to many vessels. Eleven crew, including the master, were lost when the vessel was torn in two by a torpedo from a German submarine less than 3 miles from Scarborough Castle on February 16 1917.

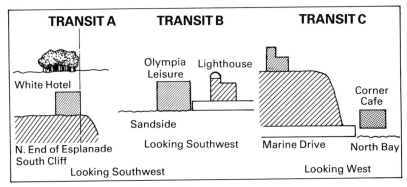

Marks for Lady Anne. (Site 128)

Today the ship lies on a sand and mud bottom, in barely 30m of water, with her upturned bow section pointing towards her stern and just abeam of the upright compound engines. The stern section is reasonably intact and straightforward to navigate by, but being close to the seabed, is better dived on neap tides when the bottom is less turbid. The remains of the massive emergency wheel are preserved at Scarborough Sub Aqua Club. Details of the ship: Engines by North Eastern Marine Engineering Company. Boiler: 1SB renewed 1906. Dimensions of the ship: 225ft long by 33ft beam, 1016 gross tons. The confirmed position for the *Lady Ann* is 54 16 56N 00 18 43W.

129 Hornsund. The 3646 ton *Hornsund* lies in just 25m of water on a sandy bottom two and a half miles east-south-east of Scarborough Harbour, and was torpedoed and sunk by German submarine on September 23 1917. A former German owned vessel captured and requisitioned as a collier by the Admiralty, the *Hornsund* is a good dive at slack water during neap tides, when bottom sediment is less disturbed. Slack here is about 2 hours after shore time but allow plenty of time to anchor in as the wreck is in three parts, due to silting. The engine stands alone, the plates having collapsed from around it. This makes a good training dive. Details: Built in Germany in 1913. Engines T.3y 27, 42.5 and 68.5-43. Dimensions of the ship: 376ft long by 51ft beam. Position of the wreck is 54 16 31N 00 18 50W.

130 Bur. This wreck is well worth a visit because of its condition – perfectly upright on the sea-bed, with only its stern damaged where it was devastated by torpedo attack on November 2 1917. The *Bur*, formerly the A. J. Hocken was a Swedish vessel of 1806 gross tons and was carrying a general cargo and timber when lost. Much of the timber slats forming her cargo are still visible in the forward holds. The wreck is in 30m rising to 25m on the deck, and is relatively easy to find in 54 16 27N 00 18 17W.

An interesting original plan of the ship is displayed at Scarborough Sub-Aqua Club and a sight of this would be very useful to both novice and seasoned divers.

Dimensions of the ship were 270ft long by 41ft beam by 18.6ft depth. Built by Grangemouth and Greenock Dockyard in 1901. Engines T.3cy 20, 32.5 and 53-36 by S H Morton of Leith. Boilers: 2SB 4CF.

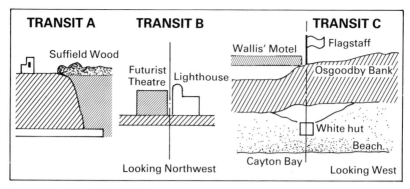

Marks for Bur. (Site 130)

131 Norhilda. A 1175 ton collier, built by Swan, Hunter and Wigham Richardson, the *Norhilda* was a fine three island vessel, torpedoed and sunk by German submarine on August 21 1917.

Today she stands upright on the sea-bed, with her high poop deck and bows intact, midships collapsed, and relatively easy to navigate round. The *Norhilda* can be found in 54 16 21N 00 17 10W, in 36m standing 6m high. This is a highly recommended dive as the vessel is still reasonably intact and stands clear of the bottom.

Dimensions of the ship: 230ft long by 37ft beam.

132 Leersum. The Amsterdam registered steamer *Leersum,* 1455 gross tons ran into the Scarborough minefield on December 16 1914, with the loss of 10 of her crew. The *Leersum,* built in 1898 by the Sunderland Ship Building Company, was en route from Rotterdam to Newcastle with a general cargo. Dimensions of the ship were 240ft long by 37ft beam. The wreck has not been positively identified but may be in position 54 16 07N 00 14 37W and known locally as the "Mast Wreck" because of the spectacular feature of the mizzen mast rising over 10m from the wreck.

Details of the ship: Built by Sunderland Shipbuilding Co 1898. Engines: T.3cy 18.5, 30 and 49-33 by McColl & Pollock, Sunderland. Boilers: 2SB 4PF. Dimensions of the ship were 240ft long by 37ft beam.

The Norhilda, *torpedoed in 1917, is a recommended dive. (Site 131)*

133 Leander. The 2968 ton Norwegian collier, *Leander* was torpedoed and sunk off Scarborough while on passage from Hartlepool to Savona by German submarine on October 20 1917.

Details of the ship: Built in 1892 by the Wallsend Slipway Company. The dimensions of the ship: 315ft long by 40.5ft beam.

General depth of water here is 48m and the wreck stands up 8m, with the stern lying over to starboard and the bow and midships twisted to port. The position of this wreck is 54 16 48N 00 14 32W.

Engines: T.3cy 23, 38 and 61.

134 Linaria. The 3081 ton Stag Line steamer *Linaria,* was mined 2.5 miles north-east of Filey on Boxing Day, December 26, 1914, so becoming another victim of the Scarborough minefield.

Built by the W Dobson Shipbuilding Company of Newcastle in 1911 the *Linaria* was 331ft long by 48ft beam. Engines: T.3cy 22.5, 36.5 and 62-42 by the North Eastern Marine Engineering Company.

135 Vaaren. She was a 1090 ton Norwegian collier, lost in the Scarborough minefield on December 16 1914 when on passage from Newcastle to Palermo with coal. There is a wreck of her approximate size in 54 16 24N 00 14 00W lying on its port side in 45m. Details of the ship: Built 1914 by Bergen Mek Verksted. Port of Registration: Bergen. Dimensions 226ft long by 37ft beam. Engine: T.3cy 17, 26 and 46-30.

WRECKS WITHOUT KNOWN LOCATIONS

Beaumanoir. The 2477 ton *Beaumanoir* was bombed by enemy aircraft off Robin Hood's Bay on June 2 1941. No positive location is given for this wreck but official sources recorded the loss as 180 degrees, 8 cables from No. 19 Buoy in Robin Hood's Bay. These were the buoys marking the safe navigational channels during the war, so for those with a war-time chart, tally-ho!

Details of the *Beaumanoir:* Built in 1920 by Murdock, Murray and Co, Port Glasgow for the Companie Nantaise des Chargeurs de l'Ouest. Dimensions: Single deck, 290ft by 44ft by 21ft. Registered Nantes. Boilers: 2SB 6CF. Engines: T.3cy 22, 36 and 59-22 by J G Kincaird.

Cap Palos. The *Cap Palos,* was a magnificent new five-masted schooner completed in 1919 as part of the post war effort to replace lost shipping tonnage. She was lost while on tow for engine repairs, having previously survived almost a year stranded on rocks in Robin Hood's Bay, a real testimony to the worth of her builders.

Parting company with her tugs in a vicious south-west gale, the Whitby lifeboat rescued the salvage crew, and was herself badly damaged while doing so. The *Cap Palos* eventually turned turtle and was found drifting upside down by a passing trawler, who attempted to tow the hulk ashore. She broke in half during the tow and the stern part was beached at Cornelian Bay in 1921. Of the remaining bow section nothing has been found. This remains a mystery wreck, as soundings indicate no targets at the charted position of 54 20 00N 00 17 45W.

Deptford. The 1208 ton Deptford, a Cory collier, built by the Blyth Shipbuilding Company, was mined 3 to 4 miles off Scarborough on February 24 1915, whilst on passage from Granton to Chatham with coal. No positive location has been recorded for this wreck. Other details: Built 1912. Engines: T.3cy by Clark of Sunderland, 19, 31 and 51-36. Boiler: 1SB 4PF.

Battersea. Victim of a collision off Scarborough, this 860 ton collier sank on February 8 1918. The wreck of the *Battersea* has never been positively located.
   Built by W Dobson of Newcastle in 1902, the ship was 215ft long by 32ft beam. Engines T.3cy 16.5, 27 and 44-30 by North Eastern Marine Engineering Company. 1SB 3PF.

Area Information and Services

Admiralty Charts. River Tees to Flamborough Head Chart No 1200, or Tees to Scarborough No 134.
Ordnance Survey. One inch series, Sheet 93.
Local Weather. Marinecall Area 3 North East Tel 0898-500 453.
Shipping Forecast. Tyne or Humber.
Coastguard. Bridlington Marine Rescue Co-Ordinating Centre 0262-672317. Scarborough (Sector Office) 0723-372323.
Weather Bulletin from HM Coastguard on VHF marine radio. Begin at 0340 hours then 4 hourly. Gale and small craft warnings issued on receipt from the Meteorological Office, repeated at 2 hourly intervals.
BS-AC. Scarborough Branch No 83. Meetings Wednesdays 9.00pm. 25 St Mary's Street. Tel 0723-372036.
Tourist Information. Scarborough Information Office 0642-471921.
Air Supplies/Diving Equipment. Sirocco/Seasports 34 Belle Vue Street Scarborough, Tel 0723-367564. Scarborough Sub-Aqua Club by arrangement, Tel 0723-372036.
Marine Engineers and Chandlers. Scarborough Marine Engineers 36 Sand Side, Scarborough, Tel 0723-375199. Northern Marine Electrics, Quay St Scarborough, Tel 0723-354480.
Outboard Repairs and Service. Yorkshire Boat Centre, Riggs Head Nr Scarborough, Tel 0723-863205. Johnson/Evinrude only.
AA 24 hour service. Middlesbrough, Tel 0642-246832 or Hull, Tel 0482-285580.
Accommodation. Information Centre, Tel 0723-372261. Caravan/Camp Sites Scarborough Borough Council, Tel 0723-366212. P Bayes, Scalby Close, Tel 0723-365908, between Scarborough and Burniston.
Launching. Robin Hood's Bay – No vehicular or launch access to day visitors due to heavy tourist pressure. Definitely not the place to take your 6 metre boat unannounced! Contact Steve and Jean Mellalieu who run the Marine Activities centre and accommodate divers and their wet gear, catering for family parties of up to 30, with a maximum of 12 divers. In the event of bad weather, other outdoor pursuits are available. BS-AC and MCS courses are run here every year. Tel 0947-880496.
Scarborough – Launching at Scarborough requires prior arrangement with the Harbour Authority. Telephone or write to the Harbour Master in advance, at the Harbour Office, West Pier, Scarborough, Tel 0723-373530.

Area 4:
Filey Brigg

This area starts at 54 16 00N and stretches south to latitude 54 11 45N, Gristhorpe to Reighton. In the middle of this stretch of coast, and indeed at the mid-point of the Yorkshire coast, is the holiday town of Filey, chiefly notable for a reef of calcareous grit which protrudes for over half a mile out to sea. Thought to be the work of the devil, this reef, known as Filey Brigg – a corruption of Bridge – has claimed the lives of many seamen, together with their ships. The Brigg is at the northern end of Filey Bay, and forms a breakwater which protects the town of Filey from the worst of the northerly gales.

It is thought that during the Roman period there may have been a harbour here; it is known that the Roman invaders did have a harbour somewhere on the Yorkshire coast, known as *Portus Felix,* which means *Peaceful Place.* It is known too that the Romans did use Filey, for they built a signal station as part of their early-warning system against Viking attacks on Carr Naze, the cliff overlooking the Brigg. The main reason for thinking that there was once a harbour here is that there is on the inside of the Brigg a reef of rocks that runs into the Bay, almost at right angles to the Brigg, and it does not look like a natural feature. Known as the Spittals, this reef only shows at low water, and even then, most of it remains covered. Some years ago, local BS-AC clubs mounted a mass dive in the area to try and find evidence of the Roman harbour, but on the appointed day, visibility was bad, and the search was inconclusive. This was not the first such search; a hard-hat diver had been employed to check the Spittals in the mid 1800's, but he found nothing either. In those days, the confident Victorians had no doubts however; they referred to the spot as The Roman Harbour, and at one time, the Filey Harbour Company was set up to rebuild a commercial harbour here. It eventually folded without laying a stone, and the local fishing cobles continued to operate from the Coble Landing, a concreted area at the foot of the cliffs where the boats were drawn up on wheels, using a team of horses. Today's coble men operate in exactly the same way, except that the horses have been replaced by ancient farm tractors. It looks quaint and picturesque, but nonetheless it is a thriving industry, and works very efficiently. The Coble Landing is in many ways the focal point of the town, and is very popular with tourists. The local lifeboat station is here, together with cafés, a bar and carpark.

The town of Filey offers no special facilities for divers; though the East Yorkshire Branch BS-AC meets and has its compressor here, many of the members live elsewhere, and their facilities can only be used by prior arrangement.

The coast to the north of Filey Brigg consists of rugged cliffs of 150ft or so, which drop sheer into the sea in places. There are rocky beaches, and offshore rocks, and generally the coast is deserted; few holidaymakers ever

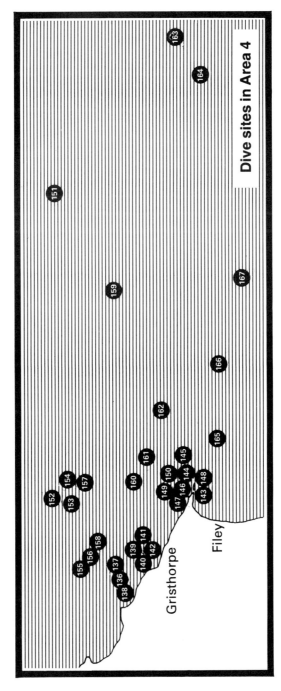

Dive sites in Area 4

visit the rocky beaches, and commercial shipping gives the area a wide berth. The only visitors to the area are local lobster and crab fishermen, together with the odd angling boat, and of course, dive boats.

There is no satisfactory access to this area by land for the diver. South of Filey Brigg is a complete contrast; there are sandy beaches and low clay cliffs which sweep round for several miles until they run into the chalk cliffs where the Yorkshire Wolds meet the sea at Bempton. Diving inshore in Filey Bay is a pointless exercise, though offshore there are many interesting wreck sites, mainly U-boat victims of WW1.

Diving the Filey area is straightforward, with few choices; the only shore diving that can be worthy of consideration is on Filey Brigg. This is no easy task, for it entails a long and difficult walk down Carr Naze from the conveniently situated North Cliff Country Car Park. As with any promontory, tidal movements here can be vicious, and a very strong current sweeps out to sea on the north side of the Brigg at some stages of tide. A better bet by far is to boat-dive the Brigg; launching can be effected by visiting boats at the Coble Landing, which is controlled by the Scarborough Harbourmaster. Engines must not exceed 12½hp however, and a fee is payable to the attendant on duty. It should be noted that there can be dangerous overfalls off the end of the Brigg when the water in the Bay is quite smooth, so small craft should take extreme care. It is not unusual for divers from Scarborough to travel by boat as far as Filey Brigg, while bound for Flamborough, and turn back because of these overfalls, which have in the past, swamped small boats. The Filey cobles do take angling parties to sea during the summer, and one skipper regularly takes diving parties too. Since he is a very experienced diver, this could well be the best way for the visiting diver to get to know the Filey area wrecks. (see Area Information)

Filey is seven miles south of Scarborough on the A165 to Hull; it is a most attractive little town, an ideal place to leave the family while the diver goes off to do his thing!

The keelboat Sincere, *wrecked at Yons Nab shows the nature of the rocky shore. She is not a dive site.*

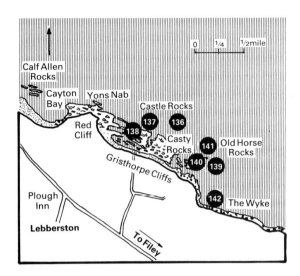

Shore Diving Sites
(all are best approached by boat however)

136 Castle and Casty Rocks. At the foot of Gristhorpe Cliffs, between Yons Nab in the north and Gristhorpe Wyke in the south, are a series of offshore reefs which make interesting diving when the weather is calm. This is lobster country, with huge tangles of kelp crowning large boulders, with sandy gullies between. The main two reefs are Casty Rocks, the southern-most, and Castle Rocks which is smaller. Behind them lie a whole group of rocks and gullies with strange names like Pudding Hole, Knotty Binks and Great Gully. At the foot of the cliffs are Gristhorpe Sands, which are so difficult to reach that holiday-makers don't bother, and it can be deserted even on a hot summer's day. The diver could spend months exploring this area. At low water, some of it dries out, but even then there are numerous gullies well worth exploring, for numerous sailing ships have come to grief here over the centuries, and they must have left some trace. In any case, the underwater scenery here is very pleasant, and the area is well worth a dive, probably after a deep dive offshore, for it is shallow here.

North of Castle Rocks are the Jenny Riby rocks, which continue on and off up to Yons Nab, the south point of Cayton Bay. Anyone wishing to explore this area would do well to get hold of the old 25" to the mile OS map of Yorkshire (North Riding) sheet XCIV. 11.

It is well worth checking out on foot at low water, for parts of the remains of the *Salient* (Site 138), *Lonicera* Lonicera (Site 137) and *Sincere* can be seen then.

Access to this area is best by boat from Scarborough, though it is possible to descend the cliffs by a mud path towards the north end of Gristhorpe Bay after leaving the A165 at Gristhorpe and driving to the cliff top via Stonepit Lane, alongside the Blue Dolphin Holiday Village.

137 Lonicera. This small Banff drifter, 82ft long and 74 tons, was built in 1911 by Chambers of Lowestoft as the *Lily Jane*. She was renamed

Lonicera, and was owned by S. Paterson of Macduff when she ran ashore in fog on the Castle Rocks, Gristhorpe on September 28, 1933. Her scant remains can be seen in a gully near the seaward side of the reef; her boiler shows on big tides, but the engines are always submerged, hard up against the outer edge of the reef. It is not worth making a particular effort to visit the *Lonicera,* but those diving this area might be interested to know of her existence.

Another fishing vessel, the Scarborough owned *Sincere* came to grief here in May of 1968; she came over the top of the reef in bad weather and got almost to the foot of the cliff at Yons Nab before she grounded. The diesel engine and other parts of her machinery are still there. This is not a dive, but divers in the area will doubtless wonder what she was.

138 Salient. This 1432 ton steamer was built by Bartram, Haswell & Co in 1879 for James Westoll of Sunderland. She was 250ft long with a beam of 34ft and a depth of 18ft, and had 140hp compound engines. During a voyage from Rotterdam to Sunderland in ballast, her shaft broke during heavy weather while off Robin Hood's Bay on March 8, 1891. *Salient* was schooner rigged, so she set sail, and headed for the safety of Bridlington Bay, running before the wind. She later accepted a tow from the steamship *Walker,* but the tow parted off Scarborough, and *Salient* proved to be unmanagable. She finally came ashore on March 9, two hours before low water, during a heavy snowstorm. The crew were able to board their own boats in the lee of the wreck, and got ashore safely. *Salient* was not insured. The wreck was subsequently salvaged by Crawford of Scarborough, who carried out the work from the shore, having a dynamite store built half way up the cliff. There is still much to see however; at low water, it is possible to walk to within a few feet of the boiler, which is on the Castle Rocks, Gristhorpe. The bottom plates are there too, and the ship's rudder lies just a few yards away. It is an interesting area to snorkel dive over at high water, but naturally, great care must be taken if a boat is brought in among the reefs. It is possible, though very difficult, to snorkel dive this area from the shore.

Salient, a steamer, whose schooner rigg failed to save her after a shaft broke. (Site 138)

139 Volunteer. Built by Morton & Co at Leith in 1861, this 607 ton brig-rigged iron screw-steamer was owned by Donald McGregor of Leith, and commanded by John Cairns. She was 208ft long with a beam of 25ft and a depth of 14ft, and had steam machinery which developed 120hp. She sailed from Leith on February 1, 1865, with a general cargo for Rotterdam, and at 01.00 the following morning was off the Yorkshire coast, making 8 knots under steam, with her foresail set. At 02.45, the lookout reported broken water off the starboard bow, and the ship struck with great force on a hidden reef almost as he spoke. Water was discovered in the fore compartment, and after making distress signals, the twenty-two crew took to the boats, landing at Filey at 09.00. The vessel quickly broke up and sank, and the underwriters suffered heavy losses.

The wreck is on a reef just a few yards south of the Old Horse reef, and the bulk of it lies on the landward side. At low water, the reef is just covered, but the kelp growing on the rocks breaks the surface. Great care must be taken approaching the reef; the area has killed at least eleven vessels, and is ready to trap yet more.

The wreck was first identified in 1969, when iron pigs were found in a gully just inside the reef; we learned that these had made up part of the cargo of *Volunteer*. Beneath these we found a battered soup ladle which bore the crest of the 1st Midlothian Rifle Volunteers – and Donald McGregor, who owned the ship, was Lieutenant Colonel of this Company. There is no large part of the ship still remaining, but enough of her is left to make for interesting diving, including her propellor and engine parts. The area is fascinating for its underwater ridges and gullies, and makes for excellent diving, with the added thrill of finding bits of the wreck among the rocks. There is a large iron anchor there too, but it is not certain that this came from the *Volunteer*.

A lignum vitae deadeye from Volunteer.

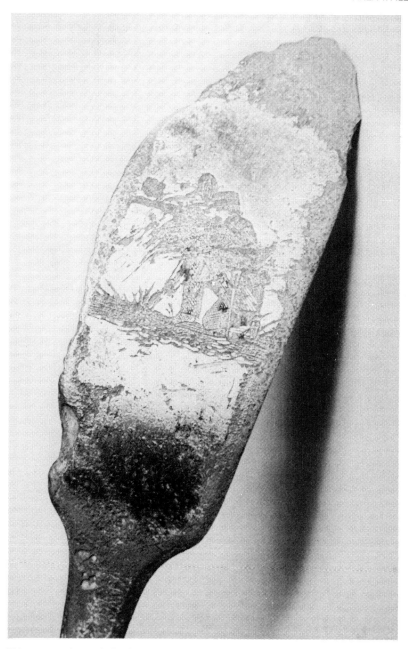

This engraved soup ladle shows a rifle volunteer, and helped to identify the wreck. (Site 139)

"The best sea boat on the North Sea run" finally came to grief on Old Horse Rocks. (Site 140)

140 John Ray. This 493 ton iron steamer was built by W.B. Thompson of Dundee in 1881 for the coal shipping company of M.A. Ray & Sons, London. She was 106ft long with a beam of 36ft and a depth of 13ft, and this enormous beam made her the '. . .ship that never rolled. . .' She was said to be the best sea-boat on the east coast run, and could make a trip in weather that '. . .would make a battleship heave-to. . .'

On January 11 1912, she ran onto the Old Horse Rocks, off Gristhorpe Cliff, and started to fill. At least twice before, this old ship had run ashore on different parts of the Yorkshire coast, and had subsequently refloated, but this time there was no escape, she broke up inside the Old Horse, and wreckage started to wash ashore soon afterwards. Captain Cook and the thirteen crew had already left in their own boat, and were picked up by a passing steamer in the prevailing thick fog.

The wreckage of *John Ray* is scattered among the rocks at the north side of Gristhorpe Wyke, between the Old Horse and the shore, with the bow section being the biggest piece. The whole area is little more than 3m deep at low water, and is rich in thick kelp that grows 2m high or more, breaking the surface in places. It is possible to take a boat in among the rocks when the weather is good and the sea calm, and it makes for very pleasant diving. Most of the wreckage is well camouflaged, and nothing stands up much over 1m high.

141 Old Horse Rocks wrecks. There are a number of other wrecks around the reef, but since it is virtually impossible to tell which bit came from which wreck, they are grouped together here under one heading.

In September of 1833, the schooner *Wilne* of Brancaster was wrecked at the foot of the cliffs inside the Old Horse, and no survivors were found. In September 1851, the Middlesbrough brig *Hambro,* Captain Storm, met the same fate in the same place. The collier brig *Beale,* a 225 ton Sunderland vessel built at Nova Scotia in 1851 struck the Old Horse and was lost on december 20 1868, without loss of life. She was 91ft long with a beam of 23ft and a depth of 15ft, and was insured for £1000. The reason for the loss of *Beale* was undoubtedly that it was thick fog at the time she struck, and this was also the downfall of the Scarborough fishing yawl *Charity,* wrecked here on January 21, 1872.

The German schooner *Emanuel* was driven ashore and wrecked here in a storm in March 1883, and the crew were able to walk ashore when the tide receded a little. The last sailing vessel to come to grief on the Old Horse reefs was another Scarborough fishing smack, the *James & Ellen,* lost in October 1897.

Two other iron vessels are mixed up with the wreckage of *John Ray* and *Volunteer,* and both were paddle steamers in use as fishing trawlers. *Chevy Chase* was a 104 ton vessel, 97ft long with a beam of 18ft and a depth of 9ft. She had been built by J. Eltringham at South Shields in 1874, and was owned by W. Adey of Sunderland. She ran onto the rocks in fog on October 6, 1886, but skipper Henry Thompson and the eight crew were rescued by a Filey coble. *Chevy Chase* was valued at £1500 at the time of loss.

Iron King was slightly larger at 112 tons, 101ft long with a beam of 18ft and a depth of 10ft. She was wrecked on the Old Horse on January 3, 1889, without loss of life, and again, fog was the cause of her loss.

Owned by F. Warren of South Shields, *Iron King* had been built nine years earlier by Eltringhams of South Shields. The similarity between the two vessels is such that it would be impossible to differentiate if any artifact should come to light from either one.

Diving the Old Horse Rocks area is not easy; outside the reef the tides are strong, and great care must be taken to avoid losing contact with the support boat. Marker buoys for each diver are an essential safety item, but are difficult to use here as they inevitably foul the huge boulders that litter the area. Maximum depth close to the reef is about 10m at low water, but much less inside the reef. Outside, the rocks are grey and somewhat forbidding, with copious growths of 'dead men's fingers', while inside the reef, there is much more colour and an abundance of thick kelp, which again makes towing a marker buoy difficult. Swimming under the kelp is worse than fighting your way through dense jungle, and often the fronds meet over your head forming a 'ceiling', but swimming over the top of it is pointless, because you cannot then see the seabed where the interest lies. It is precisely because it is difficult that this area holds such fascination; there is every chance that you might swim over a part that no diver has seen before, and make some new and exciting discovery.

Old Horse Rocks are at 54 14 06N 00 18 20W.

142 Mekong. This is probably the most dived wreck on the Yorkshire coast, for Scarborough Sub-Aqua Club have been using it as a first wreck dive for novices for over twenty years, yet it still holds surprises in store; in 1986, one local diver found a battered gold Krugerrand in the wreck. Originally called *Maund,* she was a 899 ton steam yacht, 200ft long with a beam of 30ft and a depth of 18ft. She was built by Ramage and Ferguson of Leith in 1906, and was the plaything of the wealthy. She was owned by

The wreck of Mekong, *owned by the writers of this book. (Site 142)*

Adam Singer (of sewing machine fame), was registered at Southampton, but spent most of her days on the French Riviera. Eventually she was sold to the Duc de Montpensier who renamed her *Mekong,* in 1912, presumably because he had connections with Vietnam, then under French control. In 1915, the clipper bowed yacht became *HMS Mekong* when the Admiralty requisitioned her, and put her under the command of Frank Finnis, CVO, a retired Admiral who volunteered for service at the age of 65. His job was to patrol area IX, Humber, with the 49th Patrol Unit, made up of six trawlers and the flagship *Mekong.* She was armed with two three-inch guns, and carried a crew of forty-six men.

On the night of March 11 1916, a tremendous gale blew on the north-east coast, with torrential rain, snow and hail, and the *Mekong* was battling southwards through it. At 04.50 on March 12, she struck rocks off Gristhorpe, and was driven ashore under the cliffs at Gristhorpe Wyke. Signals were made for assistance, but in the meantime, a stoker called Chapelow tried to swim ashore with a line, and was lost in the attempt. Able Seaman Roger Piper died trying the same thing, but a third man, greaser Ernest Thorne succeeded, and after climbing the 100ft cliffs, was able to raise the alarm. One other man, Quartermaster Davies died when he fell from the breeches buoy that the local Rocket Brigade set up, but the rest of the crew were brought ashore safely.

The wreck lay almost forgotten until divers from York and Scarborough started to explore the area in the late 1950's and early 60's, and found large numbers of live shells rolling around. They alerted the Royal Navy, who sadly, blew up the wreck. Today, there is little of her left other than the bottom plates and two upturned boilers, and during the summer, she usually gets buried under sand which washes into the wreck site. The winter usually scours this sand away, and in the early season, local divers root about in the bottom of the ship, which is only about 10ft deep at low water. The wreck is in fact owned by the authors of this book. It can be found close inshore, to the southern part of Gristhorpe Wyke, in between two large rock falls, and at low water, the tops of the boilers break the surface. Great care must be taken when taking a boat over the area; it would not be the first time that someone sat a boat on top of the boilers and this is not to be recommended!

143 Carnatic. On the Bay side of Filey Brigg, inside the Spittal Rocks, there is the remains of a wooden wreck in about twenty feet of water, and divers have found large copper rivets holding the planks together. It is likely that this is the wreck of the Newcastle barque *Carnatic,* a 621 ton vessel that was returning in ballast from Malta, under Captain Thomas Price. She had left on January 24, 1859, and made Flamborough Head a month later, passing it in hazy weather. The captain unfortunately mistook the lights of Filey for those at Scarborough, and as a result, ran ashore on the south side of the Brigg. The crew threw out the ballast, and local boats laid kedge anchors, but it was all in vain; the twelve year old, American built vessel became a total wreck.

A number of other wooden sailing vessels also became total wrecks on the Brigg, and since we have no positive identification on the wreckage near the Spittals, they are listed here. *Unico* was a three-masted schooner, 364 tons, carrying 600 tons of coal to Genoa from Newcastle. She was Italian, and was being piloted down the east coast by a Newcastle pilot named Corbett in January of 1871. She anchored in Filey Bay because of strong southerly winds, but a wind shift during the night caught her unawares – some say the captain and officers were drunk – and in trying belatedly to head out to sea, she struck the inside of the Brigg, and was dashed to pieces, with the loss of fourteen lives. There was just one survivor. As a result of this disaster, a Bell Buoy was put in position to mark the Brigg end for the first time.

Another Italian barque, the 594 ton *Cesare Beccaria* stranded and was wrecked on the inside of the Brigg on March 11, 1875, after a collision at sea with the steamer *Conservator.* Captain Palorino and the crew took to their own boats and landed safely; the stores were salved and sold for £200 later.

A fourth sailing ship wrecked here was the collier brig *Kirtons* of Sunderland. She struck the seaward end of the Brigg on January 5 1871, and though the crew were all saved, dare we say it – it was curtains for the *Kirtons!*

Other smaller sailing ships that were wrecked on the Brigg include the Colchester schooner *Olive Branch,* lost here on December 18 1859; the 253 ton collier snow *Seabird* of South Shields, wrecked here on January 10 1960, and the Scottish barque *Martin* which was lost with many lives here as early as 1543. Filey Brigg also became the last resting place for an unspecified number of '. . .fine ships. . .' in the gale of November, 1969, and for nine further ships in November gales of 1740, when two-thirds of the crews were lost. To go back even earlier than any of these, we know that a Flanders ship was wrecked on the Brigg in 1367; this was only recorded because she was found to be smuggling wool on which no duty had been paid underneath what was apparently a coal cargo. In 1334, an unknown vessel had stranded on rocks near Filey – which must mean the Brigg – and was immediately looted by thirty or more locals. The earliest mention of all however comes in the year 1311, when an inquiry was held to try and ascertain what had happened to '. . .a chest of gold florentines, silver coin to the value of £300, and silver in bar to a great sum, cast ashore at Fyveley, which as wreck of the sea belongs to the King. . .'

Another victim of the Scarborough minefield, S.S. Boston. *(Site 144)*

It can be seen that at least twenty-one wooden ships have been wrecked on the Brigg, and so far only one seems to have left any sign of its existence; locals have long referred to it as *Carnatic,* but you pay your money and take your choice!

144 Boston. Built at Christiana in 1905, this 1168 ton steamer was owned by Fred Olsen and registered in Norway. She was 225ft long with a beam of 34ft and a depth of 13ft. She was carrying paper pulp from Bremen to London when she struck a mine north of Scarborough on December 22, 1914, and was severely disabled. Ten of the crew left the ship and made Scarborough in their own boat; eight others stayed on board with Captain A.J. Olsen. The stricken vessel drifted south in the strong north-east-by-east wind, finally striking Filey Brigg in the late afternoon. The local lifeboat saw her down by the head, and apparently lowering her boats, and went off at 19.30. The captain and crew were landed at Filey, and the *Boston* sank in the rough seas. The wreck lies outside the Gully, between High Brigg and the birdwatcher's hut at the foot of Carr Naze.

A boiler can be seen just breaking the surface at low water on spring tides, and there is some wreckage in the Gully itself. As you would expect in a place like this, the wreck is very badly broken up, and there are no large sections of her left. Boston had T 3cy engines, 16" 27" 44"-32" by Nylands Voerksted, Christiana.

145 Lyng. This 648 ton Norwegian steamer was the mother ship to a herring fleet, and was bound for Hull from Flora with a cargo of herring barrel hoops when she struck Filey brigg on January 30, 1928. It was 01.30 when she ran aground in a slight haze, near the part known as High Brigg. Captain Ola Johansen and the 14 crew were saved, but the ship broke in half and sank shortly afterwards. The wreck lies in about 6m of water, some 30m or so off the Brigg, and unfortunately, not too far from where the sewer pipe discharges! However, if you dive when the sewer is dormant, this is an interesting dive; the ship's boiler, engine, shaft and broken propellor can be seen together with the bottom plates of the vessel. Obviously, in this depth and position, it is very badly broken up, but it does make a good dive for novices especially.

Mother ship of a Norwegian herring fleet, the Lyng, *struck Filey Brigg in 1928. (Site 145)*

Lyng was built at Greenock in 1918, and had previously carried the names *Globus, Bolam* and *Kilberry*. She was 176ft long with a beam of 30ft and a depth of 16ft, and was owned by A. Norman Larsen of Horten. She had T 3cy engines, 16" 26" 44"-26" by McKie & Baxter of Glasgow.

146 Eglantine. Built in 1878 by the Tyne Iron Shipbuilding Co, this 1312 ton steamer was owned by J. Ridley, Son & Tully and was registered at North Shields. She was 258ft long with a beam of 32ft and a depth of 21ft. The *Eglantine* was bound for Le Havre with coal from the Tyne when the captain thought he saw an enemy submarine loose off a torpedo at his ship, and in his attempt to escape into Filey Bay, he struck Filey Brigg in the early hours of April 16, 1915. Filey coastguard reported the stranding at 01.20, and the

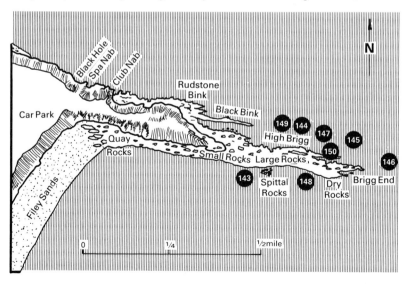

local lifeboat picked the crew up from their own boats, all landing safely at Filey. At high water that day, the ship was submerged, and she became a total wreck. *Eglantine* lies between the Bell Buoy and the end of the Brigg at low water, being slightly nearer to the Brigg. It is in about 10m of water, on a very uneven seabed, and is very broken up. Because of the rugged nature of the seabed, it is impossible to pick up on an echo sounder; there are huge boulders in the area which move about in bad weather. The bottom plates, boilers, engines, winches, anchors etc can all be seen, though nothing stands up more than a couple of metres. The tides here are particularly strong, and diving must only take place at slack water. *Eglantine* had C 2cy engines, 25" 54"-33", 2SB 4PF by North Eastern Marine Engineering of Sunderland.

147 Chilian. Owned by the Grimsby Inc Box Fishing Co, this 161 ton steam trawler was built of iron at North Shields in 1893, and was 107ft in length. She carried ten crew under Captain Little, and fished the waters off Iceland. Six of her crew died when the *Chilian* grounded in dense fog on Filey Brigg on the morning of April 9, 1894, while returning from the fishing grounds. She struck the Brigg about mid-way between High Brigg and the Brigg end, on the northern side, and the six who were lost took to the small boat as the trawler settled. The skipper and remaining crew members took to the rigging, and hung there for several hours until dawn, when they were seen and rescued.

It was half-tide when the *Chilian* struck, and by high water, she was waterlogged. Subsequently the wreck fell off a ledge into deeper water, and all hope of salvaging her was abandoned. The wreck is broken up beyond all recognition now, but bits of her remain hidden among the rocks.

148 Sleuthhound. Built of iron at Hull in 1890, this 153 ton steam trawler was 101ft long, carried nine crew, and was owned by the Humber Steam Trawling Co. On October 27, 1897, skipper Charles Neilson was bringing her home through thick early morning fog after a 'prosperous' trip, when she struck rocks, and came fast. Distress signals were made, but since the tide was ebbing, it seemed clear that they were going to have to wait until it flooded again before anything could be done. Though they were unable to see where they were at the time, they had in fact stranded on the extreme end of the Spittall Rocks, which run into Filey Bay from the southern side of Filey Brigg. By noon that day, the engine room was flooded, and local boats came off and started to ferry the trawler's catch ashore; it was a beautiful day, with the sea like glass, and many visitors came to see the sad looking *Sleuthhound*. At high water, the Scarborough harbour tug *Cambria* tried to pull her off, but failed, and the paddle trawlers *Dandy*, *Dunrobin* and *Star* were no more successful. *Sleuthhound* became a total wreck, and her stern section is still in the same place today, at the seaward end of the Spittalls, a little to the right of the rocks as you swim south on the inland side of the reef. Often a lobster will be found lurking under this section. The engines of the trawler, and some other bits of her can be found at the other side of the Spittalls, in what is known locally as Crab Hole, the area between the outer edge of the reef and the Brigg itself.

Chrysolite *ran onto Filey Brigg in 1968. (Site 150)*

149 Manx Queen. Built at Selby in 1915, this 234 ton Grimsby trawler was 120ft long, and owned by W.H. Beeley until WW1, when the Admiralty took her for an Auxiliary Patrol Vessel. She was engaged in this work when she struck Filey Brigg at 03.30 on March 1 1916, and was badly holed. At first, the stern remained afloat while the bows were hard aground, but inevitably, she filled and sank. There was no loss of life; ten of the crew were rescued by the lifeboat, and three others were brought ashore by the Rocket Brigade. For one of the crew, this was his third shipwreck in the Filey area! The wreck, which has not to our knowledge ever been positively identified, is close to that of the steamship *Boston* (Site 144), but since it is one of three trawlers in this area, all of which are completely broken up, it is going to be difficult to identify.

150 Chrysolite. This Whitby owned motor fishing vessel, registered number LH 206, was built at St. Monance in Scotland in 1947 by Walter Reekie. She was 52ft in length, and grossed 23 tons. During the late 1960's, *Chrysolite* was working from Bridlington, and on June 30 1968, she ran onto Filey Brigg in thick fog, as so many others had done before. She was soon pounded to pieces by the seas, and today there is little to see other than the remains of her engine and stern gear. Her propellor was removed some years ago. The wreck lies at the north side of the Brigg, very close to the seaward end of the sewer pipe. Not too many people dive the wreck of the *Chrysolite*!

Offshore Diving Sites

151 Tangistan. Built by W. Gray & Co at Hartlepool in 1906, this 3738 ton steamer was owned by the Strick Line of Swansea, and was 350ft long with a beam of 49ft and a depth of 16ft. She was bound for Middlesbrough with a cargo of iron ore from Spain when she became one of the earliest victims of a U-boat torpedo in this part of the world on March 9 1915, some 9 miles north of Flamborough Head. There were 38 men on board the *Tangistan,* and only one survived. The wreck is thought to be the one in position 54 15 42N 00 05 08W, with part of it in 54 16 01N 00 05 16W, but so far there is no record of any dives being done on it – it is in a little over 50m of water.

By a strange coincidence, *Tangistan* was yard number 736 at the builders; yard number 737 was the *Seistan* (Site 207) at the same yard, she was owned by the same company, and was sunk in the same way less than six miles away. *Tangistan* had T 3cy engines by Central Marine Engineering, 24" 40" 65" 2SB 6PF.

152 Bywell. There is a wreck in position 54 15 51N 00 13 33W which is thought to be the 1522 ton Newcastle collier *Bywell,* built by Blyth Shipbuilding & Drydock Co in 1913 for the Screw Collier Co. She was 245ft long with a beam of 37ft and a depth of 16ft. On March 29, 1917, she was torpedoed and sunk by a German submarine off Scarborough, while carrying a cement cargo. The wreck is in a roughly east – west attitude in a depth of 42m, and stands some 6m high. Divers have so far only seen the stern of the vessel, though the forward part is thought to be close by. *Bywell* had T 3cy engines by North Eastern Marine Engineering, 22" 33" 54", 2SB 6PF.

153 M.C. Holm. This 2458 ton Danish steamer was identified by the name on the wheel boss, discovered by Scarborough divers in 1982. Prior to this date, the position of the wreck was not known, the vessel having gone down in history as ". . .mined and sunk in the North Sea. . ." She was lost on December 31 1914, and was quite clearly another victim of the Scarborough minefield.

The *M.C. Holm* was built in 1894 by Richardson Duck & Co, and the company which owned the ship, founded by M.C. Holm in 1871, is still in existence in Copenhagen. She was 290ft long with a beam of 42ft and a

Porcelain battery case from the wreck of M.C. Holm. *(Site 153)*

depth of 17ft. The wreck now lies on an even keel in 36m of water in position 54 15 44N 00 16 24W. This is a good dive and an easy wreck to navigate underwater, being more or less in one piece, though some parts have collapsed. *M.C. Holm* had T 3cy engines.

154 Gem. This 464 ton steamer was built by J. Fullerton & Co in 1887 at Paisley, and was owned by W. Robertson of Glasgow. She was 175ft long with a beam of 25ft and a depth of 13ft, and had 80hp engines that gave her 8 knots. She was mined and sunk on Christmas Day, 1914 during a voyage from Mostyn to the Tyne with a cargo of saltash. It was a devastating explosion; the ship was blown into two pieces, and the captain and nine crew were killed.

The wreck of the *Gem* lies on a silt seabed at a depth of 40m; the bow section is on an even keel, more or less intact. The ship is broken aft of the bridge, and the stern and engines are lying some 150m away, on their port side. The wreckage has been identified as *Gem* by careful measurement, and by various fittings which are of Glaswegian origin. The bow section is in position 54 15 29N 00 15 11W while the stern is in 54 15 22N 00 15 07W. Depth is about 38m, and she stands some 3m high.

Gem had T 3cy engines by W. King & Co of Glasgow, 15" 24" 40"-33". 1SB 3CF.

155 Orianda. This 273 ton trawler was built at Selby in 1914 for the Dolphin Steam Trawling Co of Grimsby, but she had scarcely begun her fishing career when the Admiralty requisitioned her, and she changed from GY 291 to Minesweeper No. 99.

The 130ft ship was brought in to clear the Scarborough minefield in December 1914, and was to become the first sweeper to fall victim to it. She struck a mine at 11am on December 19, while steaming full ahead, and she dived beneath the waves with her masthead cutting through the water like a periscope. In less than ten minutes, she had gone, though surprisingly, only one man was lost. The rest of the crew, and skipper Lt. H.B. Boothby survived. Lt Boothby was shortly given command of a second minesweeper which was destined to meet the same fate shortly afterwards. (See *Banyers* Site 157).

The wreck of *Orianda* is in position 54 15 17N 00 18 32W within hailing distance of the wreck of the *Eli*. She is in one piece, upright on the seabed, but well sandwarped, with only the top part of her boiler and engines above the seabed.

156 Eli. This 1107 ton steamer was built by Bergens Mek Voerksted in 1908 for P. Lindoe of Haugesund, Norway. She was 229ft long with a beam of 35ft and a depth of 16ft, and had a 106nhp T 3cy engine by the builders. She was bound for Rouen with coal from Blyth when she struck a mine in the Scarborough minefield on Christmas Day, 1914, and sank in 3 minutes. Fortunately, her fifteen crew were all saved. Her wreck lies in position 54 15 12N 00 18 30W in about 20m of water in a north-west–south-east attitude. She is well broken up, lying on her port side with the starboard side plates missing for the most part. The bows are almost half buried, but fairly intact. The engines are lying flat on the seabed, with the single boiler in situ just in front of them, and a donkey boiler close by.

This wreck was known to local fishermen for many years as the 'drifter', apparently because someone trawled up a piece of wood from the area,

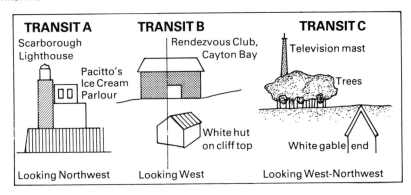

TRANSIT A	TRANSIT B	TRANSIT C
Scarborough Lighthouse	Rendezvous Club, Cayton Bay	Television mast
Pacitto's Ice Cream Parlour		Trees
	White hut on cliff top	White gable end
Looking Northwest	Looking West	Looking West-Northwest

Marks for Eli. (Site 156)

and decided it was the wreck of a wooden drifter.
Eli had T 3cy engines, 15" 26" 44"-30" by Bergens Mek Vaerks.

157 Banyers. This 480 ton Grimsby trawler was built at Beverley in 1914 for the South Western Steam Fishing Co, and was 160ft long, one of the biggest trawlers in the country at that time. She was hired by the Admiralty and put to work as a minesweeper early in WW1, and was sent to clear the Scarborough minefield that was laid by the German *Kolberg* during the bombardment of Scarborough of December, 1914. During this sweeping operation, *Banyers* struck a mine and sank rapidly, taking six lives as she sank. The CO, Lt. Boothby RNR, escaped through the wheelhouse window. This was his second sinking in this area in less than a month; he had previously been skipper of the *Orianda*, (Site 155) another minesweeping trawler that met the same fate close by on December 19, 1914. The wreck of *Banyers* is in position 54 15 07N 00 15 24W in a depth of about 36m. She lies roughly north-east–south-west, and stands some 4m proud of the seabed, on an even keel.

Lt Boothby later wrote of his experiences in a fascinating book called *Spunyarn.*

158 Garmo. Built by Earles of Hull, this 203 ton steam trawler was owned by the Ocean Steam Fishing Co. of Grimsby. Fourteen years later, she was put into service as an Admiralty Patrol Vessel and it was in this role that she met her end on December 20, 1914. She struck a mine and sank with the loss of five lives some 3.5 miles south-east of Scarborough castle. The Skipper, T. Gilbert died later from his injuries; there were nine survivors. *Garmo* lies in position 54 15 00N 00 17 55W in some 25m.

The ship was 112ft long with a beam of 22ft; her engines, by Earles, were T 3cy 11" 20" 32"-23". 1SB 2PF.

159 Birtley. Built by Wood Skinner & Co in 1906, this 1438 ton steamer was to replace an earlier *Birtley* that had been wrecked at Flamborough on November 16, 1905. Like her, this one was owned by the Burnett Steamship Co, and was 245ft long with a beam of 37ft and a depth of 16ft.

During WW1, she was armed for defence, but fell victim to a U-boat on January 4, 1918, when she was sunk some eight miles north of Flamborough Head, with the loss of all eighteen men.

Birtley, *armed for defence, was victim of a U-boat. (Site 159)*

There is a wreck in position 54 14 40N 00 08 20W which is thought to be the *Birtley;* it stands some 10m proud of the seabed in a general depth of 50m, but there is no record of it having been dived to date. *Birtley* had T 3cy engines by North Eastern Marine Engineering, 19" 31" 51". 1SB 4CF, and was capable of 8 knots.

160 Eros. This 1122 ton steamer was built in Norway in 1900, and was requisitioned by the Admiralty in WW1, under the management of Fisher Renwick & Co. She was bound for Rouen with coal from the Tyne when she was torpedoed and sunk some 1.5 miles north of Filey Brigg on August 17 1918, with the loss of the Captain and the six crew.

Eros was 231ft long with a beam of 34ft and a depth of 14ft. The wreck lies on a sandy seabed at 27m in position 54 14 12N 00 15 36W. Despite dispersal operations carried out in 1921, the wreck is in one piece, and is upright, though her well decks have become heavily sand-warped. She is small enough to be dived from bow to stern in one no-stop dive, though this of course is not the best way to see her. She was armed for defence, and though her gun has been removed, live shells can still be seen near her stern. No positive identification has been made as yet, though everything

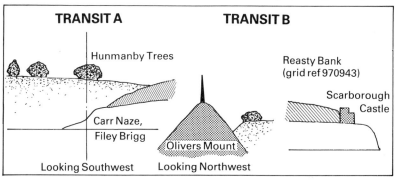

Marks for Eros. (Site 160)

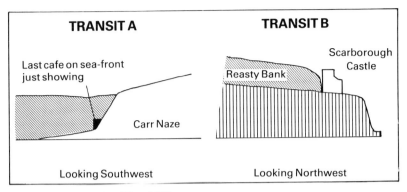

Marks for Sallogie. (Site 161)

points to this being the *Eros;* those who feel any doubt traditionally call this one the "...one boiler wreck" for obvious reasons.

Eros had Bergen built engines, T 3cy, 16" 22" 42", which gave her 97nhp and 8 knots.

161 Ballogie. Built by Short Bros at Sunderland in 1889, this 1207 ton steamer was owned by J. & A. Davidson and was registered in Aberdeen. Originally called *Mittelweg,* she was German owned until 1894, when new owners in Middlesbrough renamed her *Bull.* She was sold to Antwerp in 1912 and named *Antwerpen,* and finally became *Ballogie* in 1915 when Davidsons bought her. She was 240ft long, with a beam of 33ft and a depth of 15ft, and could make 8 knots. *Ballogie* was torpedoed by a U-boat and sunk off Filey on November 9 1917 with the loss of the captain and twelve crew. The wreck is in position 54 13 52N 00 14 52W, in about 30m of water. The bows are laid over to starboard, the midship section is broken up with the engines lying on one side. A gun was removed from the stern some years ago, and was given to a sea cadet corps. For many years the wreck was known locally as *Two Boiler wreck* for obvious reasons, but in summer of 1986, the wreck was positively identified by Filey divers Chris Truelove and Dave Hunter. *Ballogie* was carrying slag at the time of loss. She had T 3cy engines by J. Dickinson of Sunderland, 20" 33" 54"-39". 2SB 6PF.

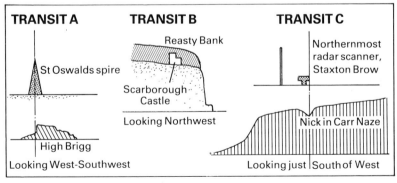

Marks for Ardens. (Site 162)

Ardens *sunk by a U-boat in 1917. (Site 162)*

162 Ardens. Originally called *Universal,* this 1274 ton steamer was built by Short Bros, Sunderland in 1878 for the Gas, Light and Coke Co, and was registered in London. She was 240ft long with a beam of 33ft and a depth of 18ft, and was armed for defence during WW1. She had more than one chance to use her gun, for *Ardens* was attacked by a U-boat on June 30, 1917. A torpedo missed her. The master was credited with having fought well against this raider, and another that attacked him on another occasion; he was awarded the DSC, and his gunners got the DSM. On August 18 1917 however, *Ardens* was attacked yet again, and this time there was no escape; she was torpedoed and sunk with the loss of one man while bound for London with gas-coal from Shields. The wreck is in position 54 13 40N 00 12 57W, by radar, 6.8 miles Scarborough Castle Headland; 1.82 miles Filey Brigg. She is in about 35m, in a most unusual attitude; she has broken amidships and folded so that the bow and stern are lying alongside each other, leaning outwards. The vessel was armed, and though the gun has been removed, live shells can still be found close to the stern section. Generally, best dive time for *Ardens* is 1½ to 2 hours before slack water at Scarborough. Visibility varies a lot here, but it can often be better here than in Filey Bay itself. Locally, this wreck is known to fishermen as "Reasty", which comes from the northernmost transit.

Ardens had engines by G. Clark of Sunderland, C 2cy, 29" 55"-36". 1SB 4PF.

163 Unknown. There is an unknown wreck in position 54 13 21N 00 00 52E in a depth of 52m that has been well broken up and scattered on the flat sand and gravel seabed, though part of it still stands some 7m high. It could be that this is the wreck of the 289 ton steam trawler *Sapphire,* built in 1913 by Cochranes of Selby, and owned by the Kingston Steam Trawling Co of Hull. She was 133ft long with a beam of 23ft and a depth of 12ft, and was less than two years old when she struck a mine and sank off Filey on March 1, 1915. One man died. *Sapphire* had T 3cy engines, 13" 22" 37" by Holmes & Co of Hull. 1SB 3PF.

Is Sapphire *the trawler at Site 163?*

164 Unknown. There is a wreck in position 54 12 53N 00 00 27W which has, for unknown reasons, gone down in records as being a Dutch trawler. The wreck is in almost 50m of water, but stands some 10m high. My guess is that this could be the wreck of *Leda,* a Dutch steamship of 1140 tons, built by Rijkee & Co at Rotterdam in 1898. *Leda* was 228ft long with a beam of 32ft and a depth of 18ft, and was owned by Koninklijke Nederlandsche Stoomb Maats. She was bound for Amsterdam with a cargo of coal from Methil when she was attacked and sunk by *UC-49* off Filey on December 6 1917, with the loss of seven lives. *Leda* is charted in a position some six miles inshore of this position, but no wreck has been found there. The ship had T 3cy engines, 17" 28"-45".

165 Amsteldam. Built by the Campbeltown SB Co in 1907, this 1233 ton steamer was owned by the South Metropolitan Gas Co and used as a collier on the east coast run. She was 230ft long with a beam of 34ft and a depth of 16ft. During WW1, she was armed for defence, but on October 18 1917 she was torpedoed and sunk off Filey by *UB-21,* with the loss of four men. The incident occurred some six miles north of Flamborough Head, in position 54 12 30N 00 14 00W, but the wreck is not in this position.

There are a number of unknown obstructions on the seabed some miles out to sea from here, and it is thought that one of these might be the *Amsteldam.* Some of them are as follows: 54 13 00N 00 05 45W in a depth of about 50m; 54 13 37N 00 06 25W in a depth of about 45m; 54 13 57N 00 05 49W in a depth of about 50m; 54 14 13N 00 09 35W in a depth of about 45m.

Amsteldam had T 3cy engines by Hutson & Son, Glasgow, 18" 27" 45"-33". 1SB 3CF.

166   Crane Barge. On February 23 1986, an unnamed dumb crane barge overturned and sank while being towed by the British tug *Eugenio.* The incident occurred in position 54 12 24N 00 11 24W but despite extensive searches at the time, the wreck has not been found, despite the fact that the crane was 20m long, and the barge was 66ft long with a beam of 26ft. What is certain is that she is there somewhere, about two miles off Filey Brigg in about 30m of water. The chances are that the wreck was not detected as a result of her being on a large rocky patch in the area; this would make sonar and depth soundings difficult to decipher. A magnetometer might help with this one.

167 Aladdin. This 753 ton steamer was built by Stavanger Stoberi & Dok in 1902, and was owned by Dampskibsalties Aladdin Stavanger. She was 195ft long with a beam of 30ft and a depth of 11ft, and was rigged as a schooner. She was torpedoed and sunk in Filey Bay on September 7 1917 during a voyage from Newcastle to Treport with coal. The wreck is charted in 54 12 00N 00 08 00W in a depth of 34m, but nothing has been found in this position. The nearest unknown obstruction on the seabed is in position 54 12 05N 00 04 10W, but since this in at 50m, no one has so far checked to see whether or not this is the *Aladdin*. The ship had T 3cy engines, 14" 23" 38"-27".

Area Information and Services

These are largely the same as for Scarborough and Bridlington areas with the following additions.
Admiralty Charts. Whitby to Flamborough Head No. 129. Filey Bay No. 1882.
Ordnance Survey. L101 Scarborough.
Tourist Information. Filey Town Hall 0723-512204.
Boat for Hire: Deep Harmony, skipper-diver John Adams, Tel 0723-514606.
Weather Area on Shipping Forecasts. Humber/Tyne.
Local Coastguard. Scarborough Sector Station 0723-372323 (Filey Sector Station now closed).
Filey Coble Landing. Controlled by Scarborough Harbour Master Tel 0723-373530.

Area 5:
Flamborough Head

This area starts at 54 11 45N and runs south to 54 06 12N, and features Flamborough Head, probably the most notable promontory on Britain's east coast. The headland is of national importance because of its wildlife and its geology, having what is generally thought to be the finest line of chalk cliffs in the country, which are home to the only colony of gannets on the English mainland. It was designated a Heritage Coast in 1979, with an information centre situated at South Landing. As part of the Heritage Coast Project, there is a programme of guided walks available free to all comers, where experienced volunteers explain various aspects of the areas heritage.

The Headland is steeped in history; it is physically separated from the rest of Yorkshire by an immense earth work known as Danes Dyke, which is known to pre-date the Danes by many centuries. The area beyond the Dyke was known until fairly recent times as Little Denmark, for the Viking invaders of the ninth and tenth centuries had made their presence felt so strongly here. The area was chosen for the site of one of the beacons that warned of the coming of the Spanish Armada in 1588, and a major navigational light has burned here since 1807.

The 400ft cliffs have long been a significant signpost for mariners, both coastwise and those coming from northern Europe, simply because they are so easy to recognise, and so difficult to confuse with any other place. Inevitably, this profusion of shipping making for the Head has led to large numbers of wrecks of all types, from the legendary *Czarina* with millions of pounds in gold, through humble colliers, Royal Navy sailing ships, torpedo victims, U-boats, fishing vessels and ocean liners. (Don't look in the text for *Czarina* though – it seems that she was just a legend!)

The earliest named wreck in the area occurred in 1348 when the King's ship *La Katerine* came ashore at Flamborough and was promptly looted by 'evil-doers'. Three sailing ships of the RN came to grief at Flamborough; the 282 tonne 6th rate *Bideford* on March 18, 1736, another 6th rater also called *Bideford,* but of 403 tonnes was lost here on December 30 1761, and the 346 tonne 16 gun *Nautilus* was lost here on February 2 1799. Sadly, none of these appears in the text as dive sites because no-one knows where they are, but they are of sufficient interest to merit a mention of their existence here.

This wealth of wrecks, together with the natural beauty of the underwater scenery has made Flamborough Head a Mecca for divers in the north of England, and sadly, this has in the past led to some degree of conflict with local shell fishermen. However, in recent years, the situation seems to have improved, hopefully as a result of a heightened awareness of each others rights and responsibilities.

This is one of the few areas on the Yorkshire coast where shore diving can be carried on, but it should be understood that this can be a very hazardous

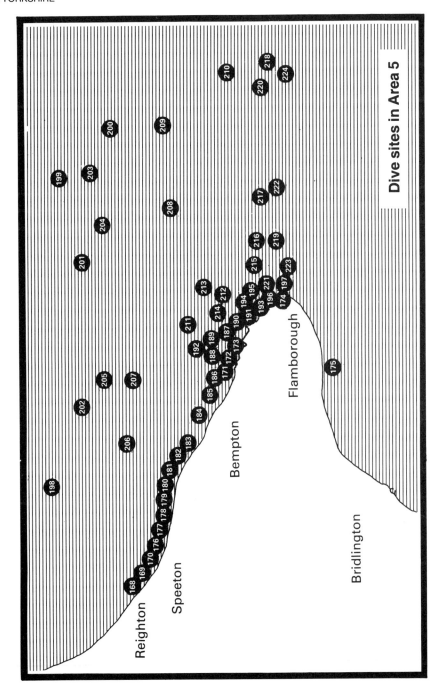

Dive sites in Area 5

business because of the peculiarities of the tidal movements here. Many divers have got into difficulties, hardly a year passes without the rescue services being alerted as a result of divers in trouble, and there have been diver fatalities here too. It would be impossible to list all the tidal movements that occur here, but during a north or north-easterly ebbing tide, half-a-mile from the rocks, the tide can still be flooding south, at certain states of tide. In some of the bays, when the tide is flooding in at the centre, currents at the edges of the bay can be sweeping strongly out to sea, and vice versa. No-one knows more about these movements than local coastguard Vic Crosthwaite, and he has expressed a willingness to advise any diver who visits him about particular problems.

Whenever shore diving is taking place, it makes sense to inform the coastguard of your intentions in any case, and it helps if divers carry floats, personal smoke floats or fluorescent dye in case of emergency. Another safety point raised by the Flamborough Coastguard is that any diver who is operating from a boat should, in the event of losing a diver, buoy the point of entry before moving off to search with the boat, for obvious reasons.

Generally speaking, shore diving is best carried out at high or low water slack, and when there is tidal movement, if you must dive at all, then think through carefully how the tide can be used to your advantage at the end of the dive. Normally, it is much better to dive from boats, with the launching sites being at South Landing, Flamborough, and at South Cliff, Bridlington. (See Bridlington chapter for details.) It is also possible to launch at Filey, and head south, but this is the longest route.

Shore Diving Sites:

168 Laura. This wreck is not a dive at all, but is included here because anyone visiting the area cannot fail to notice it high and dry on the beach, and may wonder what it is. Built by C. Mitchell & Co at Newcastle in 1880, *Laura* was a 2089 ton steamer owned by Bing & Karpeles of Trieste. She was 286ft long with a beam of 36ft and a depth of 26ft, and had compound

Laura *broke in two at Speeton Sands in dense fog. What remains of her can be seen on the beach. (Site 168)*

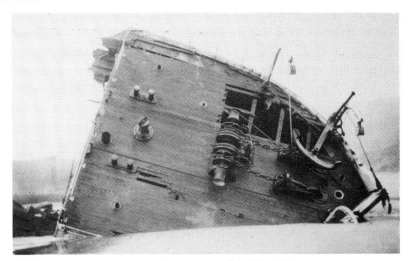

The bows of Laura, *soon after she came to grief. (Site 168)*

engines by the Wallsend Shipway Co. She ran ashore on Speeton Sands in dense fog on November 21 1897, some four miles south of Filey. There was no imminent danger, and the crew stayed aboard, while tugs assembled ready to tow her off. However, all attempts failed, and three days later, the ship broke in half, and was written off. The bottom plates, boilers, rudder-post etc can be seen today, and on big tides, it is possible to walk right round the wreck.

This site, like that of the next two, *HMS Nautilus* and *Diamond* is reached by turning off the Bridlington – Scarborough road (A165) just after Reighton village, signposted Reighton Sands. There is no launching facility here, and it is a long walk to the wreck sites – too long to carry diving cylinders. Incidentally, at low water, this is an interesting walk for days when bad weather precludes diving.

169 HMS Nautilus. On February 2 1799, the 346 ton sloop *Nautilus* came ashore on Speeton Sands, and was wrecked, without loss of life. So far, no-one within living memory has found any trace of the wreck, but it is included here because of its great appeal to divers, and the fact that there are supposed to be bronze cannon here somewhere.

Nautilus was built at Itchenor in 1784, and was one of a class of six sloops. She was 101ft long with a beam of 27ft, and was armed with sixteen 6 pounder guns. She had a complement of 121 officers and men, and was commanded by Henry Gunter RN. At the time of loss, *Nautilus* was escorting a convoy of 23 ships from Memel, Norway. There is no information available as to the precise position in which she stranded, but a local resident who was born in 1880, speaking of the *Nautilus,* said '. . .I knew a man who had seen and handled one of her big guns which had come to rest among the rocks at the foot of the white cliffs. . .' Another quote from the Parish Magazine at Speeton dated 1936 reads '. . .About a century ago, during an exceptionally low tide two brass cannon were exposed on the sands some fifty yards south of the *Laura* wreck. An attempt to salvage them at the next opportunity was baulked by that opportunity not arriving. These same buried cannon must I think, belong to the *Nautilus* and not to the Armada, though locally they were associated with the attempted Spanish invasion. . .'

(To the best of our knowledge, no serious diving survey of the area has ever been made, though we made one tentative search some years ago. A.G.)

170 Diamond. This 149 ton trawler was built at Glasgow in 1891 for the Kingston Steam Trawling Co of Hull, and was in fact the company's first ship. She was iron built, 100ft long, and had 45hp engines. On January 9 1912, she ran ashore under Speeton Cliffs while bound for Hull with her catch. The crew left in their own boat, and were picked up safely by Flamborough Lifeboat. The wreck can be seen at low water, in fact it is really a walk rather than a dive at that state of tide, but is mentioned here because parts of it never dry out, and it can be dived from seaward. The wreck can be found where the sands end and the rocky beach begins, about half a mile south of King & Queen Rocks.

171 Little Thornwick. This popular dive site is reached by taking the B1255, North Marine Road, from Flamborough village centre, turning left immediately before the Viking Hotel, formerly *Ye Olde Thornwick Hotel*. A mud path from here leads to a carpark by a café, and two separate sets of steps lead down into Little Thornwick Bay. The ones to the right lead down Thornwick Nab, and are preferred. Half way down, the path splits, with the right hand branch leading into Thornwick Bay, the left hand into Little Thornwick. After entering the water, if you swim 200m or so to the north, and about 50m from the rocks you will find wreckage; bottom plates and part of

Diamond, *a trawler ashore at Speeton Sands. Now more a walk than a dive. (Site 170)*

A big sea at Little Thornwick Bay.

an engine, with a boiler to seaward of these. It is possible that these are the remains of the 919 ton steamer *Prince Alfred,* built at Dumbarton in 1854, and wrecked north of Flamborough on January 13 1861. The ship was carrying 54 passengers, all of whom were saved, and a general cargo which was lost. The *Prince Alfred* was one of the earliest steamships to be lost off the Yorkshire coast, but since she is one of many that were lost on this short stretch, it is impossible to be sure that this is her. The area is a good dive either way; best time to dive is on the flood, so that you have help from the tide to get back ashore.

172 Thornwick Bay. The approach to this popular diving site is via the B1255, North Marine Road, from Flamborough village. A left turn immediately in front of *The Viking Hotel* takes you via an unmade road to a carpark over the Bay, passing on the way a steep sided gulley which has a path leading to the right-hand side of the Bay. From the carpark, a set of steps leads down Thornwick Nab, giving access to the left hand side of the Bay, with a set of steps off to the left into Little Thornwick (site 171). There is plenty to see in the way of marine life in the Bay, which local clubs usually dive at high water. This is partly so that the caves on the right-hand side of the Bay can be entered by snorkel divers. Diving at this side of the Bay should be avoided during the flood tide, as the unwary can be swept out of the Bay and carried down towards the Head.

173 North Landing. This north-facing Bay has been used by fishermen since time immemorial for launching their sturdy Yorkshire cobles in the quest for cod, salmon, crabs and lobsters at different seasons of the year. A popular summertime earner has been to take visitors for a trip to sea from here too. The access is very steep however, and a winch is needed for pulling the boats back up a concrete ramp to get them clear of high water. Also at North Landing is the lifeboat house, where lifeboats have been

Helicopter view of Selwicks (Silex) Bay.

housed since November of 1871. Access to North Landing is by the B1255 North Marine Road from Flamborough, but it must be made clear that it is not possible for boats to be launched here; the road from the cliff top down is far too narrow and steep in any case. Shore diving is possible from here however, and the chalk and sand seabed can lead to good visibility underwater in settled weather. At the north side of the bay on West Scar can be seen the scant remains of the Admiralty oiling vessel *Rosa,* wrecked here on April 28, 1930. It is possible to walk to parts of this wreck at low water; she is of little real diving interest.

At the south side of the bay, an interesting feature is a cave called Robin Lythe's Hole which cuts through to the open sea, and can be walked through at low tide. Divers can get through at other times, but great care must be taken to avoid being carried away with the flood when at the seaward side, off East Scar.

174 Selwicks Bay (Silex Bay). This rocky bay is just north of Flamborough Head itself, and is reached by the B1259 from the village. It affords access to shore divers via a set of steep wooden steps, and there is a large carpark at the top. The lighthouse is situated here, and there are cafés and gift shops as well as other tourist amenities. Diving here with an aqualung at low water is difficult, involving a scramble over slippery rocks for some distance. This, combined with the steep climb to the cliff top, is enough to deter all but the most determined. At high tide, diving the Bay is easier, and is interesting for the profusion of marine life, but you are not exactly breaking new ground! The tidal movements have to be carefully watched, especially when a shore diver swims out beyond the limits of the Bay proper, and especially on spring tides.

175 South Landing. This fourth place where inshore diving can take place at Flamborough was once known as a port more important than Bridlington,

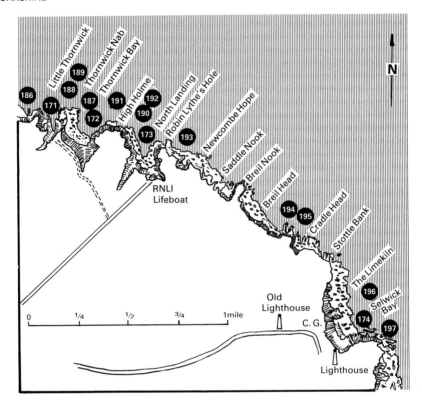

though looking at it now, this is hard to believe! There is no semblance of anything remotely harbour-like here, and no commercial craft operate from the landing today. Until comparatively recently, Flamborough fishermen traditionally kept two cobles, one each at North and South Landings, in order that they could always go to sea regardless of the wind direction. Today, a few small boats are kept here, but nothing on the scale of years gone by. The South Landing is reached by taking South Sea Road from Flamborough village. There is a carpark at the top of the cliff, by the Heritage Centre, and a gently sloping roadway down to the beach. Small craft can be launched here; permission is to be sought from the Spa Offices at Bridlington, and the local bye-laws relating to water safety must be observed (see Bridlington chapter).

Shore diving can also be carried out from here, though it might be considered more suitable as a snorkel diving site. In the days when spearfishing was considered to be an acceptable sport, South Landing was found to be quite a good site – and because of its south facing position, it is sometimes possible to dive here when a northerly wind makes most of the Yorkshire coast impossible.

The seabed off here consist of sand, stones and seaweed, and visibility can be very good in settled weather periods.

Boat Diving Sites (Flamborough area)

176 Hawkwood. Almost as strange as the story of the *Marie Celeste* is that of the *Hawkwood*, for she was abandoned by her crew who then disappeared without trace. Built at Sunderland in 1899, she was a 1155 ton steamer, owned by William France, Fenwick & Co of London, and was a well-known collier on the east coast run. She was 235ft long with a beam of 33ft and a depth of 18ft, and was valued at £14 000 in 1913. On January 12 of that year, she was seen off Flamborough Head in very heavy weather with a list to port, all her lights blazing, yet no sign of life aboard. The steamer *Newark* went as close as she dare to the *Hawkwood*, and could get no response to her signals. She noticed that some of *Hawkwood's* boats had gone, the falls were hanging down the side of the ship.

A south east gale was blowing at the time, and *Hawkwood* finally drove ashore under Speeton Cliffs, in front of Brecon Hole, a little south of King & Queen Rocks. She capsized at once, and started to break up, spewing her coal cargo onto the beach. The crew were never found; all seventeen were lost, though empty lifeboats came ashore later. It became clear in time that *Hawkwood*, like her sister ship *Monkwood* (which sank off the Yorkshire coast as *Glow* later) had an inherent design fault; the bunker space on one side of the ship was twice as great as at the other, because of an offset donkey boiler. This meant the ship had to be trimmed continuously as the fuel was burned, otherwise a list was inevitable. There is little left of *Hawkwood* today, as salvage work was carried out on her afterwards.

177 B.P. Shipbuilder. This 214 ton motor tanker carried the names *Ibis* and then *Angliran* before becoming *B.P. Shipbuilder* when she came into the ownership of B.P. Trading Ltd. She was built in 1935, and was at the end of her working life when she broke her tow off Flamborough Head on October 18 1961, and came ashore under Buckton Cliffs, about half a mile north of the *Skegness* (site 179) wreck. *B.P. Shipbuilder* soon broke up, and little remains of her today, though part of her engine breaks the surface at low water, making the wreck easy to find at that state of tide. Hardly worth a dive unless you are passing and have some air to use up!

B.P. Shipbuilder was 188ft long with a beam of 17ft and a depth of 7ft. She had 5cy oil engines by Sulzer Bros.

178 Pelican. This 156 ton iron trawler was built at Hull in 1895, was 104ft long and was owned by the St. Andrews Steam Fishing Co of Hull. She was returning from the fishing grounds when she struck Bempton cliffs in thick fog in the early hours of December 30, 1909. Blasts on her siren alerted Flamborough Lifeboat, which put off in heavy seas, and after anchoring off, rowed in towards the wreck. She was able to save the nine crew of the *Pelican* from their refuge in the rigging, the hull being submerged in broken water. Filey lifeboat stood byy offshore, while the exhausted men were brought to safety. At one stage, the lifeboat was dumped onto the trawler by a huge wave, and this resulted in damage to the rudder and the loss of four oars, but by 6am, the job was done, and the lifeboat made its way back to safety. The wreck is about 100 yards from the cliff at a point known as Weather Castle Point but there is little of her left. Tommy Round bought this as he bought most of the wrecks near Flamborough, and salvage work started almost at once with his grab boats and 'hard-hat' divers. Incidentally, one of the small boats being used to salvage *Pelican* sank full of scrap

The trawler, Skegness, wrecked with tragic loss of life. (Site 179)

some distance from the wreck, and there is no record of it being re-salvaged. It could explain the odd isolated find that divers sometimes make where there is no sign of any wreck.

179 Skegness. Built as a standard trawler for the Admiralty in 1917, this 275 ton vessel was at the heart of a disaster that still makes local people shudder after more than fifty years. Originally called *James Peake,* she was registered at Lowestoft after WW1, then later went to Hull as *Arragonite* for the Kingston Steam Trawling Co. Finally, she was sold to the Trident Steam Fishing Co, who named the 125ft ship *Skegness.* She was returning to Hull from the Faroes on September 24, 1935 when she ran ashore at Speeton at about low water 2100. The skipper, Richard Wright of Hull, sent a radio message, but indicated that he did not need assistance at that stage. However, the wind increased to a north-easterly gale which brought heavy seas and torrential rain, and the lifeboats were alerted. It was not until 2300 that the maroons went up, and Filey and Flamborough lifeboats put to sea, searching in vain for the stranded trawler. Cliff top rescue parties under the coastguard also failed to find the wreck, and by 23.30, the radio calls for help ceased. It was daylight before the full enormity of the disaster became apparent; lifeboats reached the wreck and found the funnel and wheel-house gone, and no sign of life aboard. The whole crew of eleven men had died. The bodies started to wash ashore later that day.

The wreck of *Skegness* is easy to see today; she is very broken up, and her boiler dries out at low water, though not enough to be able to walk to it. The stem post is high and dry, but the engines and after part of the ship are always underwater.

180 Wapping. This 688 ton iron steamship was built by W. Gray of Hartlepool in 1886 for F. Green & Co of London as an 'up river' collier, known to seamen as a 'flatiron' because they had low superstructure and masts that could be lowered in order to pass under the bridges on the Thames. *Wapping* was built together with *Stepney* and the slightly larger *Poplar* for the sum of £33 250 in total. All three were to be used to carry coal from the Marquis of Londonderry's purpose built Seaham Harbour to the capital. On November 29 1891, *Wapping* ran ashore in fog at Bempton, in a smooth sea. Captain R. Skelton and the fourteen crew got ashore in their own boat, and the coxswain of Flamborough lifeboat immediately set off for Scarborough in a gig in order to bring tugs to get her off the strand. Five paddle tugs visited the wreck, but found her to be already full of water, so no attempt was made to pull her off. The master had his certificate suspended for three months. There have been so many small steamships wrecked along this stretch of coast that it is impossible to say which is which, but this one may well be the wreck that is to be found at the northern end of Old Roll Up, a few yards from the wreck of *Radium* (site 181). The wreck is very badly broken up, and only the boiler is prominent, but there are bits of her hidden among the rocks, in interesting underwater terrain.

Wapping was 160ft long with a beam of 35ft and a depth of 15ft; she had C 2cy engines 27" 50"-33" by Central Marine Engine Works, Hartlepool.

181 Radium. This 3254 ton steamer was built at Irvines yard in 1906, and was 324ft long with a beam of 47ft and a depth of 14ft. She was owned by the Societe Anon Di Armamento Oceana of Trieste, and carried seventeen crew, under Captain Savo Nicorie. She was bound for Venice with coal from Newcastle when she ran ashore in fog north of Flamborough on February 17

THE WRECK BEMPTON

Carrying coals from Newcastle to Trieste, Radium *ran ashore north of Flamborough. (Site 181)*

1923. There had been a north-easterly gale for two days, and as a result, twenty foot breakers were pounding the foot of the cliffs. The vessel was holed forward and midships, and distress flares were set off at once, at about 4am. The Speeton coastguard was quickly alerted, and was successful in getting the crew off by means of lines up the 300ft cliffs. Flamborough, Filey and Scarborough lifeboats had also been alerted, and the Flamborough boat steamed through the gale to stand by for several hours. Later in the day, six of the crew reboarded the *Radium*, but by dusk they realised she was lost, and were taken off again.

The wreck lies about 50 yards offshore in the middle of a shallow bay called Roll Up, just north of Staple Nook, (or Scale Nab) and the boilers can be seen breaking the surface at low water. The wreck was heavily salvaged by the *Piscator* in the ensuing years, but what is left still makes an interesting dive, which can be combined with a dive on the *Lord Ernle,* at Staple Nook.

The water depth here is such that you can dive all day if the fancy takes you!

182 Lord Ernle. Owned by the Perihelion Steam Fishing Co of Grimsby, this 325 ton trawler had been built at Selby in 1919 and was 138ft long with a beam of 24ft and a depth of 13ft. She was returning from the White Sea on the evening of March 4 1937, when the crew, who were playing cards below, felt the vessel shiver from stem to stern at 10pm. They rushed on deck, and through dense fog, could dimly make out the huge cliffs ahead of them. The engines were put full astern, but the ship lurched over the submerged rocks. A Mayday signal was sent at once, and fires were lit on the whaleback, and on the cabin top. The fifteen men aboard must have been very conscious of the fact that when the trawler *Skegness* (site 179) had stranded close to this point eighteen months earlier, all the crew had died. Within half an hour, Flamborough Lifeboat was under way, cautiously examining the coastline through the almost impenetrable fog. She found the *Lord Ernle* at midnight, her bows touching the cliff, and her stern underwater. A heavy swell from the north-east, the aftermath of a recent gale, made it impossible for the lifeboat to go alongside the trawler in the usual way, so she anchored off, then veered down on the *Lord Ernle,* and fired a rocket line across her. One lifeboatman went aboard the trawler, and after setting up a breeches buoy, the first crewman was taken off. The lifeboat sheered, and the line parted, so more anchor line was paid out, bringing the lifeboat dangerously close to the trawler. A four inch line was put between them, and six men were saved before that too parted. On the third attempt,

Lord Ernle, *wrecked at Staple Nook. (Site 187)*

a wire rope was slung between the two, but by this time the fires had gone out, and they worked in pitch darkness until the coastguard arrived on the cliff top with a searchlight. At this time, the lifeboat was picked up by a wave and thrown onto the trawler, but it slid off again with half its rudder torn away. After 3 hours, the skipper of the *Lord Ernle* boarded the lifeboat, and coxswain George Leng was able to head for safety, having carried out a magnificent rescue for which he was later awarded the silver medal for gallantry.

The wreck of *Lord Ernle* is to be found almost touching Staple Nook, at the south end of a shallow bay, Roll Up. It is in about 6m of water, and is badly broken up, with the engine laid over to starboard. There is enough left to make an interesting dive. The wreck of *Lord Ernle* is owned by the authors of this book. She had T 3cy engines by C.D. Holmes of Hull, 13" 23" 37"-26". 1SB 3PF. N.B. Staple Nook is shown on OS maps as Scale Nab.

183 Royallieu. This 205 ton Grimsby trawler was owned by Alec. Black & Co, and had been built at Hull in 1900. She was 114ft long, had 60hp engines, and was built of iron. On April 6 1906, she stranded in fog at Bempton, and was a total loss. Filey diver Chris Baker positively identified the wreck by the yard number which he saw on the builders plate. The wreck lies close up to the cliff foot, about a quarter of a mile south of Staple Nook, where the wreck of *Lord Ernle* lies. She is close to Wandale Nab.

184 Dunstaffnage. This 1393 ton steamer was built by Mackie & Thomson at Glasgow in 1894 for the Scottish Navigation Co. She was 237ft long with a beam of 34ft and a depth of 17ft, and was a well-deck vessel. She was bound for Oporto with a cargo of coal from Sunderland when she ran aground in fog north of Flamborough on October 1, 1908. The stranding took place at Dyke End, Speeton, in front of the coastguard lookout station, and shortly after she struck, a Scottish fishing vessel passed between her and the cliffs, and remarkably, did not herself ground.

About a fortnight later, efforts were made to refloat *Dunstaffnage* but she was too badly damaged, and sank almost as soon as she was off the rocks. So far, no-one is known to have found this wreck, though Dyke End is easy enough to identify; since it is a rocky seabed here, an echo sounder is of little help, though a magnetometer would probably find the wreck. *Dunstaffnage* had T 3cy engines 17" 27" 45"-36". 2SB 4PF by Muir & Houston of Glasgow.

185 Jessie. Built by McKnight & Co at Ayre in 1901, this 332 ton steamer was 147ft long with a beam of 24ft and a depth of 10ft. She was owned by the Shields SS Co, managed by Walker & Bain of Grangemouth, when she was attacked by gunfire from a U-boat on November 11 1917. The ship was so badly damaged that she was deliberately run ashore north of Flamborough Head in an attempt to save her. Four men were killed in the attack, and the ship was doomed too. She is in chart position 54 09 36N 00 02 24W, though so far there is no record of her having been dived. There is another obstruction on the seabed about 500m north of this position which would also stand investigation.

Jessie had engines by Ross & Duncan of Glasgow, C 2cy, 18" 14". 1SB 2PF.

186 Robert Dickinson. A. Leslie & Co of Newcastle built this 1706 ton steamer in 1879, for Bell & Symonds of London. She was 261ft long with a beam of 34ft and a depth of 22ft, and had her sea trials on April 24 1879. Five days later, she left on her maiden voyage, with a cargo of coal, bricks etc. for Naples, from North Shields. She had been at sea for just twelve hours when she ran ashore in dense fog, north of Flamborough Head on April 29, 1879. A kedge anchor was laid, but efforts to refloat her failed, despite the work of a steam tug and divers sent from the Tyne. *Robert Dickinson,* insured for £25 000, broke in two in a gale in early May. The remains of the wreck are at Sanwick Nook, the third small bay north from Thornwick Bay, but time has made them scant and camouflaged.

187 Lindum. This 156 ton steam trawler was built as the *Sir Galahad* at North Shields in 1899, and was 105ft long with a beam of 21ft and a depth of 11ft. She was registered at Grimsby, owner R.D. Clarke, when she ran ashore at Thornwick Bay on October 3 1916, and was a total loss. Skipper Charlie Baker was fined £20, and had his certificate suspended for six months as a result. The ship later slid off the rocks, and now lies in about 9m of water about one cable off Thornwick Nab. The wreck is very broken up. Lindum had T 3cy engines, 12" 18" 30". 1SB 2PF.

188 Kepier. This 703 ton screw schooner was built in 1869 by J. Laing of Sunderland, and was owned by H.T. Morton of that port. She was bound for London with coal from Sunderland when she ran ashore in dense fog on Thornwick Nab on February 12 1886. At high tide, the stern to the bridge was underwater, while the bow pointed skywards. Within days, she began to break up; parts of the ships side came ashore together with sailors' chests, cargo and stores. No lives were lost in the stranding, but the vessel was doomed. The wreck is in almost the same position as *Crosby* (site 189). *Kepier* had C 2cy engines: 25", 43"-36" by T. Richardson, Hartlepool. The ship was 195ft long with a beam of 28ft and a depth of 17ft.

189 Crosby. Built by T. & W. Smith at North Shields in 1870, this 1814 ton steamer was brig-rigged, and owned by Messrs. Pile of London. She measured 273ft long with a beam of 34ft and a depth of 25ft, and was on charter to Messrs Hutchinson & Co of Hull at the time of loss. On January 9 1903, she ran ashore in dense fog half a mile north of North Landing, Flamborough, two hours before daylight at low tide. By noon of the same day, there was no trace of her. *Crosby* had left Middlesbrough the previous evening with cast-iron water pipes for Ramsgate, and the weather had been thick throughout the voyage. She struck rocks some 650 yards offshore just before 6am, and heeled over to starboard. As efforts were being made to launch the starboard boat, the *Crosby* lurched over onto port, immersing the crew, and throwing Captain Henderson into the sea. He swam to a loose ship's boat, boarded it and sculled back to the wreck, where he picked up three others, and made for the nearest landing place to the north. Meantime one man, 2nd Engineer Thomas Campbell had drowned, but the rest of the crew boarded their second small boat, and were later taken aboard the coble *Etna.* All this occurred in conditions of snow and sleet, with a strong south-easterly wind. The four men who rowed north had to face a three mile walk to civilisation when they reached a landing place, and must have been more dead than alive by the time they made it. The wreck position is a little off Thornwick Nab, but her remains are mixed up with those of *Kepier* (site 188) and it is difficult to know which is which.

190 Blonde. Built as an iron screw-schooner in 1863 by C. Lungley of London, this 613 ton vessel was owned by Danziger Rhederei Akt. Ges., Germany. She was interned at the beginning of WW1, and put to work as a collier on the east coast run. On December 28 1916, this ancient steamer ran ashore in fog at North Landing, Flamborough while carrying coal from North Shields to London. The vessel took water rapidly, and the seventeen crew and skipper Alex J. Irvine were taken off by local fishermen, led by lifeboat cox Richard Chadwick. At high water, the *Blonde* was completely submerged, and within a few days her masts and funnel were gone, and coal started to wash ashore. The master attributed the loss to the abnormal eastward set of the current . . ., but he was censured at the inquiry.

Blonde was 178ft long with a beam of 29ft and a depth of 15ft. Her engines were C 4cy 16", 36"-27" by C. Lungley of London.

191 Princess. Owned by Taylor & Sanderson of Sunderland, this 2094 ton steamer had been built by Short Bros of Sunderland in 1883, and was 286ft long with a beam of 39ft and a depth of 21ft. She was bound for Sunderland with ore from Bilbao on November 19 1893, when she encountered a violent north-easterly gale as she rounded Flamborough Head from the south. Reports at the time said that conditions were so bad that the sea was white with foam as far as the eye could see, and huge waves were breaking over the fog station, more than a hundred feet above sea level. It was about one in the morning when *Princess* found herself facing these appalling conditions, and she was driven helplessly back towards the cliffs. The crew took to the rigging when they realised what was about to happen; observers from the shore could see the ship, and attempted to fire rocket lines over her, but the wind just blew them back. The hapless vessel struck at about 2am, and went to pieces within minutes. There were no survivors from her nineteen crew.

The wreck lies between Thornwick Bay and North Landing, and for many years, her boilers could be seen at low water. She is not far from the wreck of *Caenwood* (site 192), but there is little of her left today. Three other vessels were wrecked at Flamborough in the same storm incidentally, and many other ships were lost in other parts of the Yorkshire coast that day.

192 Caenwood. Built by S.P. Austin & Son in 1902, this 1191 ton collier was owned by Wm. Cory & Sons of London, and was 225ft long with a beam of 37ft and a depth of 13ft. She was bound for Devonport with coal from the Tyne when she ran ashore near North Landing in dense fog on November 21, 1905, in a flat calm sea. The impact broke the vessel forward, and she filled almost at once. Local cobles took off the sixteen crew, and the ship broke up within seven days. She was sold for £100 to Tommy Round two days after that. The wreck is now very broken up, lying off the north-west corner of North Landing in about 10m.

Caenwood had T 3cy engines, 20" 33" 54"-33". 1SB 4PF.

193 Dundee. This 839 ton steamer was built at Kinghorn in 1890 for J. Rankine & Son of Grangemouth as a passenger steamer, the first such vessel that the company had. She measured 224ft long with a beam of 29ft and a depth of 14ft, and later came under the ownership of T. MacGill of Glasgow. In the early hours of January 26 1896, she ran ashore in fog north of Flamborough, while bound for Rotterdam with a general cargo from Grangemouth. The master sent the whole crew ashore in their own boat, but

Aground in fog, Caenwood *at North Landing. (Site 192)*

remained aboard with his officers, requesting that the local lifeboat stand by until he had effected communications with Lloyds agent. On his arrival with the coastguard officers, it was decided to abandon ship, as seas were sweeping the decks by this time, and it was evident that she was doomed. Before daylight, cargo, mainly bales of cloth, started to come ashore, and local ladies were soon on the surrounding beaches collecting the cloth, wrapping it around their bodies beneath voluminous skirts in order to carry it off under the noses of the revenue men. The wreck is a few hundred yards south of North Landing, between East Scar and Newcombe Hope, but there is nothing of great significance left due to salvage work carried out early this century.

Dundee had T 3cy engines, 19" 32" 52". 2SB 4RF 2CF by J. Scott & Co of Kircaldy.

194 Birtley. This 1029 ton collier was built by Wood Skinner & Co in 1900, and was owned by the Burnett SS Co. She measured 220ft long with a beam of 33ft and a depth of 14ft. She ran ashore a mile north of Flamborough Head on November 11 1905, while bound for London with coal from the Tyne. The sixteen crew were saved, and it seemed likely that the ship would be refloated. However, the weather worsened, and huge waves smashed over the vessel, taking away her funnel and bridge, and later breaking her back. On November 30, the wreck was sold to Tommy Round, the local salvage contractor. Captain Haddon Taylor, and the First Officer of *Birtley* had their certificates suspended for three months each. The wreck of *Birtley* is close to that of *Wandle* (site 195), and it is unclear which is which.

Birtley had T 3cy engines, 17" 28" 46"-33". 1SB 4PF by the North Eastern Marine Engineering Co.

195 Wandle. On April 29, 1916, this 889 ton collier steamer sighted a U-boat which was carrying a sail as a means of deception, and *Wandle* attempted to ram the raider, which fired at and hit the collier with her deck gun. The U-boat submerged, but the crew of *Wandle* felt sure that they had hit it as it went down. There was great excitement about the event and a big fuss was made of *Wandle* when she arrived in the Thames. However, after hostilities had ceased, it became clear that the U-boat, which turned out to be *UB-27,* was not damaged, and had dived because other British ships were approaching the scene.

The following year, while carrying out her 500th voyage with coal from the Tyne to London, *Wandle* ran ashore one mile north of Flamborough Head, which puts her between Breil Head and Cradle Head, approximate position 54 07 35N 00 05 28W. She is close to the wreck of *Birtley* (site 194), and because all the wrecks in this area were commercially salvaged by Tommy Round, it is difficult to decide which is which of them. *Wandle* was built in 1909 by W. Dobson & Co of Newcastle, and was owned by Wandsworth Gas Light & Coke Co. She was later replaced by *Wandle II,* which also sank off the Yorkshire coast as *Pitwines,* in 1941, but this wreck's position is not known.

196 Cannon. Off Selwicks Bay (Silex Bay) north of Flamborough Head can be found at least one, and probably three iron cannon, in about 15m of water. There is a single cannon straight out from the steps that lead down from the cliff top, while at the north corner of the Bay, about 50 yards offshore, is a pile of cannon shot. There is really not enough evidence to indicate what ship these could be from, but two early warships were lost near Flamborough, and by a strange coincidence, they both had the same name, HMS *Bideford.* The first of these was a 6th rate 20 gun vessel of 282 tons, built at Deptford in 1711, and lost off the Head on March 18 1736. She was 94ft long with a beam of 26ft.

The second HMS *Bideford* was also a 6th rate 20 gun ship, but she was bigger, at 403 tons. She was built in 1756, again at Deptford, and was 105ft long with a beam of 30ft. Records tell us that she was wrecked at Flamborough Head on December 30 1761.

197 Mazeppa. Palmers of Jarrow built this 1164 ton steamer in 1872, and she was owned by Renwick Wilton & Co of Newcastle. The ship was 257ft

This steamer, Mazeppa, *was rigged as a three-masted schooner. (Site 197)*

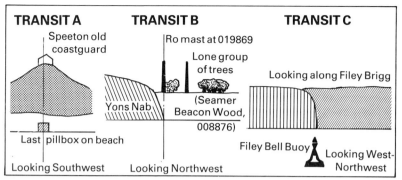

Marks for Thalia. (Site 198)

long with a beam of 30ft and a depth of 17ft, and was rigged as a three-masted screw schooner.

On the night of June 24 1908, dense fog enveloped Flamborough Head, and the *Mazeppa* ran aground during a voyage from the Tyne to Dartmouth. Another ship, the *Collingwood* ran aground that night also, and this was her second stranding here within a few months. She was refloated on both occasions, but the *Mazeppa* was not so lucky; she is still there today, though well salvaged by the local firm of Tommy Round. She lies in position 54 07 00N 00 04 09W, off the south corner of Selwicks (or Silex) Bay, on the north side of the headland. She is well broken up, and spread over a wide area of seabed, with no large pieces, and nothing standing over 3m high.

Mazeppa was fitted with C 3cy engines, 30" 55"-33". 1SB 4PF by Palmers, and a new double boiler was installed in her in 1888.

198 Thalia. This 1308 ton steamer was built in Rotterdam in 1916, and was requisitioned by The Shipping Controller soon afterwards. She was 266ft long with a beam of 39ft and a depth of 14ft, had two decks and a cruiser stern, and was armed for defence. *Thalia* was in ballast when she was torpedoed and sunk four miles east-south-east of Filey Brigg on October 8 1918, with the loss of three lives. She was in fact the last ship to be sunk by enemy action in the North Sea, during WW1. Her wreck is in position 54 11 45N 00 10 50W, in a little over 30m depth. She is pretty well all there, though fairly well broken up, and stands some 4m high. *Thalia* had engines by Werkspoor, Amsterdam, T 3cy, 20" 31" 50"-36". 2SB.

199 Commonwealth. Built by Furness Withy in 1896, this 3353 ton steamer was owned by the Commonwealth Steamship Co of London, and was 330ft long with a beam of 45ft and a depth of 19ft. She was armed for defence, but was torpedoed and sunk by a submarine with the loss of fourteen lives on February 19 1918, some five miles north-east of Flamborough Head while carrying 5300 tons of iron ore. The wreck is in position 53 11 34N 00 00 06W in a depth of 53m. She lies in a north-west–south-east attitude, and appears to be in two parts. She stands some 10m high, and one survey in 1976 concluded that the wreck of the American frigate *Bon Homme Richard* is underneath this wreck. It was not made clear at the time how this conclusion was reached, and there is no record of the wreck having been dived – possibly because the seabed here is beyond safe diving depth for

air divers. *Commonwealth* had T 3cy engines by the builders, 25" 38" 64".
2SB 6CF.

200 Riviere. Owned by the Earl Steam Fishing Co of Grimsby, this 226 ton
trawler was built at Beverley in 1916, and was 117ft long with a beam of 22ft
and a depth of 13ft. She sank after a collision in fog with the steamer
Firelight on June 10 1953 some five miles off Flamborough Head. The wreck
is in position 54 11 30N 00 01 22E, on a rock outcrop at a depth of 51m.
There is no scour, and the surrounding seabed drops away to 54m, so this
is right on the limits of safe diving.

201 Oscar (probably). Though we have no real idea as to the position of
this wreck, other than off Flamborough Head, it is included here because it
is of special interest. *Oscar* was built as long ago as 1850, making her one
of the earliest steamers ever lost in this part of the world. She was built by
Wm. Denny of Dumbarton for R. Henderson of Belfast, and was 156ft long
with a beam of 23ft and a depth of 13ft, and had a 2cy 75hp engine. She
was 330 tons gross, 198 net, and later in her career was lengthened to
160ft, and had her engine changed to a 50hp compound. In 1858 she was
sold to W. Sloan & Co, and in 1870 she was sold again to the Dingwall &
Skye Railway Co for service as a ferry. On November 9 of that year, she ran
ashore at Applecross, and was abandoned to the underwriters. A year later,
she had been refloated, and was sold to G.G. MacKay of Grangemouth who
put her on the east coast run. On July 15 1882, she was in collision with the
steamship *Breeze* of Hartlepool off Flamborough Head, during a voyage
from London to Middlesbrough. The ancient iron hull of *Oscar* took a
battering that was to prove too much, and she sank the next day. She would
make a fascinating find – and she is there, somewhere!
   There is an unknown wreck in position 54 11 01N 00 03 18W that appears
to be about the right size for *Oscar;* this one lies approximately east-west in
a depth of 45m, but there is no diving information on her as yet.

202 Mongolian. Built by D.W. Henderson of Glasgow in 1891 for the Indian
& Peninsular Steam Navigation Co, this 4892 ton ship was 400ft long with a
beam of 45ft and a depth of 23ft. She was bound for London with a general
cargo, the property of the Italian Government, from Middlesbrough when
she was torpedoed and sunk in Filey Bay on July 21 1918.
   Thirty-six lives were lost, indicating perhaps that she sank very quickly, in
a position 247 degrees, 4.2 miles from Speeton Mill, a prominent landmark.
The wreck lies in about 32m of water in position 54 10 55N 00 08 20W, and
is in one large piece. Her bow and stern are both largely intact, and though
her bulwarks have collapsed in places, it is easy to navigate the wreck by
swimming along either of her sides. She is lying upright, and her holds, 4
boilers, engine and deck layout can clearly be seen. There are numerous
cargo winches still in place, four anchors lying on her decks, and her two
masts lying partly on the wreck and partly on the sand and stone seabed. It
is possible to swim quite some distance under her whaleback bow, and
care must be taken not to do this inadvertently, since the silt kicked up by
fins is virtually impenetrable to the eye. All in all, this is one of the more
interesting wreck dives, but sadly, the visibility here is often not very good.
   Mongolian had T 3cy engines by D & W Henderson, 30" 50" 80"-60".
Lloyd's unfortunately gives no boiler details.

Mongolian, *torpedoed and sunk in Filey Bay in 1918. (Site 202)*

The ship's bell.

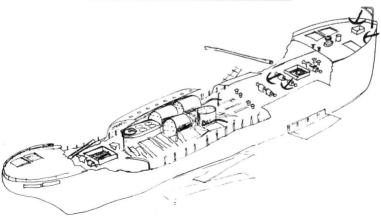

General arrangement of the Mongolian *wreck. (Site 202)*

203 Upside Down Wreck. Despite its nickname, only the forward part of the wreck fits the description. The after part of the unknown wreck is lying on its side, with a gun on its after deck. The position of this one is 54 11 11N 00 08 16W, she is just outside the wreck of the *Mongolian* (site 202), and is so close to it that the first divers on the wreck thought that they were diving that wreck, until they saw it.

It is possible that this could be the 1858 ton *Avance,* judging by the size of the wreck, and the fact that the *Avance* is charted close by in position 54 11 45N 00 11 00W – where nothing has been found.

Built by J.L. Thompson & Sons in 1883, this iron screw-schooner was formerly the *Borussia* and the *Crete.* She was 256ft long with a beam of 36ft and a depth of 17ft, and was owned by Rederi A/B Urania, Helsingborg. *Avance* was torpedoed and sunk by a U-boat in Filey Bay on June 23 1918. She had C 2cy engines, 32" 62"-39" which gave her 200nhp.

204 Bon Homme Richard (maybe). There can be little doubt that this wreck is one of the most important in UK waters, for it was the first ship in the American Navy, and its captain was America's Drake, Raleigh, Hawkins and Nelson all rolled into one.

Unfortunately, the information on the precise location of the wreck is extremely 'iffy' – in fact if we knew where it was, we would be rich men today! John Paul Jones was of Scottish descent, and during the American War of Independence, was in command of an old East Indiaman that had been sent to harass the British. In 1778, he engaged in a series of actions on the west coast that had shocked the entire nation, and made his name a household word. His greatest moment came however when he fought the Battle of Flamborough Head on September 23 1779, with a squadron of four vessels, the *Richard* and the *Alliance,* each of forty guns, the *Pallas* of 32 guns, and the *Vengeance* of 12 guns. These four attacked a convoy of merchantmen coming from the Baltic escorted by two English men o' war, the *Serapis* of 44 guns, commanded by Captain Richard Pearson, and the *Countess of Scarborough,* 22 guns, commanded by Captain Piercy. In a long and fierce battle, the merchant vessels escaped unscathed, but the American fleet gained the upper hand, and to save lives, *Serapis* eventually struck, and was boarded by John Paul Jones. Meanwhile the *Bon Homme Richard* was abandoned, on fire and waterlogged, eventually sinking to become Yorkshire's most illustrious wreck.

There is an obstruction on the seabed in position 54 10 36N 00 02 00W which has been linked to the John Paul Jones ship; it is in about 47m of water, and looks about 150ft long on sonar. There is no record of anyone having dived this obstruction so far; it is not easy to locate on an echo sounder, and it may well turn out to be just a pile of stones, or a sand ridge. On the other hand . . . Another survey team that looked for the American Navy's first ship concluded that it lay, by coincidence, directly underneath the wreck of a WW1 merchant shipwreck, that of the *Commonwealth* (site 199). One day of course, the wreck will be found, for the one thing that is certain is that it is there somewhere! There are no guarantees with the two alternatives given here, but so far, neither position has been proved to be wrong.(See back cover)

205 Trongate (possibly). There is a bad obstruction in position 54 10 32N 00 07 10W which may well prove to be *Trongate,* which is currently charted as being in position 54 10 35N 00 07 40W, but so far there is no record of her having been dived. The ship was a 2553 ton, owned by Turnbull Scott Shipping of London, and built for them by Thos. Turnbull & Co of Whitby, in 1897. She was 310ft long with a beam of 44ft and a depth of 20ft, and was valued in 1911 at £13 000. She loaded coal at Newcastle for France, and was torpedoed and sunk by *UC-71* on September 22 1917, some five miles north of Flamborough. One report says that Captain H.M. Brown and the entire crew took to their boats and were all rescued, while another source suggests that two men died in the sinking. *Trongate* had T 3cy engines by Blair & Co of Stockton, 23" 37" 61"-39". 2SB 6CF.

206 Hercules. Built at Whitehaven in 1881 for R.P. Houston & Co of Liverpool, this 1095 ton steamer later was sold to German owners, but was then put back under the British flag when she was requisitioned in 1915. She was attacked by a U-boat on August 26 1917, in the North Sea, but the torpedo missed, and *Hercules* lived to fight another day. A second attack on her succeeded however on March 25 1918, when she was sunk with the loss of one life four miles north-north-west of Flamborough Head. It was a torpedo that got her, and *Hercules* did not use her own gun – the attack came too suddenly for that. She was 221ft long with a beam of 34ft and a depth of 17ft.

The wreck lies in position 54 10 19N 00 09 33W, in about 30m of water. She is broken up, but appears to be all there, and stands some 4m or so clear of the sand and silt seabed. Visibility is often very poor on this one. *Hercules* had engines by Jones of Liverpool, C inverted 2cy, 27" 54". 1SB.

207 Seistan. This 4238 ton Strick Liner was built by W. Gray & Co at Hartlepool in 1907 as *Saint Rene*, later renamed *Headley* and finally *Seistan*. She was 364ft long with a beam of 50ft and a depth of 18ft, and was registered at Swansea. Her 408nhp engines gave her a speed of 10 knots, but this did not save her from being torpedoed and sunk by a U-boat with the loss of five lives on October 23 1917, some three and a half miles north-west of Flamborough Head. Captain R. Forbes was among the survivors. The *Seistan* was yard number 737 at the builders; by a strange coincidence, yard number 736 at the same builders was *Tangistan* (site 151), another Strick Liner, and she was also torpedoed and sunk within 6 miles or so of *Seistan*, earlier in WW1.

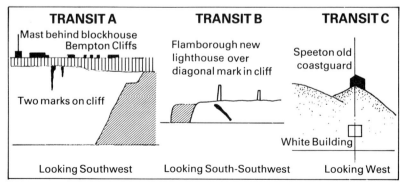

TRANSIT A	TRANSIT B	TRANSIT C
Mast behind blockhouse Bempton Cliffs	Flamborough new lighthouse over diagonal mark in cliff	Speeton old coastguard
Two marks on cliff		White Building
Looking Southwest	Looking South-Southwest	Looking West

Marks for Seistan. (Site 207)

The wreck is in position 54 10 05N 00 07 10W, in a depth of about 33m. The wreck is all there, and makes an impressive dive, with the bow and stern sections prominent, and the midships section broken up and scattered. The stern section is the highest part of the wreck, standing up some 10m or so, and leaning over to starboard. The propellor was removed in the 1970's by divers, but one blade broke off, and is still buried in situ. Close by are several rounds of ammunition from the ship's gun, which was mounted on the poop deck. There is a large spare propellor lying forward of this section, made of cast iron. Unfortunately, underwater visibility is often very poor on this wreck, except after a prolonged period of calm weather and slack tides. *Seistan* had engines by Central Marine Engineering Works, T 3cy, 26" 43" 72"-45". 3SB 9RF.

208 Chicago. This 7709 ton steamer was built by Earls of Hull in 1917 for Ellerman Wilson Line of Hull, and was 446ft long with a beam of 57ft and a depth of 31ft. She was armed for defence during WW1, but this did not prevent her from being attacked by a U-boat on July 8, 1918, carrying oil fuel, some 4 miles north-east of Flamborough Head. The wreck lies in position 54 09 28N 00 01 32W, in a depth of about 40m. She is in a northeast–south-west attitude, and has a least depth of 36m.

Three men were lost in the sinking. *Chicago* had T 3cy engines, 28" 46" 79"-54". 3SB 12CF, giving her 685nhp.

209 Charing Cross. Built by Palmers & Co at Howden in 1892, this 2534 ton steamer was owned by the Charing Cross SS Co of Cardiff, and was 300ft long with a beam of 40ft and a depth of 21ft. She was a collier, and was armed for defence in WW1, but was attacked and sunk by a U-boat on July 1 1918, some 4 miles off Flamborough Head. The wreck lies in about 48m of water in position 54 09 18N 00 01 11E, and is known to fishermen as a bad obstruction. There is no record of her having been dived.

Charing Cross had T 3cy engines, 22" 36" 60". 2SB 6CF.

210 Grekland. This Swedish steamer of 2744 tons was built as *St. Eric* in 1905 by J. Blume & Co at Sunderland, and was 314ft long with a beam of 46ft and a depth of 20ft. She was torpedoed by a U-boat on June 29, 1918, off Flamborough Head, and her wreck is thought to be the one in position 54 08 34N 00 03 07E in approximately 46m of water. All that is known at present is that there is a bad obstruction in this position; no dives have been recorded on the wreck to date. *Grekland* had T 3cy engines, 23" 38" 62". 2SB 6PF, by Dickerson of Sunderland.

211 Greltoria. This 5143 ton steamer was built in 1917 by the Northumberland Shipbuilding Co of Newcastle for Griffiths Lewis S.N. Co of Cardiff, and was 375ft long with a beam of 51ft and a depth of 32ft. She was less than a year old when she was torpedoed and sunk close to Flamborough Head on September 27 1917. One report suggests that she was carrying coal at the time; another says that she had a general cargo. The wreck, owned now by Bridlington Diving Services, lies in position 54 08 30N 00 05 25W in a depth of about 27m. She is lying on a silty seabed, and the wreck is in fact heavily silted over, making visibility very poor here. *Greltoria* had T 3ct engines, 25" 41" 69"-48". 3SB 9CF by North Eastern Marine Eng. Co of Sunderland. The ship was armed for defence.

212 Middlesbro'. This 989 ton steamer, often wrongly referred to as

The strange and tragic mystery of Malvina *and* UB-107 *is still unsolved. (Site 213)*

Middlesbrough, was built in 1924 by Hawthorn Leslie & Co at Newcastle, and was owned by the Tyne-Tees Steam Shipping Co. She was 225ft long with a beam of 32ft and a depth of 14ft. Bound for London with a cargo of girders from the Tees, she came too close in and struck a submerged rock off Flamborough Head on December 9 1939. Water poured into the engine room and stokehold at over a foot a minute, and the crew were obliged to take to their small boats. They were picked up by a passing steamer, and by the local lifeboat, which landed several survivors, then went back to the scene only to find that the *Middlesbro'* had gone down. The incident occurred during pitch darkness. The wreck was positively identified by diver Gordon Wadsworth, who saw the makers plate on the wreck in position 54 08 24N 00 04 36W. She is broken up, lying on her port side with the uppperworks on the coarse sand and gravel seabed. The ships double bottom stands some 4m high in places, in a seabed depth of 32m. *Middlesbro'* had engines by the Shields Engineering Co, T 3cy 19" 31" 50"-33". 2SB 6CF.

213 Malvina/UB-107. This combined wreck site is one of the strangest and most tragic that can be found, for even now, almost seventy years after the event, no-one knows how two crews were lost in one place, probably at the same time. The *Malvina* was a 1244 ton iron screw-schooner built at Glasgow in 1879 by J.G. Thompson. She was 254ft long with a beam of 31ft and a depth of 18ft, and was owned by the London & Edinburgh Shipping Co of Leith. On August 2 1918, she was attacked and sunk by a U-boat

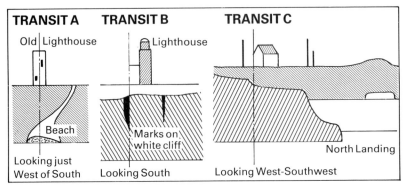

Marks for Malvina. (Site 213)

some little distance north-north-east of Flamborough Head, and the captain and thirteen crew were all killed. At the time of loss, she was carrying a general cargo, and was armed for defence. Five days earlier, an apparently unconnected incident had occurred off Whitby, when the armed yacht *Vanessa* and three armed trawlers came across a German submarine, thought to be the *UB-107*, commanded by Von Prittwitz. This vessel had undertaken two unsuccessful cruises off the east coast earlier in the year, and had left Zeebrugge on July 26 for a third attempt to destroy British shipping. She never returned home, and *Vanessa* was credited with having sunk her with depth-charges off Whitby. British divers failed to locate the wreck of *UB-107* at the time however, but her wreck was estimated to be in position 54 23 30N 00 24 20W.

In 1985, a group of visiting divers were helping a local fisherman by diving on a wreck off Flamborough known as *Porter Packet* in order to free his lobster pots, when they realised that they were diving on a submarine wreck. Further dives established that the propellor was still in place, and it bore the distinctly engraved legend *UB-107*. There was still no positive identification of the steamer that *UB-107* was tangled up with, but examination of the boilers and engine led us to believe that it was in fact the *Malvina*. Divers from Filey finally came up with the evidence during summer of 1986 when they discovered a steel plate partially buried under the bows of the steamer, but with enough of it showing to make out the letters 'Mal . . .'.

Because there were no survivors from either vessel, we can only speculate as to what terrible events took place on that day in August 1918, and no-one to date has been able to decide whether the U-boat is lying under, over or even through the wreck of *Malvina*, but it seems likely that they went down together. It is conceivable that the stricken U-boat might have collided with the wreck a day or two after *Malvina's* sinking, but this seems less likely.

The two wrecks are in position 54 08 15N 00 04 24W, in a depth of about 25m, and are lying more or less at right angles to each other, with the U-boat disappearing into the steamer near the engines of the latter. The steamer's engines are laid well over, immediately behind the two boilers, and when last seen, were draped with old trawl nets. The bows are a little way off, and near the fo'csle divers have found plates, dishes and porcelain ink bottles, but nothing so far that gives a clue as to why she was

UB-110, the same class as UB-107, was sunk in 1918, then raised and towed to Whitby. (Site 213)

nicknamed *Porter Packet*. Diving here must only be attempted at slack water, which occurs about the same time as low water Scarborough, or even a little before. When the tide starts to flow, it runs very fast, very quickly, even on neap tides, and will catch out the unwary. Great care must be taken; this is not a dive for novices.

Malvina had T 3cy engines by the builder, 25" 43" 68". 2SB 6CF. *UB-107* was 510 tons displacement, 4 bow torpedo tubes, 1 stern tube. This U-boat incidentally, had earlier sunk *Chloris* (site 270), *John Rettig* (site 266), *Crimdon* (site 57) and *Kalo* (site 272) off the Yorkshire coast. (See separate entries.)

214 Harbourne. Built by S.P. Austin in 1893, this 1158 ton collier was owned by J. & C. Harrison, and was 244ft long with a beam of 34ft and a depth of 17ft. She was bound for London with a cargo of coal from Blyth when she came into collision with the steamer *Eppleton* off Flamborough Head on March 29 1894. *Harbourne* sank, but fortunately all the crew were saved. The wreck is thought to be the one in position 54 08 00N 00 05 12W, but so far there are no records of her having been dived.

Harbourne had T 3cy engines, 18" 30" 49". 1SB by J. Dickinson.

215 Apollonia. Built by Reinherstieg Schiffswerft at Hamburg in 1891 as the *Venetia,* this ship had no less than six names in her 26 year career. She became the *Bellagio* in 1900, *Paros* in 1905, *Galata* in 1906, and *Apollonia* in 1913. Her sixth name was given to her by divers who discovered the wreck in the 1970s; they named her *The Bombship* – which gives an idea of what she was carrying!

Apollonia was 334ft long with a beam of 40ft and a depth of 24ft, and grossed 2861 tons. She was originally a passenger liner on the Hamburg – New York run, but ended her days in the ownership of the Sicilia Soc di Nav, Palermo. She was carrying munitions when she was sunk off Flamborough Head on March 1 1917. There is some doubt as to the cause of loss; one source suggests that she struck a mine, while another says that she was torpedoed by the German submarine *U-32*. Either way, Flamborough lifeboat was launched, and was able to save seven lives.

The wreck is in position 54 07 32N 00 03 41W in a depth of about 21m. She is in a north-west–south-east attitude, on a rocky shelf, and is very broken up, with a high point about midships. Diving on this wreck should only be undertaken at slack water here; this occurs about one hour before slack water at Bridlington. *Apollonia* was fitted with T 3cy engines.

216 Unknown. In position 54 07 25N 00 02 44W is the wreck of an unknown vessel which measures approximately 215ft by 36ft, in a depth of 28m. She is lying north-south, and though well broken up, stands some 6m clear of the seabed. This position is close to where the 'A' type Standard ship *War Crocus* was sunk, two and a half miles east by north of Flamborough Head. *War Crocus* had a particularly brief and inglorious career; she was built in 1918 by W. Gray & Co of Hartlepool for The Shipping Controller, and was launched in time to be taken over on July 7 1918. She sailed that evening, and early the following morning was sunk by a torpedo, fortunately without loss of life.

War Crocus, 5296 tons, was 400ft long with a beam of 52ft and a depth of 28ft. She had T 3cy engines, 27" 44" 73"-48". 3SB 9CF by Central Marine Engineering Works. However, other reports say that *War Crocus* sank four miles east by north of the Head, in position 54 08 00N 00 01 30E, which would put her almost out of diving depth for air diving.

217 Cambrai. Built in 1875 by Schlesingers of Newcastle, this 963 ton steamer was originally named *Louise,* and was owned by Cie Des Bateaux a Vap du Nord. She was 219ft long with a beam of 30ft and a depth of 18ft, and was rigged as a screw schooner. She was attacked and sunk by a German submarine on August 8 1918, off Flamborough Head. The wreck lies in position 54 07 23N 00 01 32W in a depth of 38m. She is very broken, lying almost north-south, with the high points some 4m clear of the seabed. *Cambrai* had engines by T. Clark of Sunderland, C 2cy, 28" 53".

218 Arctic. This iron trawler was built at Hull in 1888 and grossed 154 tons. She was owned by the Grimsby Steam Fishing co, was 101ft long, and had 45hp engines. In the early hours of January 20, 1909, she collided with the Grimsby steamer *Haverstoe* while returning from Iceland, some 6 miles east-by-south of Flamborough Head. It was clear weather at the time; the two ships simply passed too close together, and the propellor from the *Haverstoe* ripped through one of the trawlers plates, and she sank within four minutes. Two fishermen were lost, eleven others escaped with their lives.

The wreck of *Arctic* is thought to be the one in position 54 07 12N 00 06 35E in a depth of 50m. She is lying roughly east-west on a smooth gravel seabed, and stands some 4m high. There is no record of her having been positively identified as yet.

219 Goodwood. This 2796 ton collier was built by S.P. Austin & Son at Sunderland in 1937, at a cost of £56 000 for W. France, Fenwick & Co and was reckoned to be the best collier on the east coast run at the time. She was 306ft long with a beam of 44ft and a depth of 19ft, and had her engines aft. *Goodwood* was to earn the distinction of being the first ship to be sunk in the North Sea in WW2.

She was torpedoed and sunk off Flamborough Head on September 10

North Landing, where some shore diving can take place. (Site 173)

1939, while in convoy. No lives were lost despite the speed of the sinking, but Captain Hewson had both legs broken in the attack. The U-boat attacker was sunk by one of the escort vessels, and was salved later; papers recovered from it were of such value to our forces that it was decided that it was worth the loss of the *Goodwood* in return for them! The wreck, which is owned by a team of divers, is in position 54 07 10N 00 02 47W in a depth of 28m. It lies in a north-west–south-east attitude on a smooth, hard bottom, and is in two parts. The main part of the wreck is lying on its port side, well broken up, with parts flattened right down to the seabed.

Goodwood had T 3cy engines by North Eastern Marine Engineering, 18" 29" 52"-39". 2SB 6CF.

220 Graafgeld. On January 15 1917, five Norwegian seamen were brought ashore at Bridlington in an exhausted state; they had been in the sea for an hour following the sinking of their ship, the 728 ton *Graafgeld*. These five were the lucky ones; there had been thirteen men aboard the ship, the other eight, including the captain, were lost. The ship had struck a mine about a mile and a half east of Flamborough. Unfortunately, this ship is not listed in Lloyd's Register, hence the lack of detail here. The wreck is in position 54 07 06N 00 01 02E in a depth of 45m. She is in one piece, lying almost east-west on a smooth gravel bottom, and stands some 6m high, with no scour.

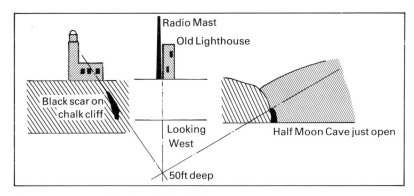

Marks for Hospital Ship. (Site 221)

221 Hospital Ship. Lying in just 16m of water off Selwicks Bay is an old steamship wreck whose identity has not yet been established, but which is known locally as the hospital ship. There are no records of where this name came from, incidentally.

The wreck is completely broken up, but the two boilers, engine parts and bottom plates are clearly visible among the rocky gullies that form the seabed here. Part of a ship's bell was found here among the wreckage recently, and this bore a string of indecipherable letters, preceded by a letter *H.* This might we be from the *Harbourne,* charted in position 54 08 00N 00 05 12W (Site 214).

222 Gunhouse wreck. This is the name given to an unknown wreck in position 54 07 02N 00 00 56W, in a depth of 37m. Whatever it is, it is big, at over 400ft in length, and stands some 10m high. It is in two main parts, with the high point near the break, and it lies in a north-west–south-east attitude on a smooth gravel seabed.

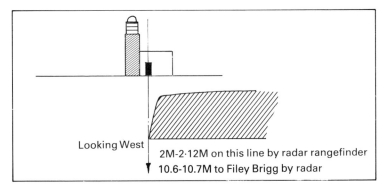

Marks for Gunhouse wreck. (Site 222)

223 Lady Josyan. Pearce & Co of Stockton built this 1054 ton steamer in 1872, and she was 225ft long with a beam of 30ft and a depth of 17ft.

She was owned by R. Gordon of London, and was carrying coal from the Tyne to the capital when she came into collision with the *Hero* of Middlesbrough off Flamborough Head. The incident, which took place on October 26 1884, resulted in the loss of *Lady Josyan*. The wreck is thought to be the one in position 54 07 00N 00 04 00W, but so far there is no record of her having been dived, even though there is only about 25m of water here. *Lady Josyan* had C 2cy engines, 26" 52"-36" by Day, Summers Co.

224 Kilrea. Built by the Dundee Shipbuilding Co in 1912, this 767 ton steamer was owned by R. & D.A. Duncan and registered at Belfast. She was originally called *Wanstead,* being renamed *Teesdale* and finally *Kilrea*. She was 190ft long with a beam of 30ft and a depth of 12ft, had three masts and aft engines. On February 15 1944, she sank after a collision off Flamborough Head. The wreck is in position 54 06 57N 00 01 59E in a depth of 46m. She is lying roughly north-west–south-east on a smooth gravel bottom, with high points at each end standing almost 5m clear of the seabed, with no scour. *Kilrea* had T 3cy engines, 16" 27" 44"-30" by G.T. Grey of Shields. 1SB 3PF.

Area Information and Services

These are the same as for Bridlington area, with the following additions;

Local Coastguard. Sector station, Flamborough, Tel 0262 850203 during business hours.
Heritage Coast Project Officer. Tel 0262-678967.
Camping. Sea Farm Camp Club, Flamborough, Tel 0262-850053.

Area 6:
Bridlington Bay

This area starts at latitude 54 06 12N in the north, and reaches south to latitude 54 48 41N an area known as Bridlington Bay. Its northern extremity is boardered by the white cliffs of Flamborough Head, which affords protection to the small fishing port of Bridlington, nestling in the north-west corner of the Bay. From here, the coast curves gently in a south-south-easterly direction, and is notable for having one of the longest unbroken stretches of sandy beach in England. The hinterland, an agricultural area bounded by the Yorkshire wolds, is still known by its ancient name of Holderness.

Bridlington Bay provides a marked contrast with the more northerly parts of the Yorkshire coast, for there are no rocky beaches or cliffs, just clay, mud and sand. Consequently there is no kelp or other weed, and this in turn means that there is little in the way of "scenic" diving from the shore once you move south of the chalk headland at Flamborough. The seabed over

The great gale of 1871 wrecked more than 30 ships in Bridlington Bay. It is doubtful whether anything of them is left for the diver.

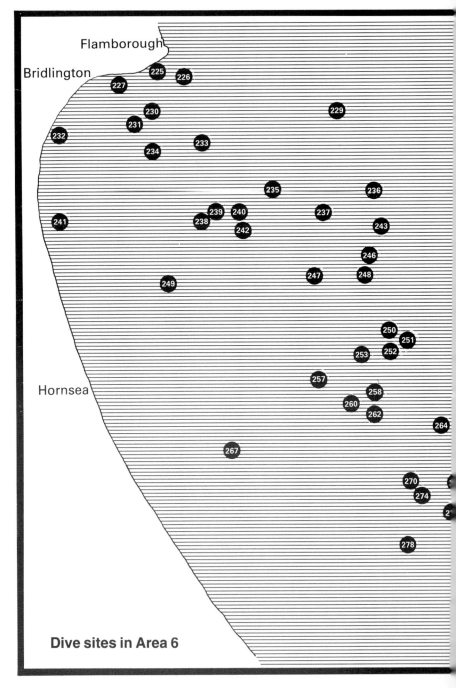

Dive sites in Area 6

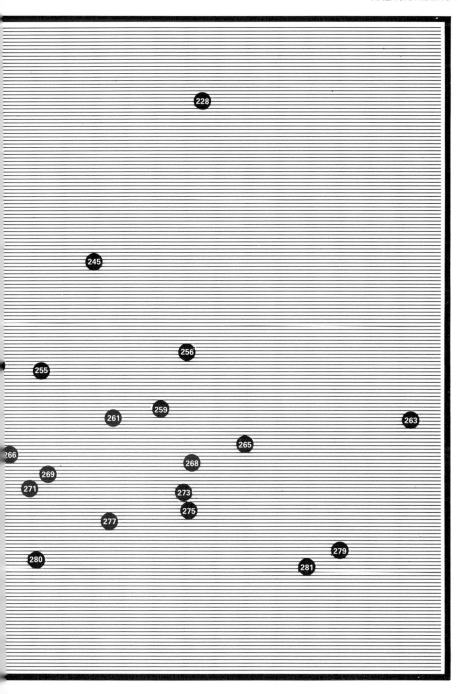

Looking into Bridlington Bay from Dane's Dyke.

the whole area is composed of sand, shingle, clay, gravel and broken shells. Generally speaking, the further south you go, the shallower the depths become. Off Flamborough Head itself, the 30m depth contour passes little over a mile offshore, while off Hornsea, some twelve miles to the south, the 30m contour is twelve miles offshore.

What this area lacks in underwater scenic beauty, it more than compensates for by its abundance of shipwrecks, most of which are relics of the two World Wars. Many of these have been dived, but many more remain unsullied by the wreckhunter's hand. Diving the area is quite straightforward with clearly defined launching areas for small boats, and with a number of charter boats available at Bridlington. Normally these are used to take angling parties, but since the anglers are keen to fish on wrecks, the skippers are able to meet the needs of divers too. There is currently only one charter skipper here who takes divers only.

The East Yorkshire Borough Council controls launching slipways at South Landing, Flamborough, and at South Cliff, Bridlington, and applications to use either of these should be made either to the Foreshores Officer, The Spa, Bridlington, or to the Inspector on duty at the South Cliff launching site. There are strict rules governing every aspect of safety, from clear identification marks on the vessel to safety equipment carried, and a requirement for third party insurance cover. All boats launched must leave their trailers on the beach, where they can be clearly seen, and all boats must return to the shore an hour before sunset. The season for launching from either of these slips extends from Good Friday to 31 October in any year. Copies of the regulations can be obtained from The Spa, South Marine Drive, Bridlington, YO15 3JH.

Bridlington Harbour is controlled by a body of commissioners, not by the local authority, and does not offer launching facilities for visiting boats. .

A third launching facility for the north end of Bridlington Bay is provided by the South Shore Boat Club, Wilsthorpe, Bridlington – not to be confused with the South Cliff launching site. The two are just a few hundred yards apart.

Bridlington itself is a typical east coast holiday town which offers all the amenities and accommodation you would expect to find in such a place. From the divers point of view, air is available at Sea Diver the only diving equipment dealer in the town. Bridlington is fed by two main roads, the A165 from Scarborough and the north, and the A166 from Driffield and points west.

Three miles southwards from Bridlington, the next launching site is at the tiny village of Fraisthorpe. A narrow winding road leads to a small carpark from which access to the beach can be gained by small boat trailers. the access is controlled by the owners of Auburn Farm, who for a modest fee will unlock the gate for divers, who must be self-sufficient. For a somewhat less modest fee, the owners will offer the services of a tractor to rescue you if your towing vehicle gets stuck in the sand!

Hornsea is the only other coastal town in the area; it is a small holiday town some 15 miles south of Bridlington by road. Although there are no special facilities for divers in the town, there is good access to the sea. At the end of New Road is a concrete ramp which is open to all users, and is currently free of charge. Hornsea Coastguard use this ramp to launch their own 5.4m Avon Searider – the only coastguard boat in use on the Yorkshire coast. About 200 yards south of this slip is a second one, the Town Launching Site at the end of Sands Lane, where there is a gap in the sea defence wall. This is where the local fishing boats operate from, and again there is free access to all users at present. During the last two years, work has been carried out on the groynes on the beach, and the end of each line of groynes now carries a marker, making it much safer for boats operating from here. There are no particular dangers offshore.

At the time of writing, few divers take advantage of the launching facilities in Hornsea, though local Police diving teams do come here from time to time. The Hornsea Coastguard Sector Station is manned during business hours, and divers planning to launch here should make their intentions known. Without exception, the coastguards welcome telephone enquiries or information from divers, and are only too plesed to offer help and advice. It is foolish not to use their good offices. Divers who are perhaps travelling

A submarine, UB-122, of the type which operated in this area.

seventy or eighty miles to the coast should always telephone Humber Coastguard before setting out in order to ascertain sea conditions, in order to save a wasted journey.

Hornsea is approached by the B1242 from Bridlington, the A1035/B1244 from Beverley, or the A165/B1243 from Hull.

Shore Diving Sites:

None in this area.

Boat Diving Sites

225 Mary. Built at Helsingfors in 1884, this 1124 ton steamer was owned by Helmsing & Grimm, and was registered at Riga, Russia. She was 233ft long with a beam of 31ft and a depth of 16ft, and was rigged as a screw-schooner. On March 2 1916, she ran ashore between Flamborough Head and South Landing, Flamborough during the hours of darkness. The *Mary* was holed, and her bottom badly damaged, but the crew would not leave when the local lifeboat arrived. Later, a heavy north-west gale sprang up, and the ship began to break up. There was 12 feet of water in the after part of the ship when the lifeboat *Matthew Middlewood* took off the 19 crew, leaving the *Mary* to her fate. The vessel had C 2cy engines, 26" 51"-33" by the builders.

226 Thea. A victim of the Smithic Sands was this 273 ton Belgian vessel, built at Ostend in 1929, and owned by J. Holdenberg of Groningen. She was 115ft long with a beam of 23ft and a depth of 8ft, and was powered by a six-cylinder diesel engine. On April 27 1946, she capsized and sank on the Smithic with the loss of two lives.

Captain Jan Bergema, his wife, and the rest of the crew took to the small boat, and rowed ashore, making a landfall at Barmston, a few miles south of Bridlington.

The wreck is in position 54 05 58N 00 03 59W, a little to the south of the north-cardinal North Smithic buoy. She lies on the eastern side of a sandwave in a depth of about 10m. The seabed is irregular, and the wreck is partially buried, but different parts scour out at different times.

227 Akranes. This 358 ton Grimsby trawler was named after a place in Iceland, where she was a regular visitor before WW2. The vessel had been built in 1929 at Selby for the Consolidated Fisheries Co, but was requisitioned by the Admiralty, and was made flagship of a group of three minesweeping trawlers, whose duties were to keep clear the swept channel between Flamborough Head in the north and Sheringham in the south. She was commanded by Lt. W.A.C. 'Bobby' Harvey, RNVR, who had previously been blown up by a mine in the Humber aboard the minesweeping trawler *Sea King*.

Akranes was anchored off Danes Dyke, south of Flamborough Head on the night of July 4 1941, with the trawlers *Sandringham* and *Almandine* after a days sweeping. It was a glorious night, with a mirror-like sea. RAF bombers were heard overhead on their way to attack German targets, and *Almandine* was on guard duty, with her guns manned, and both she and *Akranes* had their small boats tied alongside as was their normal practice. Just after the midnight news on the radio, the rattle of gunfire was heard,

The wreck of L'Avenir *is believed to be near* Akranes. *(Site 227)*

and there was a great roar overhead as the deck of *Akranes* was splintered, and two loud explosions followed. The guards had actually seen the aircraft approaching, but had assumed it to be a British 'plane limping home in distress. Their mistake cost dear, for though two bombs missed the ships and another did not explode, cannon fire from the plane sank the *Akranes,* leaving her wheelhouse top and fo'csle head just awash. The crew were able to escape in their own boat. Divers found shortly afterwards that there was an unexploded 500lb bomb inside the *Akranes;* it had gone through the side of the ship, and had sunk her without going off. The wreck is in position 54 05 45N 00 07 33W in less than 6m of water at low water. She is well broken up, but is still an interesting dive for novices. **L'Avenir.** Early on the morning of February 19 1906, this 553 ton Belgian steamer came ashore in fog close to South Landing Flamborough. She was refloated soon after-

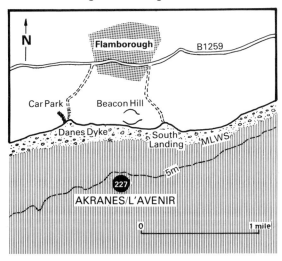

wards, but was found to be making water, so was beached again some distance to the southward, where she became a total wreck. Owned by F. Alexander of Antwerp, she was an iron three-masted vessel, 200ft long with a beam of 26ft and a depth of 14ft, and was carrying herring barrel hoops from Nantes to Peterhead. She was an old vessel, having been built by Pearse & Co of Stockton in 1865. The wreck was subsequently bought by a Sunderland broker, who removed most of the ship. She is mentioned here however, because a large anchor and chain close to the wreck of *Akranes* is thought to have come from *L'Avenir.* It is possible to dive this area from the shore, but this is not recommended, since tidal movements here can be dangerous.

228 Kieldrecht. Built in 1916 by Van der Giessen & Zonen at Krimpen, this 1284 ton steamer was requisitioned by the Shipping Controller in WW1. She was 237ft long with a beam of 36ft and a depth of 16ft, was registered at London and managed by R. & J.H. Rea. On June 15 1918, she was sunk by *UB-107* off Flamborough Head while in convoy. Her wreck is thought to be the one in position 54 05 16N 00 27 26E in a depth of 51m. This wreck lies roughly north-west–south-east on hard ground, and stands some 5m high, with no scour. So far the wreck has not been positively identified. *Kieldrecht* had T 3cy engines, 17" 29" 46"-36". 2SB 4CF by Alblasserdam Msch Fab. Incidentally, *UB-107* was herself sunk within a few miles of this position a month or so later (site 213).

229 UB-75. This 520 ton U-boat left Borkum on November 29 1917, under the command of Ober Leutnant F.R. Walther and attacked shipping off Whitby in early December; the steamers *Aigburth, Highgate, Lampada* and *Venetia* were all sunk in that area between December 5-9 by torpedoes. After these attacks, *UB-75* vanished. She was due back at her base on December 13, and when she failed to arrive, it was assumed that she had fallen foul of mine-nets, laid to trap U-boats, off Flamborough Head. There is a wreck in position 54 04 42N 00 05 39E which is thought to be the *UB-75*; the wreck is in two parts in a north-west–south-east attitude at a depth of 47m. It stands some 6m proud of the smooth gravel seabed, and is about the right size for a U-boat at 182ft long with a beam of 19ft. *UB-75* carried four bow torpedo tubes and one stern tube, but carried no mine-laying equipment.

230 Unknown. In position 54 04 37N 00 05 46W there is a wreck lying north-south in a depth of about 7m, with a 1m scour. There is little of it showing above the sand, but what there is covers an area of about 20m by 6m. This could be all that remains of the ill-fated Glasgow steamer *Bordeaux,* which sank with all hands on November 29, 1897, close to the sandbank known as the South Smithic, off Bridlington. A violent north-north-westerly gale blew that day, and the 333 ton vessel sought shelter in Bridlington Bay, during a voyage from Methil to London in ballast. Watchers from the shore could tell that the ship was already in difficulties, as she was '. . .pitching fearfully. . .' and shortly ran ashore south of Flamborough Head, drifting off and evidently in a sinking condition soon afterwards. Distress signals were sent up, and Flamborough lifeboat was launched but returned as she was unable to face the huge seas. Bridlington lifeboat was not launched; the secretary decided that it would be suicidal to attempt a rescue. The *Bordeaux* sank during the early hours of the morning, and at daylight, her two masts could be seen from the shore. This disaster greatly upset the local people when they realised what had happened; young men burned effigies of the lifeboat secretary in the street for his decision not to launch. In fact, the subsequent inquiry vindicated his '. . .brave decision. . .' though the Flamborough lifeboat was censured for failing to launch when the *Bordeaux* was seen close to the cliffs earlier on.

There is another possibility that the wreck in this position could be that of the 58 ton steam drifter *Research* which also went down with all hands. This disaster took place on November 25 1925, when the hapless vessel sank on the Smithic Sands in a blizzard, killing five men from the same Filey family.

231 Girl Ita. This British motor fishing vessel foundered on September 1 1976, without loss of life. She was 100ft long with a beam of 26ft and a depth of 13ft. The wreck lies in position 54 04 37N 00 06 08W, in a north-east–south-west attitude, in a depth of about 5m with a 1m scour. She is on the Smithic sands, a little to the west of the unknown wreck thought to be the *Bordeaux* or the *Research*.

232 Potomac. This brig-rigged screw steamer was built by the London & Glasgow Engineering Co of Glasgow in 1872, for the Mercantile Steamship Co of London. She was 263ft long with a beam of 33ft and a depth of 25ft, and grossed 1832 tons. During a voyage from Odessa to Aberdeen, she was found to be leaking badly, and had to be towed into shallow water off Bridlington on November 11, 1893. The vessel could not be saved; she sank in position 54 04 13N 00 11 26W, about 7 cables south-south-east of the pier light at Bridlington. Local boats managed to salvage some of her wheat cargo, but much of it was lost. In 1971, the salvage company Risdon Beazley sent their *Topmast 18* to salvage and disperse the remains of *Potomac,* and they left it almost buried in a depth of about 3m. It is now described as a foul area but, like most shallow wrecks in this part of the world, from time to time the sand washes away and exposes parts of the wreck.

The wreck lies less than a quarter of a mile from the low water mark on the south beach. *Potomac* had 150hp engines by the builder, C 2cy 31" 54"-33".

233 Biesbosch. This 484 ton steamer was built in 1916 by J.T.H. Wilmink & Co at Groningen and was registered in Amsterdam. She was owned by N.V. Hollandsche during WW1, and was 152ft long with a beam of 25ft and a depth of 12ft. On December 29 1923, *Biesbosch* was carrying a cargo of iron and steel when she discovered a leak while off Flamborough Head. She was in Belgian ownership at the time, under Captain J.B. Outryve and eleven crew. The vessel anchored inside the Headland while efforts were made to cure the leak, while keeping the pumps running. At 20.00 that night, it was clear that they were losing the battle to save the ship, so the crew abandoned into their own carefully provisioned boats. They rowed to a safe spot close to Bridlington harbour where they anchored until daylight, and then entered the harbour. Local fishermen set off to see if they could salve the derelict, but the weather worsened; a strong south-easterly wind brought heavy seas. The following day, tugs arrived, but despite a thorough search, could find no trace of the *Biesbosch,* which was presumed to have foundered during the night.

The wreck lies in position 54 03 43N 00 02 42W in a depth of 24m. She is in a north-south attitude, on a smooth gravel seabed, and largely intact. There is little scour, and parts of the wreck stand some 4m high. Biesbosch had T 3cy engines by Landweer & Zonen.

234 Brabant. Built at Fredrikstaad in 1907, this 1492 ton Norwegian steamer was owned by A.S. Ganger Rolfe, and was 241ft long with a beam of 35ft and a depth of 17ft. She was carrying 696 tons of woodpulp when she struck a mine and sank south of Flamborough Head on January 15 1917. At the time, her two masts, funnel and upper works were visible above the surface, and the position was noted as 3.4 miles 111 degrees from Bridlington Quay light. She is in position 54 03 31N 00 05 42W, at a depth of about 6m, in a 2m deep scour, with a least depth of 5.3m over her. The wreck is silting up rapidly. *Brabant* had engines by the builder, T 3cy 18" 29" 50".

235 Feltre. There are two conflicting reports on how this 6455 ton ship came to be sunk off Flamborough Head, though what *is* certain is that she was sunk there, for the wreck has been positively identified by the bell which bears the ship's original name, *Rhenania*. She was built by Bremer Vulkan, Germany, in 1904, and was 409ft long with a beam of 53ft and a depth of 28ft, and was designed to carry over 260 passengers for the German–Africa Line. She was laid up in Naples at the outbreak of WW1, but was then requisitioned by the Italian Government and put to use as a cargo ship. One source says that she was then sunk by a mine on May 25, 1916, six miles off Flamborough Head, while another – and believed to be more reliable source – says she was torpedoed by a German U-boat off the Head on August 26 1917.

The wreck of *Feltre*, known locally as *Cap Morel* or *Cattermole* to fishermen, is in position 54 02 06N 00 01 44E in a depth of 36m. She is lying almost north-south, and is in one piece, though she is starting to break up. There is little scour, and the wreck stands some 7m proud of the seabed. *Feltre* was unusual in that she had quadruple expansion steam engines, delivering 387nhp.

236 Manchester Engineer. This 4465 ton steamer was built by the Northumberland Shipbuilding Co in 1902 for Manchester Liners, and was 360ft long with a beam of 48ft. She was armed during WW1, but was chased by a U-boat in the Arctic in June of 1917. On this occasion, she escaped, but a U-boat got her two months later during a voyage from Shields to France with coal. The attack came on August 16 1917 some four and a half miles south-east of Flamborough Head, but fortunately there were no lives lost. There is a bad obstruction in position 54 02 02N 00 07 56E which is thought to be the *Manchester Engineer;* this wreck lies north-west–south-east in a depth of 49m on a smooth seabed. The wreck is over 300ft in length, has its bows to the north-west, and stands some 9m high. Though no positive identification has taken place as yet, it seems clear that this must be the right ship. *Manchester Engineer* had T 3cy engines, 25" 41" 69" by Richardson of Sunderland, 3SB, 9CF.

237 Ville de Valenciennes. This 1734 ton steamer was owned by Cie Des Bateaux a Vapeur du Nord, and was built by J. Readhead & Sons in 1897. She was 274ft long with a beam of 35ft and a depth of 16ft and was registered at Dunkirk. She was sunk by a torpedo from a U-boat on

September 22 1917, some 11 miles south-east of Bridlington. The wreck lies in position 54 01 46N 00 03 06E in a depth of 39m. She is in one piece, in a north-west–south-east attitude, and stands some 7m high, on a firm seabed with little scour.

Ville de Valenciennes, a collier, had T 3cy engines by the builder, 23" 37" 61"-39".

238 Nitedal. Owned by T. Sagen, this 1714 ton Norwegian steamer was built by Laxevaags Maskin & Jernskibs in 1903, and was originally called *Hero.* She measured 268ft long with a beam of 39ft and a depth of 17ft, and was built of steel. *Nitedal* was carrying 2500 tons of coal when she was torpedoed by a U-boat on October 20 1917, some 6 miles south of Bridlington. She is reported to have sunk in less than three minutes. The wreck is said to be in position 54 01 12N 00 02 08W, but so far no divers have confirmed this. The depth here is about 18m.

Nitedal had engines by the builders, T 3cy 19" 31" 51"-33". The same position is given for the wreck of *Leka,* (site 239).

239 Leka. This Norwegian steamer was owned by C.T. Gogstad and had been built in 1892 by Richardson Duck & Co at Stockton. She was 270ft long with a beam of 37ft and a depth of 17ft, and had a gross tonnage of 1845 tons. Originally called *Zoe,* she was registered at Christiana, and was iron built.

Leka was carrying iron ore when she was torpedoed by a U-boat on September 24 1917, south of Flamborough Head. She is reputed to have sunk in exactly the same position as *Nitedal* (site 238), 54 01 12N 00 02 08W. Clearly, there is a fascinating project waiting here, to determine which – if either – of these unfortunate vessels occupies this spot. *Leka* was fitted with engines by Blair & Co of Stockton, T 3cy 21" 35" 57"-36". 1DB 4CF.

240 Tredegar Hall. This 3764 ton steamer was built at Sunderland in 1906 by Doxford & Sons for E. Nicholl of Cardiff, and was London registered. She was 342ft long with a beam of 47ft and a depth of 25ft, and was armed for defence in WW1. She was torpedoed and sunk with the loss of three lives on October 23 1917, south-east of Flamborough Head while carrying a cargo which included iron ore. The wreck has been known for some years as the Ore ship, for obvious reasons; she is in position 54 01 07N 00 00 18E in about 22m of water. She is fairly well broken up, but appears to be all there. The two boilers are upended on the seabed, and between them and the 15ft diameter iron propellor is a large mound of the ore cargo. *Tredegar Hall* had T 3cy engines by the builders, 26" 46" 68"-42".

241 Sote. This 1353 ton steamer had no less than six names during her career; she was built by Kish Boolds & Co at Sunderland in 1883 as *Nantes Hambourg,* renamed *Ville de St. Nazaire, Herleve, Ellerker, Orion,* and finally *Sote.* She was 249ft long with a beam of 34ft and a depth of 19ft, and was owned by Angf. Aktieb Thule of Sweden.

On May 25 1918 she was torpedoed off Bridlington while carrying a cargo of wood, paper and iron, and was quickly taken in tow. Efforts to beach her failed, and she sank in position 54 01 00N 00 11 00WW, 182 degrees, 3.65 miles from Bridlington Pier Light. Some of her cargo was salvaged later, and dispersal took place on the wreck. She is in some 7m or so of water, off Hamilton Hill, Barmston, and is heavily sand-warped, but may well be worth a dip when the sea has been calm for a spell. *Sote* had C 2cy engines by G. Clark of Sunderland, 33" 62"-42".

242 Brema. Built at Rostock in 1904, this 1537 ton steamer was owned by a German company and registered in Bremen as the *Mecklenburg,* but was taken as a war prize, and put into use as an Admiralty collier under the name *Brema.* She was 261ft long with a beam of 38ft and a depth of 17ft.

On August 19 1918, the Germans claimed her back when a U-boat torpedoed and sank *Brema* some 7 miles south of Flamborough Head, fortunately without loss of life. The wreck lies in position 54 00 48N 00 00 17W, in 22m of water, with no scour. She lies almost east-west, and though broken up, stands some 7m proud of the seabed in places. It has not been positively identified as the *Brema* at this stage however.

Brema had engines by the builder, A.G. Neptun, Rostock, T 3cy 20" 32" 52"-36".

243 Dryade. Built at Rostock in 1906, this 1833 ton steamer was requisitioned by the Admiralty in WW1 for use as a collier, managed by Everitt & Newbiggin. She was 252ft long with a beam of 37ft and a depth of 15ft. On December 8 1917, she was sunk after a collision some 10 miles south-east of Flamborough Head during a voyage from the Tyne to London with coal. Her wreck is thought to be the one in position 54 00 46N 00 08 04E, in a depth of 42m. Lying roughly south-east–north-west, this large wreck is broken at the forward hold, and stands some 8m proud of the seabed.

Dryade had T 3cy engines, 17" 30" 48"-33" by A.G. Neptun, Rostock.

244 Chant 63. This 405 ton Ministry of War Transport vessel was built in 1944, and was 131ft long. She was bound for Portsmouth from Middlesbrough when she capsized and sank off Bridlington on June 5 of the same year, and her fourteen crew were rescued by Bridlington Lifeboat. There is a small intact wreck in position 54 00 26N 00 14 43E which is thought to be *Chant 63;* the wreck lies in 50m of water in a south-east–north-west attitude on an undulating sandy bottom, and stands some 6m high. There is no record of her having been dived as yet.

245 Virginian. Built in 1906 by Cook Welton & Gemmell at Beverley, this 211 ton trawler was owned by the Onward Steam Fishing Co of Grimsby and was 115ft long with a beam of 22ft and a depth of 11ft. She sank after a collision with the *Empire Rapier* some 30 miles north-north-east of the Humber on November 5, 1946. Her wreck is thought to be the one in position 53 59 47N 00 20 39E, in a depth of 50m. The wreck is well broken up, lying roughly east west on a smooth gravel seabed, from which she stands less than 2m proud. No positive identification has taken place on this one yet. *Virginian* had T 3cy engines, 12" 21" 34"-24" by C.D. Holmes of Hull.

246 Staxton Wyke. Built at Beverley in 1937 as *Lady Hogarth,* this 472 ton trawler later became *Kingston Emerald,* and in 1951, *Staxton Wyke* when she was bought by the West Dock Steam Fishing Co. She was 164ft long with a beam of 27ft and was registered at Hull. On August 23 1959, she was in collision with the MV *Dalhanna* some 10 miles south of Flamborough during a thick fog. The sea was calm, yet the trawler sank in less than two minutes, taking five men's lives. The sixteen survivors were taken aboard the steamer, and later transferred to the local RNLI lifeboat. Several searches at the time failed to locate the wreck, but she is now thought to be the wreck in position 53 59 47N 00 07 28E. This wreck lies in a depth of 36m, stands 4m high and 50m long; exactly right for the *Staxton Wyke*.

247 Diana. Built in Norway in 1904, this armed British steamer of 1107 tons was 225ft long with a beam of 32ft and a depth of 14ft. She was torpedoed by a U-boat, thought to be *UB-108,* some 10 miles south-south-east of Flamborough Head on June 7 1918, while carrying a coal cargo. Her wreck is thought to be the one that lies in position 53 59 19N 00 04 34E in a depth of 32m. This wreck lies almost east-west, in a slight scour, some 6m proud of the seabed. There is no record of any positive identification of her as yet. *Diana* had T 3cy engines by the builder, Bergens Mek Vaerks, 17" 28" 46"- 33".

248 HMS Fairy. This 355 ton 'C' class destroyer was one of 38 such ships built between 1896 and 1901 at an average cost of £60 000 each. Capable of 30 knots, these three-funnelled steamers carried one 12 pdr gun, five 6 pdrs, and had two 18" torpedo tubes. *Fairy,* under the command of Lt G.H. Barnish was senior officer's ship of a convoy escort guarding thirty merchant ships as they rounded Flamborough Head in the early hours of May 31, 1918. It was an overcast night with a smooth sea, and *Fairy* was to seaward and abaft the beam of the rear ship in the convoy. At 0205, the alarm was sounded, and a submarine was seen off the port bow, some 300 yards away. *Fairy* attacked what turned out to be *UC-75,* and after ramming and sinking her, crumpled her own bows '. . .like tinfoil. ..' as far back as the bridge. Clearly doomed, *Fairy* tried to reach the shore, but at 0305 she sank in 16 fathoms. The crew, and the survivors from the *UC-75,* were picked up by the Greyhound. Lt. Barnish was awarded the DSO for his fine effort in protecting the convoy and sinking a U-boat. (See site 257).

The wreck of *Fairy* has never been positively identified, but is thought to be the one in position 53 59 02N 00 07 16E in 34m of water. This wreck lies roughly north-east–south-west and stands in a slight scour, some 4m proud of the surrounding seabed. *Fairy* was built at Fairfield, and was 209ft long with a beam of 21ft.

Weymouth type cruiser, HMS Falmouth, *of the 3rd Light Cruiser Squadron. (Site 249)*

249 HMS Falmouth. This Weymouth class cruiser of the 3rd Light Cruiser Squadron was commanded by Captain J.D. Edwards, and had a complement of 376. She carried eight 6" guns, four 3 pdrs, and two 21" torpedo tubes. Her 22 000 ihp turbine engines gave her a speed of 27 knots, and she ws 453ft long, with a beam of 48ft and a depth of 15ft. She was built by W. Beardmore in 1910, and her displacement was 5250 tons. At 16.45 on August 19 1916, the 3rd Light Cruiser Squadron ran into a submarine trap off Flamborough Head, and *U-66,* commanded by Ober Leutnant Von Bothner hit *Falmouth* with two torpedoes, one at the bow and one at the stern. A destroyer screen, by use of depth charges, kept *U-66* and *U-49* (O/L Hartman) from moving in and finishing *Falmouth* off. After two hours, the U-boats backed off, and *Falmouth* was able to make six knots under her own power towards safety. The next day, despite a screen of six destroyers, *U-63,* commander Otto Schultz, got in two more torpedoes, and *Falmouth* sank some eight hours later. There were no fatalities, though one stoker died later from injuries received in the attack. The wreck lies in position 53 58 56N 00 04 30W in 16m of water, in a north-south attitude. After the war, dispersal operations took place, and four tons of gelignite laid the vessel low, as well as removing her bronze propellors. There is still much to see however, and though *Falmouth* is hardly recognisable as a ship anymore, she makes a fascinating dive. As recently as 1986, a steel plate bearing the ship's name in brass letters was found on the wreck, and sadly, was damaged by souvenir hunters. The wreck is on a sand and shingle bottom, with a scour on the landward side.

250 Markersdal. Built by Burmeister & Wain at Copenhagen in 1907, this 1640 ton steamer was named *Haakon* and then *Ellen Jensen* until Akties Dampsk Rodby Havn gave her the name *Markersdal*. She was 270ft long with a beam of 39ft and a depth of 18ft, and was in use as a collier. On June 30 1917, she was torpedoed and sunk by a U-boat some 9 miles east of Hornsea in a depth of about 32m. The wreck lies north-west–south-east in position 53 57 07N 00 08 52E, in two halves. The northern half stands up the highest at almost 6m, and there is a scour about 2m deep in places. *Markersdal* had T 3cy engines by the builders, 18" 29" 50"-33". Her boiler details are not recorded in Lloyd's register.

251 UC-39. On February 8 1917, this U-boat, under the command of Ober Leutnant Ehrentraut, was in the act of shelling the steamer *Ida* when she was surprised by the British destroyer *HMS Thrasher,* who attacked with guns and depth charges. The *UC-39* dived, but the damage she had sustained forced her to surface again, as water was pouring into her control room. *Thrasher* immediately opened fire again, killing Ehrentraut. The master of the Swedish ship *Hanna Larsen* emerged from the conning tower hatch bearing a white flag; he had been a prisoner aboard the U-boat since his own ship had been sunk further south earlier that day. The seventeen crew of the U-boat were taken prisoner, but *UC-39* sank while being towed in by the destroyer *Itchen*. Four months later, the wreck was located by another destroyer, and divers found the U-boat, already covered in barnacles. The *UC-39* was 420 tons displacement, carried 18 mines in 6 chutes, and had 2 bow and 1 stern torpedo tubes. The wreck is in position 53 56 46N 00 10 01E in a depth of about 36m, lying almost east-west. The forward hatch is open, and though there is a lot of silt, shells can be seen inside. The propellor of the U-boat, clearly marked with its number, is in the

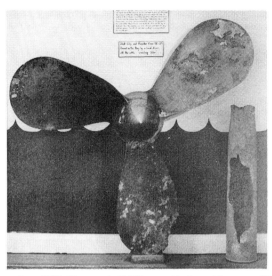

The propeller of UC-39, *now in Bridlington Harbour Museum. (Site 251)*

Bridlington harbour museum. *UC-39* had sunk several vessels off the Yorkshire coast earlier incidentally; *Hurstwood* off Whitby on February 5; *Corsican Prince* (site 67) off Whitby on February 7; *St. Ninian* (site 68) off Whitby the same day, and *Hanna Larsen* off Spurn Point on February 8, her swansong.

252 Ragnhild. Built at Flensburg in 1895 as the *Finland*, this 1495 ton steamer later became the *Carbonia* and then *Ragnhild* when she came into the ownership of the Pelton SS Co. She was armed for defence in WW1, but was torpedoed and sunk by a U-boat in Bridlington Bay on September 3 1917, with the loss of the captain and fourteen crew. The wreck is thought to be that which lies in position 53-56-28N 00 09 04E in a depth of 33m. The wreck lies north-west–south-east and stands about 3m clear of the seabed, with little scour. Ragnhild had T 3cy engines, 16" 26" 43"-33" by her Flensburg builders.

253 Stanburn. Originally named *Hebburn,* this 2881 ton steamer was built by Wood Skinner & Co at Newcastle in 1924. She was renamed *Stanburn* when she was bought by the Stanhope Steamship Co in 1937, and was 334ft long, with a beam of 45ft and a depth of 22ft. On January 29 1940, *Stanburn* was attacked by a German aircraft who bombed and machine-gunned her until she sank. One report suggests that the enemy's plane then machine gunned the survivors in their small boat. Whether this is true or not, there were only three survivors out of a crew of twenty-eight men. The fortunate three were picked up by the steamer *Gripfast,* which had survived a similar aircraft attack. There is a large wreck in position 53 56 23N 00 07 20E which is thought to be the *Stanburn;* it lies almost north-south in 31m, and is largely intact, standing over 5m high. *Stanburn* had T 3cy engines, 23" 38" 65"-42". 2SB 8CF by North Eastern Marine Engineering.

254 Dana. Built by J. Blumer & Co at Sunderland in 1883, this 1620 ton steamer was owned by R. Gohle of Sweden. She was 258ft long with a beam of 36ft and a depth of 16ft, and had previously carried the name *Clieveden*. She was torpedoed and sunk by a U-boat on November 11 1917, some fourteen miles off Hornsea. Her wreck is thought to be the one that lies in position 53 56 09N 00 14 55E in a north-south attitude in 47m, but she has not been positively identified as yet. She is on a smooth gravel seabed, and stands about 6m high at the most.

Dana had C 2cy engines, 32" 60"-39". 2SB 6PF by North Eastern Marine Engineering.

255 Lady Anstruther. There is a wreck in position 53 55 58N 00 17 39E which is thought to be the 527 ton steamer *Lady Anstruther,* sunk after a collision in August 1947. She was 167ft long with a beam of 27ft and a depth of 11ft, and was owned by the Nobel Explosive Co. Registered at Glasgow; she was an aft-engined ship, built by Dublin Shipbuilders Ltd in 1922 – so she might have an interesting cargo! The wreck lies in a north-east–south-west attitude in 46m of water on a sand and gravel seabed, and stands some 3m high. *Lady Anstruther* had engines by W. Beardmore & Co. T 3cy 14" 24" 40"-27". 1SB 3CF.

256 Harnis. This 783 ton motor vessel was owned by Larsen Reederei of Flensburg, West Germany, and had been built at the same place in 1953. She was 197ft long, with a beam of 34ft and a depth of 14ft, and had her engines aft. *Harnis* was bound for Whitby with pig iron from Ymuiden, Holland, when she was run down in fog on February 25 1975, by a Russian fishing vessel. The *Harniss* sank quickly with the loss of one life; five survivors were landed later by the Russian ship *Gordyy*, while the local rescue services knew nothing of the event. The wreck of *Harnis* is thought to be the one in position 53 55 48N 00 23 54E in a depth of 46m. The wreck in this position lies roughly south-east–north-west, and stands some 3m clear of the seabed, in a slight scour. So far, there is no record of it having been dived.

257 UC-75. This minelaying submarine, like all those in her class, had two bow and one stern torpedo tubes, and carried eighteen mines in six chutes, each of which passed right through the hull. She displaced 420 tons. *UC-75* was commanded in the early part of 1918 by the submarine ace Ober Leutnant Johann Lohs, who sank the steamer *Gascony* off the Sussex coast on January 6 of that year. (See *Dive Sussex*)

On May 22, *UC-75* was under the command of O/L W. Schmitz, who took her from her base at Bruge to attack shipping in Bridlington Bay, after laying mines off the Humber. At 01.55 on May 31, 1918, *UC-75* was about to attack a convoy when she was accidentally run down by the steamer *Blaydonian,* who immediately alerted her escort, the ancient 370 ton destroyer *Fairy*. The Captain of HMS *Fairy* found it hard to believe that any enemy submarine would appear on the surface in the middle of a convoy, so after challenging her twice, rammed the submarine's stern, in order that the crew – who might just be British – would be able to escape. A voice from the submarine shouted *Kamerad!* but at the same time, *UC-75* fired a round with her deck gun. *Fairy* then closed on the U-boat, firing forty rounds before she rammed close to the deck gun. Several of the enemy submariners were picked up by *Fairy* before *UC-75* sank. One of them was the captain. The impact had been too much for the *Fairy* however; she had twice rammed a target newer and larger than herself, and her bows had opened up. She too sank within an hour. (Site 248)

The wreck of *UC-75* has never been positively identified, but is thought to be the one in position 53 55 31N 00 04 43E. The obstruction in this position lies almost north-south in 26m, stands some 4m high, and about 150ft long, but there is no record of her having been dived as yet.

258 SNA III. This strangely named steamer was built by the Great Lakes Engineering Works of Michigan in 1915 as the *International,* later renamed *Clinchfield* and finally *SNA III* when she came into the ownership of the French Societe Nationale d'Affrements. She was a 1709 ton steamer, 256ft long with a beam of 43ft and a depth of 17ft, and had her engines aft. She was carrying a coal cargo from the Tyne to Rouen when she was sunk by a U-boat torpedo some 10 miles east of Hornsea on September 26 1917. The wreck of *SNA III* is in position 53 54 53N 00 07 38E, in a depth of about 28m. She lies roughly north-east–south-west, with her highest point of about 5m at the north end. One diver who saw the wreck claims that she has a bronze propellor still in place. *SNA III* had T 3cy engines, 16" 26" 45"-17". 2SB 4CF.

259 Realf. Built by Kocksums MV Aktieb and owned by A/S Asplund, this Norwegian motor ship was 468ft long with a beam of 60ft and a depth of 35ft, and grossed 8083 tons. She was an aft engined tanker, designed to carry petroleum in bulk, had two decks and a cruiser stern. On December 1 1939, she struck a mine some 15 miles off Hornsea, and sank shortly afterwards. The wreck of *Realf,* owned by diver Terry Dealtry of Bridlington, is in position 53 54 38N 00 25 04E in a depth of about 44m. She lies roughly north-west–south-est, with high points at either end standing some 9m proud of the seabed. Parts of the wreck are partially buried, and the scour is over 2m deep in places.

260 Unknown. There is a wreck in position 53 54 22N 00 06 35E in a depth of about 27m which was originally thought to be *Orsa,* (site 298) but which still awaits identification. The wreck has a large boiler and a prominent bow section, but the rest of it is very broken up. It lies almost east-west, with the highest part standing over 4m proud of the seabed, with little or no scour.

261 Briton. This 134 ton Grimsby trawler was owned by Baxter & Green of that port, and had been built of iron at Middlesbrough in 1891. She was captured and sunk by gunfire from an enemy submarine on September 25 1916, the day after the whole of Scarborough's trawling fleet had been wiped out by submarines further north. *Briton,* fishing number GY 374, was reported sunk some 18 miles south-east by east of Flamborough Head. Her wreck is thought to be that which lies in position 53 54 13N 00 21 57E, in an almost north-south orientation, in 46m depth. So far there is no record of her having been dived.

262 Celtic. This 170 ton iron screw ketch was owned by the Grimsby Steam Fishing Co and was built by Earles of Hull in 1889. She was 106ft long, with a beam of 20ft and a depth of 11ft. On December 1 1906, she was run down by the steamship *Jagersborg* some 15 miles north of Spurn Point during fog. The wreck lies in about 26m of water in position 53 54 11N 00 07 45E, but is difficult to find as she is well flattened to the seabed. It was positively identified by diver Pete Fergus, who saw the telegraph, unusually, made of steel, reading 'slow ahead'. *Celtic* had T 3cy engines by Earles; 10" 20" 32"-22". 1SB 2CF.

263 Rochester. This 165 ton trawler was built at Govan in 1898, and was owned by the Consolidated Fisheries Co of Grimsby, though the ship was registered at Lowestoft as *LT 153*. She was built of steel, and was 104ft long. The *Rochester* was mined and sunk south of Hornsea on July 27 1944. Her wreck is thought to be the one in position 53 54 00N 00 42 30E at a depth of about 35m. She is so far offshore however – about 27 miles – that she is unlikely to be of much interest to sport divers.

264 Togston. Owned by G.V. Turnbull of Leith, this 1057 ton steamer was built in 1909 by Osbourne Graham & Co of Sunderland, and was 210ft long with a beam of 33ft and a depth of 14ft. She was attacked and sunk by a German submarine on October 18 1917, while carrying a cargo of coal from the Tyne to London. Five men were lost in the torpedo attack by *UC-47*. The wreck lies in position 53 53 59N 00 12 07E, at a depth of 32m. She lies north-west–south-east on a sandy bottom, with a 1m scour, and stands some 4m high.

Togston was armed for defence, and had engines by Richardsons, Westgarth & Co of Sunderland, T 3cy 16" 27" 44"-30".

265 Unknown. During WW2, this obstruction was depth charged as it was thought to be an enemy submarine, but pieces of wood floated to the surface after the explosions, but to this day, no-one knows what wreck this is in position 53 53 14N 00 30 04E. Since the depth of water here is about 45m, sport divers have not bothered with it so far. The wreck lies in a north-east–south-west attitude on a sandy bottom, and is apparently intact, standing up some 7m. It covers an area roughly 75m by 12m.

266 John Rettig. Another victim of the raid by *UB-107* on July 27 1918, this 1809 ton steamer was owned by Angf. Aktieb Gefle, Sweden, and had been built in that country in 1915. She was 265ft long with a beam of 42ft and a depth of 20ft. She was carrying a general cargo at the time of loss, and the wreck lies in position 53 53 08N 00 15 13E, in 40m of water. The wreck stands about 7m high, and lies in a north-east–south-west attitude, with high points at each end. *UB-107* sank *Chloris* (site 270) and *Crimdon* (site 57) that same day, *Kalo* (site 272) a few weeks earlier, and was herself sunk at about the same time, all off the Yorkshire coast. *John Rettig* had Fredrikstad built engines, T 3cy 18" 29" 50"-36".

267 Longbenton. Built at Blyth in 1898, this 924 ton steamer was owned by Harkers of Swansea, and registered at Newcastle. She was 211ft long with a beam of 30ft and a depth of 14ft, and was in use as an Admiralty collier during WW1. On June 27 1917, she was torpedoed by a German submarine 12 miles south by west from Flamborough Head, while southbound with 1000 tons of coal. The wreck is thought to be that which lies in position 53 53 07N 00 00 18W, in a depth of 14m. This wreck lies in a north-north-east–south-south-west attitude, and stands some 4m high. There is a scour to the east side, and the wreckage stretches out for some distance.

Longbenton had engines by the North Eastern Marine Engineering Co, T 3cy 17" 28" 46"-30". 1SB 3PF. The wreck is owned by diver Pete Fergus, skipper of the dive boat *Storm Drift*.

268 Corhampton. This Cory collier was a 2495 ton steamer, built by S.P. Austin & Son, Sunderland in 1933. She was 292ft long with a beam of 42ft and a depth of 19ft. She was disabled during a voyage from Blyth to London, and while under tow, was bombed by a German aircraft on November 15 1941. She sank some 26 miles north-east of Spurn Point. Her wreck is shown on Danish fishery charts as being in position 53 52 45N 00 26 45E, in a depth of about 20m, but to date, there is no record of this having been verified by divers. *Corhampton* had her engines aft, built by North Eastern Marine Engineering at Sunderland they were T 3cy 18" 30" 51"-36".

269 J.B. Paddon. This 570 ton steamer was built at Ardrossan in 1914 as the *Starbeam*, for Stephenson Clarke. She was bombed and abandoned in position 53 55 00N 00 16 00E on December 27 1941, and she sank shortly afterwards. The wreck is thought to be that which lies in position 53 52 26N 00 18 11E, in a depth of 40m. This wreck lies almost north-south, and stands up about 4m with no scour.

J.B. Paddon had T 3cy engines, 13" 22" 36"-24". 1SB 3CF, by Lidgerwood of Glasgow.

270 Chloris. Originally called *Mary Horton,* this 984 ton steamer became *Pegwell,* and finally *Chloris* under the ownership of T.H. Hutchinson of Glasgow. She was built at Montrose in 1904, and was 210ft long with a beam of 33ft and a depth of 14ft. During WW1, she was armed for defence, but was attacked and sunk by the submarine *UB-107* on July 27 1918, the same day that *John Rettig* and *Crimdon* were sunk by the same raider.

Chloris was carrying a general cargo which included timber at the time, and reports say variously that either one man or three men were lost in the sinking. Revenge came quickly however, for the *UB-107* was herself sunk close at hand soon afterwards. (Site 213.)

There is a wreck thought to be the *Chloris* in position 53 52 03N 00 10 17E in a depth of 27m, with a 1m scour. The wreck is lying roughly north-east–south-west, and is fairly well intact, standing some 6m proud of the seabed. *Chloris* had engines by the North Eastern Marine Engineering Co of Sunderland, T 3cy 16" 25" 42"-33". 2SB 4PF.

271 Varangmalm. Built in 1919 by Awuijk & Zonen A/S Malmfart, this 3618 ton steamship was originally *Zwart Zee,* later changed to *Ovedbent* then *Hadjipateras* and finally *Varangmalm.* She was 361ft long with a beam of 48ft and a depth of 23ft. On October 29 1939, she struck a mine and sank off Hornsea. There is a wreck in position 53 51 50N 00 16 51E which is thought to be the *Varangmalm;* the wreck is lying east-west on a sand and gravel seabed at a depth of 38m, with no scour. She appears to be lying on one side, and stands some 6m clear of the surrounding seabed. Her engines were T 3cy, 24" 40" 67"-45".

272 Kalo. Built in 1903 by Furness Withy at Hartlepool, this 1957 ton steamer was owned by Dannebrog Steamship Co of Copenhagen. Originally called *Estonia,* she was 281ft long with a beam of 42ft and a depth of 18ft. She had a coal cargo aboard when the German submarine *UB-107* torpedoed her on June 13 1918, killing three of her crew, some 18 miles south of Flamborough Head. An armed trawler took the *Kalo* in tow, but she sank in position 53 51 47N 00 12 37E, where the wreck can be found today. She is in 28m of water, lying north-west–south-est, with the bows south-

This Danish steamer, Kalo, *was another victim of* UB-107. *(Site 272)*

east. The seabed is rippled sand over gravel, and part of the wreckage is covered, but there is little scour. There are high points at bow and stern standing 6m or so clear of the seabed, and there is more wreckage to the east of the main bulk of the wreck.

Kalo had engines by the Central Marine Enginering works of Hartlepool, T 3cy 21" 33" 56"-36". 2SB 4CF.

UB-107, the submarine that sank the *Kalo,* went on to sink *Chloris* (site 270), *John Rettig* (site 266) and *Crimdon* (site 57) all on the same day, July 27 1918, and was herself sunk by armed trawlers that same day, off the Yorkshire coast (site 213).

273 British Prince. This Rio Cape Liner was built by W. Doxford & Son in 1935, and grossed 4979 tons. Originally called *Sutherland,* she had her name changed to *British Prince* in 1936. The ship was 412ft long with a beam of 54ft and a depth of 26ft, had one deck and a cruiser stern. On September 26, 1941, she was bombed and sunk by enemy aircraft while carrying a cargo of copper. The wreck lies in position 53 51 40N 00 25 22E, in 40m of water. With such a cargo it is inevitable that salvage operations would be carried out, and in fact Risdon Beazley worked on the wreck between March 1949 and September 1951, and again in April 1976. The wreck is lying upright, but in two pieces; the northern part lying south-east–north-west and the southern part almost south-north. There is no scour, and parts of the wreck stand up more than 10m from the seabed. She covers a large area of the seabed, as one would expect from a comparatively large vessel.

274 Ellington. Owned by J.A. Davidson, this 703 ton steamer had been built in 1882 by D. Baxter & Co of Sunderland, and was registered at Aberdeen. She was 184ft long with a beam of 30ft and a depth of 13ft. She was armed for defence during WW1, but was sunk by other than enemy action; she collided with the French steamer *Cabourg* off Flamborough Head on November 16 1917, while bound for St Malo with pitch from Leith. The wreck is in position 53 51 37N 00 10 26E, in about 28m of water, and has been positively identified by Humber Divers. There is no scour, but the wreck is very broken up, standing only a metre or so clear of the seabed. The 4.7" gun that she carried has been removed.

Ellington was an old ship, and had engines by Baird & Barnsley of North Shields, C 2cy 24" 48"-33". 1SB 3PF.

275 Botanic. Cochranes of Selby built this 348 ton trawler for the City Steam Fishing Co of Hull in 1928, but in WW2, she was taken over by the Admiralty for use as a minesweeper. She was 140ft long with a beam of 24ft and a depth of 13ft. On February 18 1942, she was bombed and sunk by a German aircraft, on the same day that the *Warland* met the same fate a few miles to the southward. In all probability, the same aircraft sank both ships. (See *Warland*.) The wreck of *Botanic* is in position 53 51 15N 00 26 38E in a depth of 38m. She is lying almost east-west, upright, with little scour, standing some 5m high in places. When built, she had engines by C.D. Holmes of Hull, T 3cy 13" 23" 37"-26". 1SB 3PF.

276 Cadmus. Built in 1911 by Irvines at West Hartlepool, this 1879 ton steamer was owned by J. Gaff & Co, and was registered at Sydney, New South Wales. She was 279ft long with a beam of 40ft and a depth of 18ft, and was armed for defence in 1917. She was torpedoed by a German submarine 20 miles south of Flamborough Head on October 18 1917. No lives were lost in the sinking. The wreck lies in position 53 50 55N 00 12 27E, in a north-east–south-west attitude, in a depth of 25m. She is in two main parts, with loose coils of steel wire and other debris lying between them, together with empty 18 pounder shell cases, which made up much of her cargo. It has been commercially salvaged, but there is so much dangerous cargo lying about that the Hydrographic Dept. have considered declaring it a prohibited wreck for sport divers.

Cadmus had engines by Richardson Westgarth & Co, T 3cy 20" 33" 54"-36".

277 Kimberley. Built at Selby in 1902, this 190 ton iron trawler was owned by the Diamond Steam Fishing Co of Grimsby, and was 110ft in length. On March 29 1941, she was attacked and sunk by bombs from a German aircraft while fishing 22 miles south-east of Flamborough Head. There is a wreck in position 53 50 42N 00 21 49E which is thought to be the *Kimberley;* the wreck is lying on its side in a north-south attitude, in a depth of 40m. The wreck stands some 6m high at its after end.

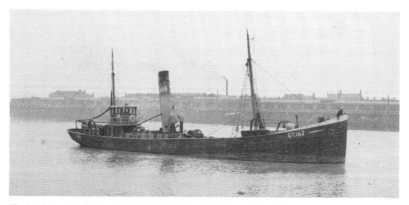

Kimberley, attacked and sunk by bombs in 1941. (Site 277)

278 Upminster. Owned by the Hudson Steamship Co of London, this 2176 ton steamer had been built by Osbourne Graham & Co at Sunderland in 1917. She was 280ft long with a beam of 40ft and a depth of 18ft. On May 2 1928, while bound for Methil in ballast from London, she was in collision with the steamship *Lanrick,* and sank shortly afterwards. The wreck lies in position 53 49 46N 00 09 37E, in a depth of 26m, with a least depth of a little over 18m. She is lying almost north-south, with the bows to the north, and there is little scour. The forward part of the ship is very broken, and partly buried, with the high points of the wreck being midships and aft. *Upminster* had engines by Richardsons, Westgarth & Co, T 3cy 21" 34" 56"-39". 2SB 4CF.

279 Kos 16. This strangely named whaling ship was built in 1932 at Middlesbrough for the Norwegian Hvalfangerslsk Kosmos II A/S, who owned a fleet of identical ships, named *Kos 1* to *Kos 18.* During WW2, the 258 ton ship was sunk in a collision while in use as a British Admiralty trawler, on August 24 1941. She measured 120ft long with a beam of 24ft and a depth of 14ft, and burned oil fuel. Her wreck is thought to be the one in position 53 49 24N 00 35 35E, in a depth of about 38m. She lies in a slight scour in a north-west–south-east attitude, on a smooth gravel bottom close to a ridge, and is apparently intact. *Kos 16* had engines by Smiths Dock Co, T 3cy 14" 23" 39"-24".

280 Unknown. There is a wreck in position 53 49 23N 00 17 21E which was thought to be the *Juno,* a Finnish steamship sunk in October, 1939, but divers have since established that the *Juno* is in fact in 53 44 54N 00 17 49E. (Site 295.) This unknown wreck is in two main parts, lying in a slight scour in a depth of 32m, with nothing standing much over 2m proud of the seabed.

281 Gluckauf. The 1915 ton German steamer *Gluckauf* sent out an SOS message on February 9 1939, after a collision in fog some 6 miles north-east of Spurn Head. Humber lifeboat raced to the scene, to find on arrival that most of the crew had been taken aboard the 7813 ton French steamer *Rhea,* and that the *Gluckauf* had in fact collided with a sunken wreck, the *Katina Bulgaris* (Site 338), which had herself been sunk after a collision the previous day.

Gluckauf, built in 1912 by S.P. Austin & Son at Sunderland as *Rondo,* was 266ft long with a beam of 38ft and a depth of 18ft. At the time of loss, she was owned by Gluckauf Kohlen Handels MBH, and was bound for Rostock from Immingham. The charted position of the wreck is 53 49 12N 00 34 00E, in a depth of about 35m, with a least depth of 21m. There is some doubt as to whether the wreck in this position is in fact the *Gluckauf;* this position is some 13 miles north of the *Katina Bulgaris* wreck site. Clearly, more diving is needed here.

Gluckauf had engines by G. Clark of Sunderland, T 3cy 20" 33" 54"-39".

Area Information and Services

Admiralty Charts. Flamborough Head to Blakeney Point, No. 1190. Flamborough Head to Withernsea, No. 121. Bridlington Bay, No. 1882.
Ordnance Survey. L101 Scarborough. L107 Kingston-upon-Hull.
Local Weather. Marinecall Area East, Tel. 0898-500 454.
Weather Area on Shipping Forecasts. Humber.
Local Coastguard. Humber District Headquarters (at Bridlington) Tel. 0262-672317. Hornsea Sector Station, Tel. 0964-534533. In emergency call 999. Weather bulletins from HM Coastguard on VHF marine radio begin at 0340, then four-hourly. Gale and small craft warnings issued on receipt from Met. office, repeated at two-hourly intervals.
BS-AC Branches. East Yorkshire Branch, Filey, No. 176. Dry meetings held Crown Hotel, Queen Street, Filey, Friday 8.30pm year round, Tel. 0723-512148. Training sessions currently held at Bridlington Leisure World, The Promenade, Bridlington, Tel. 0262-606715, Monday 8.00pm winter only. Air is available by arrangement at £1 per bottle. Visiting divers are welcome to attend wet or dry meetings, and on club dives by prior arrangement.
Other Clubs. Driffield and District Divers Sub-Aqua Association No. 443. Dry meetings held Downe Arms, Little Driffield, Tuesday 8.00pm, fortnightly in winter, weekly in summer. Tel. 0377-42243. Pool training held at Driffield Sports Centre, winter only, 8.00-10.00pm Saturdays. The club is three years old, has its own compressor in Driffield, and welcomes visiting divers. Contact can be made through Brian Wheeldon, currently ADO, Tel. 0377-43606.
Tourist Information. Bridlington 0262-678255; Hornsea 0964-532919.
*Air Supplies:*Sea Diver, 7 Rope Walk, Bridlington, Tel. 0262-606388. Air to 3,500psi, open 7 days in summer, 9-5. Diving equipment sales and repairs.
Boats for Hire:Kiwi, Skipper Phil Rylatt, proprietor of *Sea Diver,* 6 diver capability. Tel. 0262-606388/675721. *Our Freda,* SSSSper Chris Wright, 12 diver capability, Tel. 0262-677530. *Eva Ann,* Skipper Dave Screeton, 12 diver capability, though the vessel is licenced to carry up to 46 passengers. Normally fully booked up with angling parties, but often available for evening dives. Tel. 0262-676597. Ted. Newby, Tel. 0262-676551, handles a number of large angling boats which can also take diving parties by arrangement.
Outboard Repairs, Supplies and Servicing. Hull Boat Centre (see Spurn Area).
AA 24 hour Service. York, Tel. 0904-27698.
Bridlington Harbour. Tel. 0262-670148.
Accommodation. Plenty of all types available, see *Tourist Information.*
Boat Clubs. South Shore Boat Club, Bridlington, Tel. 0482-811406.

Area 7: Spurn

This area runs from latitude 53 48 41N to latitude 53 34 00N, Aldbrough to the Humber. The southernmost part of the Yorkshire coast, known officially now as North Humberside, consists of clay cliffs and sandy beaches which terminate in Spurn Point, a most unusual geographical feature. This three mile long spit of sand and shingle curves round like a talon into the Humber estuary, and is only a matter of yards wide in places. Periodically, the sea breaks through the narrow northern end of the spit, forming an island which then washes away completely. As more sand and shingle wash down the coast as a result of the erosion that takes place here, the spit reforms, the whole process taking two or three centuries. No one can predict when the cycle will begin again, but perhaps it is significant that Humber Coastguard have recently moved their headquarters from a building on Spurn Point to another one at Bridlington, some thirty miles to the north!

Today, Spurn Point is a nature reserve, owned by the Yorkshire Wildlife Trust and looked after by warden Barry Spence. There are restrictions on access to the Point, and boats on trailers are not admitted.

It has to be said right away that the underwater scenery off the southern Yorkshire coast has little to commend it in the way of natural beauty, and the

Spurn Point with wreckage of the trawler Saltaire. *(Not a dive site)*

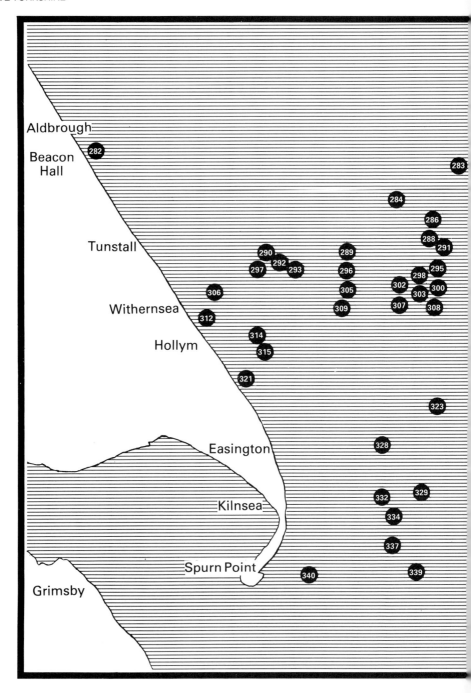

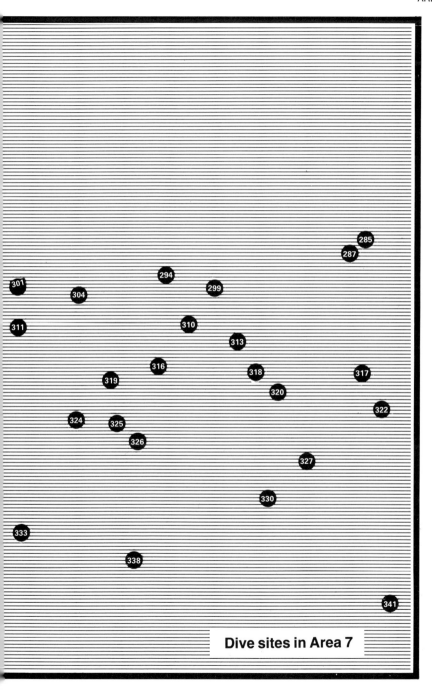

Dive sites in Area 7

marine biologist might do well to dive the more northern parts of the coast. However, for the wreck-hunter, this is a happy hunting ground, where wrecks abound in shallow and usually clear water. The snag is that the wrecks are hard to find, since transits are difficult on this fairly featureless coastline, and many of the best wrecks are out of sight of land. To be successful here, the diver must rely largely on electronic aids to navigation, and perhaps the best course of action is to charter a large boat with a diving skipper, and make a mini-expedition of it. The comparatively long distances, together with the difficulty of pinpointing the wrecks, can make this area a little daunting otherwise.

Most of the wrecks are the result of enemy action in the two World Wars, but the sheer volume of shipping using these waters over the years has inevitably meant that there were many losses due to collisions, groundings and other peacetime causes. Many of the wrecks have had dispersal operations carried out on them, but in most cases little has been actually removed, leaving them interesting to divers. Dispersal was necessary because of the shallowness of the water; many of the wrecks off the Humber had their masts and superstructure above the surface at the time of sinking. The area does however, contain some large and deep holes in the seabed, the best known being the Silver Pit, named after the wall-to-wall fish it contained when it was discovered in the mid-nineteenth century. It was on discoveries like this that the great trawling industries of Hull and Grimsby were founded though sadly, these have now declined almost to the point of extinction. Inshore fishing is still big business however, and many of the wrecks in the area will be found to be festooned with lost fishing gear.

Another notable feature of the maritime scene here is the proliferation of offshore gas drilling-rigs and platforms; the West Sole and Rough Gas fields have been producing for some years now, with pipelines coming ashore at the Easington Natural Gas Terminal. The West Sole field is some thirty miles off-shore, yet the water depth around it is less than 30m.

There are two quite distinct ways of diving this area, one of which, as mentioned earlier, is to charter a large boat from either Hull, Bridlington or Scarborough and make a two or more day expedition of it. Most of the writers' diving here has been done this way. The alternative is to launch a small, fast boat that is capable of dealing with the quite long distances involved. Road access to the area is not particularly good; the A1033 from Hull to Withernsea is the main route to the coast, with the B1445 taking you down the coast to the villages of Easington and Kilnsea, and on to Spurn Point. Coming down from Bridlington and the north via the B1242 can be tedious, as the road winds and twists needlessly as it goes round the edge of individual fields. The best launch sites are those at Withernsea, where there is currently no charge for visiting boats using the slipways. One of these is next to the boat club on Queens Promenade, and the other is on the Central Promenade, by the old pier towers. Withernsea itself is a small seaside holiday town offering the usual amenities and accommodation of all types, but there are no diving facilities on offer to visitors. Launching is also possible at Easington beach, beyond the caravan site, though an off-the-road vehicle is required since the access is deeply rutted; the locals use a tractor. Further south at Kilnsea there is a launching site on the inside of Spurn Point at Tommy Burkitt's slip, some 200 yards north of the Crown and Anchor pub. Since this access leads to miles of mudflats at low water, it holds little appeal for divers other than the proximity of the excellent pub, where food and accommodation are available.

Further north, there is a boating compound at Sand-le-Mere, Tunstall, where launching can be accomplished by use of a tractor or landrover. Camping and caravanning facilities are offered here too. Generally speaking however, there seems little advantage in using any of the slips other than those at Withernsea unless you are taking advantage of the camp sites offered at the other launching points mentioned here. If you are lucky enough to meet up with the Withernsea based divers, they will even show you where the wrecks are!

Shore Diving Sites

The only inshore dive site of real interest is the wreck of the *Earl of Beaconsfield*, which is capable of being reached from the shore. However, access to that part of the beach is so difficult that even this one must really be considered a boat dive.

Boat Diving Sites

282 Earl of Beaconsfield. During the transitional period from sail to steam, many sailing vessels were adapted to become steamers, but this one made the transition in reverse! *Earl of Beaconsfield* was an iron vessel, built by Todd & McGregor of Glasgow as the steamer *Cuba* in 1864. She was 338ft long with a beam of 42ft and a depth of 27ft, and had four masts. Originally owned by Cunard, by 1882 she was owned by D. Brown of London, and had her steam engines removed. It was as a 2488 ton four-masted iron sailing ship that she ran ashore near Aldborough, six miles north of Withernsea on November 6 1887, during fog. She was bound for Hull with grain from Calcutta at the time, and the first local people knew about the stranding was from a fishing smack which sent its small boat ashore to alert the authorities. A telegram was sent to the agent for the company in Hull, the Earl of Beaconsfield Shipping Co, of London. Several small boats put off, and found the master ditching cargo, having raised steam in the donkey boiler to operate the ships own lifting gear. Three tugs were in attendance by the fourth day, but the ship was still hard aground on a sandbank, about a quarter of a mile offshore. The 27 crew were taken off by the local pulling lifeboat after rockets had been fired from the ship during strong easterly winds. All efforts to get her off failed; she is still there today, and parts of the wreck can be seen at low water. There is enough wreckage there to make an interesting dive – portholes were still being found until recently – but she is not easy to get at. There is no easy route from the cliff top, and she is quite a way from the nearest launching site. However, after a prolonged period of settled weather, the inshore visibility can be good enough to make this a fascinating dive.
N.B. This wreck is inside Cowden Gunnery Range – see Restrictions in Introduction.

283 Sota Eduardo. This 800 ton general cargo ship was built at Bilbao in 1974 for Eduardo de la Sota Proveda S.A., Spain, and was 200ft long with a beam of 34ft and a depth of 15ft. She capsized and sank while under tow during a voyage from Spain to Scarborough on July 19 1985, carrying a cargo of chipboard. The wreck is in position 53 48 41N 00 19 09E in a depth of 33m. She lies north-south, with the bows to the south, on her port side. She stands some 10m proud of the surrounding seabed, and is already showing signs of being covered by silt. The *Sota Eduardo* was driven by a 1125bhp 16cy Caterpillar diesel, aft in the ship.

284 Unknown. Humber Divers found a wreck in position 53 47 15N 00 15 31E which has so far not been positively identified. A small vessel, it was armed with a small gun on the stern, indicating a war loss. It lies roughly north-east–south-west in a depth of about 22m, with the boiler and engine standing up some 3m or so. Little scour has taken place on the wreck; clearly, more diving is needed on this one.

285 Pilsudski. At 14 294 tons gross, the *Pilsudski* is the largest wreck known to be off the Yorkshire coast. Owned by the Gdynia-America Shipping Line, she was 499ft long, with a beam of 71ft and a depth of 32ft. She was built in Italy in 1935, by Cantieri Riuniti dell Adriatico, and was powered by two nine-cylinder Sulzer diesels which gave her a service speed of over 18 knots. When pressed, she could exceed 20 knots. Named after a famous Polish General, *Pilsudski* was sister to the *Batory,* and they were the pride of the Polish merchant fleet at a time when owning transatlantic luxury liners was a symbol of national status for any western country.

Pilsudski made her maiden voyage to New York via Montreal in September 1935, and in the ensuing years, made twenty transatlantic trips a year, carrying up to 770 passengers each time. When the German invasion of Poland took place on September 1, 1939, *Pilsudski* was homeward bound from America, and was diverted to Britain. Less than three months later, on November 26 1939, she struck a mine and sank off Withernsea while bound for Australia from the Tyne. Ten lives were lost.

The wreck of *Pilsudski* is in position 53 45 45N 00 45 40E, in a maximum depth of 33m, and she is a most impressive dive. Most prominent is the bow section, which is laid over to port at about 45 degrees, and broken off just aft of the foc'sle. Three separate decks can be seen and entered, though extreme caution must be exercised. There are toilets and showers still in place, with large tiled areas, and a number of portholes in place which can be opened from the inside. On the starboard side, the embossed letters of the name can be discerned, together with the decorative scroll work which adorned the bow. Strong tidal currents sweep round the bow, even it seems, at slack water. At any other time it is quite impossible to swim round the bows at seabed level because the currents are so strong. There are overfalls on the surface above the wreck when the tide ebbs or flows. The bows stand some 9m proud of the surrounding seabed, but aft of this section, the wreck is much lower and more broken up, with much of interest for the diver. The stern section – which will not normally be reached in the same dive – stands almost upright, some 5m proud of the seabed, and is partially buried, with neither of the ship's propellers showing above the sand and shingle. The base section of a gun lies on the seabed to port, but there is no sign of the gun barrel. Again, there is much to see forward of the stern section, including a huge stockless anchor that looks like new.

The problem with this fine dive site is that the wreck lies some 25 miles offshore, and almost 18 miles from Flamborough Head. The best way to visit her is to mount a mini-expedition using a large boat from Hull, Bridlington or Scarborough.

The largest known wreck off the Yorkshire coast – the Pilsudski. *(Site 285)*

286 Magnolia. Built at Beverley in 1909, this 260 ton steam trawler was originally named *Kong Frederik III*, but when she came into the ownership of T.W. Baskcomb of Grimsby her name was changed to *Magnolia*. She was 125ft long with a beam of 22ft and a depth of 12ft. After springing a leak, she sank while under tow of the trawler *Rose of England* off Withernsea on August 20, 1952.

There is a wreck in position 53 46 11N 00 17 36E which is thought to be the *Magnolia*, lying on the north side of a clay ridge at a depth of 19m. The wreck is lying roughly north-west–south-east, with the bows to the west, and has her engine and boiler still standing, roughly 4m proud of the seabed. More diving is needed, but all the indications are that this is the *Magnolia*.

The engines fitted to *Magnolia* were built at Grimsby, T 3cy 12" 22" 35"-21".

287 Vereingte. In position 53 45 54N 00 43 33E is the wreck of a 102 ton German vessel described as a *lighter*, but Mr. J.B. Wilson who dived it mentions the vessel has a boiler. I have so far failed to find this vessel in Lloyds Registers, but the wreck lies in roughly 30m of water in a north-west–south-east attitude, and though the stern is well broken up, the boiler and bow section are more or less intact.

288 Modiva. Owned by I.A. Christensen, this Norwegian steamer had been built by the Antwerp Engineering Co in 1911, and grossed 1276 tons. She was 229ft long with a beam of 35ft and a depth of 15ft. She had a cargo of coal aboard when she was mined ten miles off Withernsea on January 31 1917. The wreck lies in position 53 45 48N 00 17 27E in a depth of about 20m, and was positively identified during the summer of 1986. Though very broken, the whole ship can be recognised; the bows are there with two stockless anchors, the holds are flattened to the seabed, but the engine, boiler and donkey boiler are prominent. The propellor shaft can be followed right to the stern gear, and the stern lies over to port. Items of interest include two spare folding anchors, two winches aft, and a spare propellor lying just aft of the engines.

The bell of Modiva, *mined off Withersea. (Site 288)*

Modiva had engines by the North Eastern Marine Engineering Co of Newcastle, T 3cy, 17" 28" 46"-33". 1SB 3CF.

289 Paraciers. This French steamer must hold the record for the largest number of previous names, having been called *Tidjitt, Syra, Halifax City, Syracusa,* and *John Cockerill* before finally settling on *Paraciers*. It will be interesting to see what name the ship's bell carries, should it ever be found. Built in France in 1894, she was a 2542 ton ship, 321ft long with a beam of 40ft and a depth of 24ft. She was sunk by a U-boat off Withernsea on September 17 1917, while bound for her home port of Boulogne with coal from Newcastle. The wreck is lying in position 53 45 22N 00 12 42E in a depth of 19m, with a slight scour to the south. She lies over on her side, in a north-west–south-east attitude, very broken up, with her bows to the north. The highest point on the wreck, just over 3m, is the after part.
Paraciers had T 3cy engines, 26" 43" 69"-43".

290 German Aircraft. In chart position 53 45 20N 00 08 12E is the wreckage of an unknown German aircraft; a radial engine marked BMW was found in this position by Mr. D.G. Bailey. During WW2, many German bombers, mainly Heinkels, attacked shipping entering or leaving the Humber, as well as dropping bombs on Hull and the surrounding area. This is clearly the remains of one that did not escape our defences at the time. The remains lie about 300m north of the wreck of *Otis Tetrax* (site 293).

291 Horsted. This 1670 ton Stephenson Clarke collier was built by the Burntisland SB Co in 1936, and was 256ft long with a beam of 37ft and a depth of 16ft. She was part of an East Coast convoy when she was attacked by a U-boat on December 4, 1939, and sunk by a torpedo off Withernsea. Three men were killed, two others died later, but Captain Hunter and the survivors were picked up by the warships escorting the convoy, one man having survived for almost an hour in the icy water. The wreck of *Horsted* is thought to be that in position 53 54 11N 00 17 56E, in two distinct pieces in a depth of 20m. The northern piece is the biggest, covering an area of 100sq m or so.

Horsted was fitted with T 3cy engines, 17" 29" 48"-33". 2SB 4CF by Rowan & Co of Glasgow.

292 Empress. Built in 1893 by Furness Withy at Hartlepool, this 2918 ton steamer changed her ownership and her name to *Cadiz,* then later changed again to *Empress* when she was bought by the Amaryllis Shipping Co of Cardiff. She was armed for defence in WW1, but was mined and sunk with the loss of five lives on July 31 1917, while carrying 5760 tons of coal down the Yorkshire coast. She sank some four miles off Withernsea, with her two masts showing above the surface.

Empress was 314ft long with a beam of 41ft and a depth of 21ft. There is a wreck lying in position 53 45 09N 00 09 21E which is thought to be – and is large enough to be – the *Empress,* but so far, no positive identification has taken place. The water depth is only around 15m here, so she is obviously waiting to be dived again.

Empress had engines by T. Richardson of Hartlepool, T 3cy 21" 38" 62"- 42". 2SB 6CF.

293 Otis Tetrax. Owned by the Dutch company of Hudig & Pieters, this 996 ton steamer was built in Holland by J. Meyer in 1916, and registered at Rotterdam. She was 215ft long with a beam of 32ft and a depth of 17ft. Although armed for defence as she went about her work as a collier in WW1, this did not prevent her from being attacked and sunk by a German U-boat on August 20, 1918. She went down off Withernsea, without loss of life. The wreck is in chart position 53 45 04N 00 08 12E in about 13m of water.

Otis Tetrax had Dutch built engines, T 3cy 18" 29" 47"-35". 2SB 4CF.

294 Unknown. Lying in position 53 45 00N 00 33 02E is the wreck of a small vessel, measuring roughly 50m long by 15m wide, in a depth of 30m. She is lying north-west–south-east on the edge of some rough ground, and has been the cause of many a lost trawl net. This one needs more diving information. It is possible that this could be the 165 ton trawler *Falmouth,* sunk by our own mines on April 12 1945 – but see the unknown wreck in position 54 44 46N 00 35 41E.

295 Juno. Built as *Lormont* by Hawthorns & Co, Leith in 1920, this 1276 ton ship was owned by Moss Line Ltd of Liverpool, but was sold to Finnish owners in 1934 and renamed *Juno.* She was 245ft long with a beam of 39ft and a depth of 16ft. On October 30 1939, the ship struck a mine and sank while bound for Viipuri, Finland, with a general cargo. There was some doubt about whether or not the ship had been torpedoed; either way, four ships' lifeboats and two timber liferafts washed ashore near Withernsea, together with various bits of wreckage. The wreck lies in position 53 44 56N 00 17 49E, in a depth of 20m. She is heavily dispersed, with the two boilers out of line, the propellor shaft, stern gear and engines listing to starboard on a sand/stones/shells seabed. The bows are also lying over to starboard, separated from the wreck by a short distance. There is much to see, including winches, masts and some cargo – though it is doubtful whether you will still find any of the tin ingots that were on her original manifest. Among the other items she had aboard were hides, aeroplane parts, electric motors, welding equipment and pen nibs! The boilers on the wreck are 2SB, 6CF, but unfortunately, Lloyds Register does not record the details of the boilers on *Juno,* so we cannot use that to check her identity. *Juno* had engines by Hawthorns, T 3cy, 21" 35" 59"-39".

296 Georgios Antippa. Built as the *Prins Willem II,* this 1960 ton steamer later became *Elpiniki* and finally *Georgios Antippa.* She was 272ft long with a beam of 36ft and a depth of 20ft, and was built in Holland in 1890. On November 28 1917, while operating as an armed British merchant vessel, she was torpedoed by a German submarine in position 53 44 55N 00 12 31E. She sank without loss of life, in a depth of 22m. Steve Cooper of Withernsea discovered a wreck in this position which is almost certainly the *Georgios Antippa;* the wreck is armed with a 90mm cannon, and a machine gun. So far only the forward part of the wreck has been dived, the rest lies a little distance away. The highest point on the dived part stands almost 6m proud of the seabed, in a slight scour.

When built, the ship was fitted with T 3cy engines, 22" 34" 56"-40" and in 1909 she was fitted with a new double boiler.

297 Lyra. This 1141 ton Norwegian steamer was owned by C.T. Gogstad & Co and had been built in that country in 1917. She was 238ft long, with a beam of 36ft and a depth of 17ft. She was less than a year old when she was torpedoed by a German U-boat on November 4 1917, while carrying a cargo of nitrate of soda and aluminium ingots.

The wreck lies in about 15m of water in position 53 44 54N 00 07 25E, and was positively identified by local diver J. Boddy. She is well dispersed, with only the engine and boiler standing proud of the seabed, and evidence of the aluminium ingots lying around.

Lyra had Norwegian built engines, T 3cy, 16" 25" 42"-30".

298 Orsa. Built by the New Waterway Shipbuilding Co in 1925, this was a 1478 ton steamer owned by Clydesdale Shipowners Co. She was 250ft long with a beam of 37ft and a depth of 16ft. On October 21 1939, she was mined and sunk with the loss of sixteen men, while bound for Bordeaux with coal from the Tyne.

There is a wreck in position 53 44 47N; 00 16 58E which is likely to be the *Orsa;* the engine cylinder diameters match those known to be fitted to the ship, but sadly, Lloyd's register does not mention the number and type of furnaces/boilers that *Orsa* had. The wreck has 2SB, 6PF. She lies over on her starboard side, and though badly broken, stands almost 4m high, and is an interesting dive. The engines are lying flat on the seabed, and one of her boilers is upended.

Orsa had engines by the builder, T 3cy, 18" 30" 49"-36".

299 Unknown. In position 53 44 46N 00 35 41E is the wreck of an intact vessel, thought to be a trawler, in a depth of about 30m. The wreck is about 120ft long, and is lying roughly east-west, with the bows to the west. Until recently, one of the msts was still in position, reaching to within 14m of the surface.

This could be the wreck of the 165 ton steam trawler *Farmouth,* owned by the Consolidated Fisheries Co of Grimsby, and built at Govan in 1897. The ship measured 104ft in length, with a beam of 21ft and a depth of 11ft. She sank close to this position after striking one of our own mines on April 12 1945.

300 Portia. Owned by J. Lund & Co, Norway, this 1127 ton steamer had been built by Trondhjems Mek Verksted in 1914, and was 226ft long with a beam of 36ft and a depth of 16ft. She had 1600 tons of coal aboard when she was mined and sunk off Withernsea on February 1 1917.

The wreck is in position 53 44 44N 00 17 01E, lying roughly north-south in a depth of 20m with a slight scour, and no part of the wreck standing up more than 2m.

Portia had T 3cy engines, 17" 27" 46"-30", built by Trondhjems Mek Verksted.

301 British Councillor. At 7048 tons, this tanker was one of the larger ships to be wrecked off the Yorkshire Coast, following a torpedo attack from a German U-boat on February 2 1940. Owned by the British Tanker Co of London, she had been built in 1922 by Sir J. Laing & Son at Sunderland. She measured 440ft long, with a beam of 57ft and a depth of 34ft.

The wreck of *British Councillor* lies in position 53 44 42N 00 24 05E, in a depth of 27m, with a slight scour. The wreck is well dispersed, over a wide area, with the bulk of it lying north-west–south-east, and no part of it standing more than 4m high.

The ship was built with two steam turbines, producing 642nhp, geared to one shaft, by G. Clark of Sunderland, with 3SB 12CF.

302 Corinth. There is a wreck in position 53 44 41N 00 16 02E which is thought to be the 3669 ton steamer *Corinth,* owned by the Corinthian Shipping Co of Liverpool. Built by Thompson at Sunderland in 1904, she was 346ft long with a beam of 51ft and a depth of 23ft. During a voyage from Blyth to Rochefort with 5500 tons of coal, she was captured by an enemy submarine who sank her with bombs on November 11 1916, some 28 miles south of Flamborough Head.

The wreck is lying roughly north-east–south-west in a depth of 20m, and is in three main pieces with the engine section being the highest, at 5m or so clear of the seabed. She is well broken up, and more diving is needed to try and identify this wreck positively.

Corinth had T 3cy engines by Dickenson, 24" 40„ 66". 2SB 8PF.

303 Modig. This 1704 ton steamer was built in 1913 by Nylands Verksted, and was owned by I.A.N. Christensens Rederi, Norway. She was 265ft long with a beam of 40ft and a depth of 19ft, and carrying 2400 tons of coal when she struck a mine and sank on December 21 1916, some eight miles off Withernsea.

The wreck of *Modig* lies in position 53 44 30N 00 16 42E, in a depth of 20m, with no scour. She is lying in a north-south attitude; is badly broken up, and one of her 2 boilers is half buried in the sand and stony seabed.

Modig had engines by Nylands Verksted of Xania, T 3cy 19" 31" 51"-33".

304 Grangemouth. Built in 1908 by the Grangemouth and Greenock Dockyard Co, this 1419 ton steamer was owned by G. Gibson & Co of Leith. She was 275ft long with a beam of 36ft and a depth of 17ft. On March 22, 1939, she collided with the trawler *Sudanese,* while bound for the Tees with a general cargo from Antwerp. There were seventeen people aboard the steamer, including four passengers, who thought that the likelihood of war with Germany had become a reality in the confusion! The Grangemouth was badly damaged, and the passengers and crew abandoned the ship and were taken aboard the *Sudanese.* Later, some of the crew reboarded the stricken steamer, and a tow was set up. The tow rope broke, and another was established to a Grimsby tug, but the *Grangemouth* sank before she could be towed to safety.

The wreck lies in position 53 44 29N 00 27 50E, in a north-east–south-west attitude, in 28m of water. The forward part of the ship is fairly intact, while the stern half is well broken up. Parts of the mid section stand some 8m high.

Grangemouth had engines by Dunsmuir & Jackson of Glasgow, T 3cy 25" 42" 68"-45".

305 Whitemantle. During a voyage from the Tyne to London with coal, this 1692 ton steamer struck a mine and sank with the loss of fourteen lives, six miles off Withernsea. Built in 1920 by Wood Skinner & Co, she was 260ft long with a beam of 38ft and a depth of 16ft, and was owned by the Gas Light & Coke Co. She is thought to be the wreck in position 53 44 24N 00 12 44E, in a depth of about 17m. The wreck lies roughly east-west, with the bows to the east and shallowest point. She is well broken up, on a flat seabed with little scour.

Whitemantle had engines by North Eastern Marine Engineering Co, T 3cy 20" 33" 54"-36". 2SB 6CF.

306 Henry Woodall. This 625 ton collier was built by Hawthorn Leslie on the Tyne in 1935, for Stephenson Clarke. She was 177ft long, with a beam of 28ft and a depth of 11ft. On May 10 1940, she was mined and sunk three miles east of Withernsea, with the loss of seven men. Captain Bain was among the survivors.

The wreck, which is owned by local divers, is in position 53 44 20N 00 05 00E, in a depth of about 11m. She is well dispersed, with the stern section completely separated from the rest, and stands a maximum of 3m clear of the seabed.

Henry Woodall had engines by North Eastern Marine Engineering, Sunderland, T 3cy 13" 22" 36"-24".

307 Unknown. In position 53 44 13N 00 15 52E is the wreck of an unidentified trawler of about 250 tons, approximately 100ft in length. The boiler, engine, stern-tube, propellor shaft and stern gear are present, and there is a winch forward. The wreck is in a depth of about 17m, and was discovered by Steve Cooper. There are a number of trawler wrecks in this vicinity that have not yet been found; one that sank near this position was the River Don, a 202 ton Grimsby trawler, 115ft in length, that foundered on October 27 1931. She had been built for the Admiralty as Patrick Borrow at Montrose in 1917. It could well be this ship that Steve has located.

308 Unknown. In position 53 44 07N 00 16 32E lies the wreck of a steamer that is well broken up, and has little remaining forward of her two boilers. Aft of the boilers are her engines, propellor shaft and stern gear, together with a large amount of flattened plate. She lies at a depth of approximately 20m, and evidence has been found to the effect that she was built by W. Gray of Hartlepool. Unfortunately, there is no record of any of Gray's ships having been lost close to this position, but there are on record nine ships built by this company that were subsequently lost '. . .in the North Sea. . .' My guess is that this wreck could be that of the 2494 ton Hildawell, sunk by a German submarine on December 20, 1916, with the loss of the captain and twenty-one crew. This ship had carried a cargo of iron ore; there are indications of iron ore on the wreck. The wreck has two single boilers, each with two corrugated furnaces, and the boilers are much further apart than is the case with most wrecks. She has clearly been heavily dispersed.

The collier Henry Woodall, *was mined and sunk with loss of seven men. (Site 306) Painting by Peter L Bailey.*

309 Derwent. One of the most exciting finds off the Yorkshire coast in recent years was the discovery of the wreck of the *Derwent,* made by a group of divers from Withernsea and Hartlepool, and passed to the present writer by Rob Dawson. The Scarborough Steam Shipping Co had been formed in Scarborough in 1881, to run a steamer between the North East, Scarborough and London, carrying passengers and cargo. Their first ship, the steamer *Balaclava,* proved a success, and the company ordered a brand new vessel to be called *Derwent,* from W. Gray & Co of Hartlepool, at a cost of £8100. The 417 ton vessel was delivered in October 1884, and she made 51 voyages between the North East and London in the next year. On October 23 1885, she left Hartlepool with a coal cargo under Captain Henry Price, and was not heard of again. She disappeared during a force 10

Bell of the Derwent, *which was lost in a gale in 1885. (Site 309)*

storm, and the only clues were a lifebelt with her name that washed up in Lincolnshire, and a bucket, also named, which came ashore near Spurn Point. At the subsequent inquiry, it was revealed that the ship had sailed with just 19 inches of freeboard, but this was considered adequate. Twelve men were lost with the *Derwent;* there were no survivors. The wreck was found and positively identified in 1986, in position 53 44 02N 00 12 36E. She is well broken up, in about 15m of water, but there is plenty left of her to make an interesting dive. The *Derwent* was 158ft long with a beam of 25ft and a depth of 12ft. Her engines were by T. Richardson, C 2cy; 70nhp.

310 Vechtstroom. Originally called *Energie II,* this 845 ton steamer was built in Holland in 1918 for NV Hollandsche Stoomb Maats. She was 201ft long with a beam of 30ft and a depth of 13ft, and had her engines aft. She was carrying a coal cargo when attacked by a German aircraft on September 22 1941. *Vechtstroom* was sunk in position 53 43 29N 00 34 04E, in a depth of 28m. The wreck is lying with her bows to the north-west, broken amidships, stern pointing almost due south. She is in a slight scour, on a firm sand and clay seabed.

Vechtstroom had T 3cy engines, 16" 25" 41"-27" by Burgerhouts, Rotterdam.

311 Unknown. In position 53 43 26N 00 24 11E lie the remains of an old steamship, standing some 4m high in a depth of 25m. The wreck appears to be about 50m long, and is flattened, apart from the engine and boiler. A bell was found by Humber Divers, and the letters '. . .ARNSTRV. . .' remained on it. So far, all efforts to identify the vessel have failed.

312 Crux. Built at Govan in 1896, *Crux* was a 132 ton trawler owned by the Grimsby & North Sea Steam Trawling Co. She ran ashore in a gale on January 10 1912 at Out Newton, four miles south of Withernsea, and one man lost his life. The local lifeboat was launched through heavy surf, and after a dangerous voyage, was forced to turn back. Meantime the rocket brigade made contact with the wreck, and succeeded in rescuing Captain Warner and nine crewmen.

The wreck is in position 53 43 12N 00 04 00E, with a least depth of 3m over her. She lies at right-angles to the shore, in a scour, with only her bottom plates, boiler, engines and propellor shaft evident.

313 Jersey. During WW1, many steam trawlers were sunk by bombs placed aboard them by raiding U-boats off the Yorkshire coast. *Jersey,* a 162 ton Grimsby trawler, was one of these. She was fishing some 16 miles off Spurn Point in company with another Grimsby trawler, the *Rado* (site 320), when an enemy U-boat surfaced alongside, forced her crew to abandon ship, and then scuttled the trawler, on October 4 1916. Owned by Hagerup, Doughty & Co, *Jersey* was 104ft long, and had been built at Govan in 1896. The wreck lies in position 53 42 54N 00 37 18E, in 27m of water, in an east-west attitude, and is partly buried.

314 Canada. Among the largest ships ever wrecked off the Yorkshire coast was the 11 108 ton Danish motor vessel *Canada,* which left King George V Dock in Hull on November 3 1939, and struck a magnetic mine off Holmpton, Spurn Head, the same day. The 64 crew members, 5 of them women, took to the lifeboats, for the ships' number two hold was completely wrecked, and the ship seemed doomed. The lifeboat containing Captain

Scuttled by a U-boat crew, the steam trawler Jersey. *(Site 313)*

Knudson circled the ship, and he decided to re-board with a skeleton crew, but after five tugs had failed to move the ship, they too left. The wreck lies in position 53 42 19N 00 07 05E in about 13m of water, with a least depth of 2m over the wreck. She lies north-south, with the bows north, and is well broken up. The wreck has been well known to local divers for many years, and because it is still a danger to navigation, it is marked by a large wreck buoy. In 1972, a team of divers removed the propellor from this wreck, without, unfortunately, informing the owners, Trinity House, who had plans of their own for the bronze artifact. The *Daily Express* of August 24 1972, put it in a nutshell with their headline '. . .Seabed pirates steal ten tons of loot. . .' The matter was eventually resolved however; it is not easy to land a ten ton

M.V. Canada *struck a magnetic mine off Spurn Head. (Site 314)*

175

The superstructure of Canada *before she finally sank. (Site 314)*

propellor without anyone noticing it, and the divers responsible were brought to book. Most people who were aware of the incident at the time secretly admitted that it had been a fine piece of salvage work!

The *Canada* had been built in 1935 by Nakskov Skibs A/S, and was 469ft long, with a beam of 64ft and a depth of 36ft.

315 Georgios. This Greek steamer, a 2216 ton vessel, had been built by F. Kruppe at Kiel in 1910 as the *Dr Adolf Schmidt*. She was renamed *Else* and later *Batna,* under French ownership for a time. On November 14 1939, while loaded with esparto, she struck the wreck of the Danish steamer *Canada* off Withernsea, and stuck fast, with 20ft of her bow over the wreck. Amazingly, there were no casualties; 22 crew were taken off and landed at Grimsby by the Humber lifeboat. Attempts to refloat the *Georgios* failed, and she now lies in 13m of water, just outside the *Canada* wreck, in a north-west–south-east attitude. The ship was 286ft long with a beam of 43ft and a depth of 19ft. Her engines, by Krupps, were T 3cy, 20" 31" 53"-38".

316 Homer. This 1308 ton steamer was built by J. Readhead & Co on the Tyne in 1881, and was owned by Dick & Page of London. She measured 250ft long with a beam of 34ft and a depth of 17ft. On February 15 1901, she was in collision with the Russian barque *Hopper* off Spurn Head while bound for the Tyne with steel from London. At the moment of impact, an able seaman named McAllister leapt from the *Homer* onto the Russian ship, and at the same time, the captain of the Russian vessel leapt aboard the *Homer.* It transpired that the AB had made the wiser decision; he was to be the only survivor from the *Homer,* his sixteen shipmates going down with the ship, together with the unfortunate Russian. The *Hopper* had been bound for the USA in ballast at the time, and though she searched in the dark, could find no trace of the *Homer* after the two vessels drifted apart.

The wreck is in position 53 42 05N 00 32 30E, lying north-east–south-west, with the bows to the south, in 26m depth. The boilers and engines are the highest point on the wreck, standing some 4m high. *Homer* had engines by Readhead & Co, 2C 30" 57"-36". 2SB 4PF.

317 Keynes. This 1706 ton Stephenson Clarke collier had been built by Wood Skinner at Newcastle in 1915, and was 260ft long with a beam of 38ft and a depth of 16ft. On the morning of January 11 1940, she was attacked by a German aircraft which dropped a number of bombs that missed, and was finally driven off by machine-gun fire from the ships' only gun. A second attack was made that afternoon, and this time the raider scored several hits, injuring crewmen, and sealing the fate of *Keynes.* British fighter planes alerted by the radio operator drove off the German aircraft and a British warship picked up the *Keynes* crew.

The wreck is in position 53 42 04N 00 44 57E in a depth of 26m, lying north-west–south-east, with the engine section being the highest point on the wreck. She has an iron propellor, and is usually festooned with lost trawl nets. There is a half model of *Keynes* in the Trinity Maritime Centre Museum at Newcastle.

Keynes had T 3cy engines, 20" 33" 54"-36". 2SB 6CF by North Eastern Marine Engineering Co Ltd.

318 Corland. Originally named *Buffs*, this 3431 ton steamer carried a portrait of the King of Denmark, who was honorary Colonel of the Buffs. She was a collier, owned by W. Cory & Sons of London, and was 341ft long with a beam of 47ft and a depth of 23ft. She was built by S.P. Austin & Son at Sunderland in 1917. During a voyage from Blyth to London with coal, she was attacked and sunk by German aircraft on February 5 1942, in position 53 41 57N 00 38 21E. The wreck now lies in a depth of 27m, heading roughly north-south, with the bows to the south, and some 7m clear of the seabed at the highest point. *Corland* had engines by Richardson Westgarth & Co of Sunderland, T 3cy 24" 40" 65"-42". 2SB 8PF.

319 Revello. The night of December 6/7, 1959, brought terrible gales to the North Sea, and many ships were wrecked as a result. Among them was the 230 ton Grimsby trawler *Revello,* which sprang a leak and had to be abandoned some ten miles from Spurn Light Vessel. The eleven crew were picked up from their rubber dinghy by the Newcastle steamer *Baluchistan* and landed safely at Hull. The wreck is lying in 24m of water in position 53 41 23N 00 29 50E in an east-west attitude, with high points at each end standing almost 5m clear of the seabed.

320 Rado. A German U-boat captured this Grimsby trawler while she was fishing some 15 miles north-east by east of Spurn Light Vessel on October 4 1916, and sank her by placing bombs aboard after allowing the crew to escape in their own boat. Built of steel at Hull in 1903, *Rado* was a 182 ton ship, 105ft long, owned by G..F. Sleight. The wreck is thought to be the one in position 53 41 25N 00 35 41E, in a depth of 26m. More diving information on her is needed. Another trawler, the *Jersey,* was sunk close by on the same day by the same raider.

A terrible gale in December 1959 caused the loss of Revello. *The crew were saved.*
(Site 319)

321 Dryburgh. At 2.15pm on November 11 1939, this 1289 ton steamer struck the wreck of the *Canada* (site 314) off Holmpton, and was badly holed. Her distress signals were answered by the Spurn Lifeboat and the tug *Yorkshireman* which took the *Dryburgh* in tow, pulling her off the wreck with the intention of beaching her. However, the *Dryburgh* was already doomed; she filled up, capsized and sank about half a mile inside the *Canada*. Built by the Campbelltown Shipbuilding Co in 1919, *Dryburgh* was owned by G.Gibson of Leith, and was carrying a cargo of coal and horseflesh at the time of loss. She was 230ft long with a beam of 36ft and a depth of 16ft.

Steve Cooper of Withernsea has located a wreck which is almost certainly the *Dryburgh* in position 53 41 18N 00 06 29E, in about 15m of water. The wreck is virtually complete, with her back broken, and stands some 7m high at the stern and midships.

Dryburgh had engines by Ross & Duncan, Glasgow, T 3cy 18" 30" 50"-33". 2SB 6CF.

322 Revigo. This 230 ton trawler was owned by G.F. Sleight of Grimsby, and had been built at Beverley in 1907. She was sunk by a mine on September 7 1914, some 25 miles off Spurn Point. Her wreck is thought to be the one in position 53 40 51N 00 48 46E, lying roughly east-west, in 32m of water. Further diving is needed on this one.

323 Giuseppe. This one is something of a mystery, and has so far eluded positive identification. A bell was found bearing this name on a steamship wreck in position 53 40 35N 00 18 27E. The engine and boilers are there, together with the sternshaft and propellor, lying almost north-south on a gravel seabed. Parts of the wreck stand almost 5m high, in a depth of about 17m. More diving is needed on this one in order to try and date the wreck, for *Giuseppe* was not an unusual name; there are many in Lloyd's Register over the years.

324 Norfolk Coast. Owned by Coast Lines Ltd of Liverpool, this 782 ton steamer had been built by Harkess & Co at Middlesbrough in 1910, and was 195ft long with a beam of 30ft and a depth of 12ft. She was armed for defence during WW1, but this did not prevent her from being attacked by *UB-30* on June 18 1918, while bound for the Tyne. A torpedo sank her in position 53 40 10N 00 28 02E with the loss of eight lives.

The wreck lies roughly south-east–north-west, in some 20m of water, standing roughly 4m high at the boilers. The wreckage covers an area of approximately 90m by 20m, with little scour, and a liberal covering of lost fishing nets.

Norfolk Coast had aft engines by Richardson Westgarth & Co, T 3cy 16" 27" 44"-30". 2SB 4CF.

325 Benmacdhui (II). This 6869 ton Ben Line steamer survived an air attack off Yarmouth in February 1941, but was sunk by a mine on December 21 of that year some 10 miles east-north-east of Spurn Point. Two men died when the ship sank while en route for Hong Kong from Immingham. Built by Russell & Co of Aberdeen in 1911, she was originally named *Archimedes,* later changed to *Den of Airlie* and then *Benmacdhui*. She was 434ft long with a beam of 54ft and a depth of 35ft.

The wreck lies in position 53 40 09N 00 30 24E, in 21m of water with almost 3m scour, and is in two parts. She lies roughly north-west–south-east, with about 15m separating the bows and forward part of the ship from the boilers, engines and stern section. She lies upright, with the bows to the north, and a salvage contract is held by Humber Divers, who have salvaged much of the cargo.

Benmacdhui has engines by D. Rowan & Co of Glasgow; T 3cy 27" 46" 76"-51". 3SB 9CF.

326 Unknown. In position 53 39 35N 00 31 32E can be found this unidentified steamship, in some 19m of water. The wreck lies roughly north-west–south-east, and appears to have been carrying iron ore. It is well broken up, with only the engine and boiler still standing, reaching almost 4m from the seabed.

327 Catford. This 1568 ton steamer was built at Dublin in 1919, and was owned by the South Metropolitan Gas Co. She was bound for the Tyne in ballast from London when she was mined and sunk on May 31 1943, in position 53 38 56N 00 41 16E. One source says that five lives were lost; another says that there were nine fatalities. The ship was 240ft long with a beam of 36ft and a depth of 19ft.

The wreck lies in a north-south attitude, bows north, in 25m of water. She is upright, though very broken up, and there is a scour to the west.

Catford had engines by J.G. Kincaid & Co of Greenock, T 3cy 18" 30" 50"-33". 2SB 6CF.

328 Saltoun. This 727 ton steamer was built in Holland in 1918 as the *Princenhage I,* but had her name changed to *Saltoun* when she was bought by G. Gibson of Leith. She was sunk in a collision with the steam trawler *Prince Leo* on November 7 1927, while carrying pig-iron, in position 53 38 54N 00 14 56E. *Saltoun* was 184ft long with a beam of 29ft and a depth of 12ft, and had her engines aft.

The wreck is in 16m of water in a slight scour, lying north-north-east–south-south-west, with her bows to the south. She is very broken up, and partially buried, with a lot of cargo lying about.

Saltoun had Dutch built engines, T 3cy, 14" 20" 39"-24".

329 Ionic. After a collision with the Hull trawler *Hornbill* on March 7 1928, the Grimsby trawler *Ionic* was taken in tow, but sank off the Humber before reaching safety. The 159 ton trawler was 110ft long with a beam of 22ft. The wreck of *Ionic* lies in position 53 37 34N 00 17 33E, in a depth of about 14m of water. She lies north-west–south-east, bows to the south-east, and is almost buried.

Built by Earles of Hull in 1890, *Ionic* was an iron vessel owned by the Grimsby Steam Fishing Co.

330 Royston. On May 4 1941, this 2722 ton collier was attacked by enemy aircraft 17 miles east of Kilnsea. One bomb fell on her port side, three landed amidships, and one struck the starboard beam. Despite this battering, *Royston* survived until the next day, when she finally sank while under tow, in position 53 37 32N 00 39 35E. Built by Smiths Dock Co at Middlesbrough in 1929, she was owned by Witherington and Everett of Newcastle, and was carrying 4300 tons of coal at the time of her loss. She was 305ft long with a beam of 45ft and a depth of 21ft.

The wreck lies in 20m of water in an east-west attitude, with the bows to the west; she has high points at each end, and there is little scour. *Royston* had 266nhp engines, T 3cy 21" 35" 57"-42". 2SB 6CF.

Benvolio *was another victim of a German mine. (Site 331)*

331 Benvolio. This 352 ton trawler was built by H. Cochrane & Son at Selby, for Hull Owners, but was later sold to Grimsby where she fished as GY 183. She was requisitioned by the Admiralty, and was sunk by a mine on February 23 1940, with the loss of all ten crew.

The wreck lies on the edge of a sand hole, and is difficult to find with an echo sounder, as the edge of the hole gives a much sharper reading. The seabed depth at the wrecksite, position 53 37 32N 00 20 52E, is between 25 and 30m. The bow section is more or less intact, the stern part lies on its starboard side some 15m away.

332 Dido. This Wilson Liner was built by Earles Shipbuilding Co at Hull in 1896, and had a gross tonnage of 4769 tons. She was 401ft long with a beam of 48ft and a depth of 29ft. On February 26 1916, she was mined and sunk 4 miles north-north-east of Spurn Point, with the loss of twenty eight men, including Captain Taylor. The Belgian steamer *Martha* which was close by picked up three survivors, and landed them at Hull. The wreck lies in position 53 37 18N 00 15 15E, in 15m of water, in an east-west attitude. She has been thoroughly dispersed, and is spread over an area of about 200m by 30m, with nothing standing more than 2m high. One large piece of wreckage lies some 50m to the west of the main wreck.

Dido had engines by Earles of Hull, T 3cy, 25" 40" 70"-48".

333 Ophir II. On September 7 1941, this 213 ton Grimsby trawler was mined and sunk in the Northern Approach Channel to the Humber. She had been built in 1906 for the Forward Steam Fishing Co of Grimsby by Cochrane & Sons of Selby. She was in Admiralty service at the time of her loss.

The wreck lies in position 53 36 53N 00 25 05E, in a depth of 20m, with a slight scour. She lies roughly north-west–south-est, and is well broken up, in three main pieces, with no part standing more than 4m high. *Ophir II* had engines by C.D. Holmes of Hull, T 3cy, 12" 22" 35"-24".

334 Unknown. In position 53 36 39N 00 15 58E lies the wreck of a twin screw vessel, in a depth of 14m with a slight scour. The wreck was armed, and is in an east-west attitude, roughly. There are live shells scattered about the seabed. Steve Cooper of Withernsea who found the wreck estimates her size at about 500 tons.

335 Barrage balloon platform. Originally thought to be the wreck of the trawler *Benvolio* (site 331), the obstruction in position 53 36 31N 00 21 01E proved to be a concrete structure used to anchor barrage balloons during WW2. The structure was demolished by explosives, and is now scattered over a wide area, with no part standing higher than 2m.

336 B.O. Borjesson. Originally called *George Harper,* this was a 1586 ton Swedish steamer, built by A.G. Neptun, Rostock, in 1907. She was 261ft long, with a beam of 38ft and a depth of 16ft. She was mined and sunk with the loss of six lives on November 19 1939, in position 53 36 08N 00 20 43E.

The wreck lies in a slight scour on a flat seabed, in a depth of about 17m. *B.O. Borjesson* had T 3cy engines by A.G. Neptun, Rostock, 18" 30" 48"-33".

337 Fermo. Following a collision with the Norwegian steamship *Breidablik,* the 175 ton trawler *Fermo* sank three miles north-east of the Humber Light Vessel. Built at Beverley in 1898, she was owned by the Ocean Steam Fishing Co of Grimsby, and was 100ft long.

The wreck lies in position 53 35 43N 00 15 57E, on a flat seabed, with no part of the wreck standing more than 3m high. Diver Steve Cooper positively identified the wreck when he saw the name on the bows in 1986.

338 Katina Bulgaris. Built as *Grelwen* by Richardson Duck & Co of Stockton in 1912, she became *Tonwen, Tavian* and then *Katina,* before adopting her final name. She was owned then by N.T.H. Bulgaris and registered in Andros, Greece. She was 390ft long with a beam of 53ft and a depth of 26ft, and her gross tonnage was 4567 tons.

At 12.16 on February 8 1939, she collided in fog with the American steamer *Meanticut* of New Orleans, while bound for Buenos Aires with coal from Hull. Humber lifeboat went to the rescue, together with two tugs, but the *Katina Bulgaris* sank before they arrived. The crew had already been taken aboard the 6061 ton *Meanticut.*

The wreck is in position 53 35 28N 00 31 20E, and for many years it was buoyed, being a danger to navigation. Dispersal operations carried out by Humber Divers have now left the wreck standing no more than 4m high. She lies roughly east-west, very broken up, in a depth of around 17m with a flat seabed.

339 Albania. On October 23 1939, this 1241 ton Swedish steamer was mined and sunk off Spurn Point while bound for Gothenberg from London. Built at Tonning in 1903, she ws 238ft long with a beam of 35ft and a depth of 15ft. So far, no positive identification of the wreck has taken place, but there is a wreck in position 53 34 50N 00 17 18E which may well be the *Albania,* in 36m of water.

Albania had engines by Schorner & Jensen, T 3cy 20" 32" 53"-36". 2SB 4CF.

340 Amenity. This 297 ton motor vessel was built in 1928 by Fellows & Co of Great Yarmouth, for F.T. Everard & Sons of London. She was mined and sunk on November 15 1940, on the edge of a sandbank known as the Binks, east of Spurn Point. She is lying in position 53 34 34N 00 10 49E, in a depth of approximately 13m. The ship measured up at 115ft long, with a beam of 23ft and a depth of 9ft. Her five cylinder oil engines were built by Plenty & Sons, Newbury.

341 William Balls. During dense fog off the Humber on July 4 1893, this ship collided with the 2293 ton steamer *Elba,* and both vessels subsequently sank.

William Balls was a 1612 ton steamer, built by J. Readhead at Shields in 1883, and owned by W.D.C. Balls of the same port. Fortunately, no lives were lost during the collision, which occurred on a voyage to Southampton with coal from Shields. The ship was 259ft long with a beam of 37ft and a depth of 18ft.

There is a wreck in position 53 34 27N 00 47 01E, lying roughly east-west on a flat seabed at a depth of 48m, and it is thought that this could be the *William Balls.*

The vessel had engines by Readheads, C 2cy, 30" 58"-36".

Area Information and Services

Admiralty Charts. Entrance to the River Humber Chart, No. 109. Flamborough Head to Blakeney Point, Chart No. 1190. Flamborough Head to Withernsea, Chart No. 121.

Ordnance Survey. 1:50 000 L107 Kingston-Upon-Hull. L113 Grimsby.

Local Weather. Marinecall area East, Tel. 0898-500 454.

Shipping Forecast. Humber.

Local Coastguard. Humber District HQ (Bridlington), Tel. 0262-672317. Sector Station Hull Marina, Tel. 0482-23307. In emergency call 999.

Weather Bulletins from HM Coastguard on VHF marine radio. begin at 03.40, then 4 hourly. Gale and small craft weather warnings issued on receipt from Met. Office, repeated at two hourly intervals.

B.S.-A.C Hull Branch. Meet 7-8pm Tuesdays at South Hunsley swimming pool, Ellerton, Brough, followed by meeting at local pub (venue currently being changed). Approximately 150 members, about half of whom dive regularly. Most diving done at Flamborough where club owns two wrecks. Three inflatable boats; visiting divers welcome provided they have evidence of qualifications. D.O. Trevor Jones. Air available by arrangement.

Tourist Information. Hull 0482-223344. Withernsea 0964-612284.

Air Supplies. Sub Sea Services, Railway Street, The Boatyard, Hull. Tel. 0482-227464. Open 09.00-17.30 six days. Hull Dive Centre Unit 9 Factory Estate, English Street, Hull. Tel. 0482-25772.

Outboard repairs, supplies & service. Sub Sea Services (see above) Hull Boat Centre, Spyvee Street, North Bridge Road. Tel. 0482-29602.

Inflatable spares repairs and sales. Humber Inflatables Ltd. 246 Wincolmlee, Hull. Tel. 0482-226100.

AA 24 hour service. 0482-28580.

Dive Boats. None available south of Bridlington at time of writing.

Hull Marine. Tel. 0482 25048.

Diving School. Sub Sea Services (see above) all B.S.-A.C. courses.

Accommodation. See Tourist information. Crown & Anchor, Kilnsea B&B or camping, Tel. 0964-650276. Easington Beach caravan site, Tel. 0964-650293. Sand-le-Mere caravan site, Tel. 0964-670403.

Boat Club. Withernsea, Tel. 0964-612922.

Index

Numbers given in this index refer to **site numbers** in the text. Entries in italics are names of wrecks. Wrecks not positively identified are not generally indexed, except as Unknowns.

Buddy Excellence by A.P. Valves

BUDDY COMMANDO. Fitted with Quick Release Shoulder Adjusters. Both sizes come complete with new 0.4L-232 BAR, lightweight Aluminium AIR cylinder; AP3 Direct Feed and Back Pack.

BUDDY SEA KING DELUXE. British Design Award Winner 1987 — Presented by HRH Duke of Edinburgh. Comes complete with new, lightweight, 0.4L-232 BAR Aluminium AIR cylinder; AP3 Direct Feed and Back Pack.

BUDDY ARCTIC. A versatile ABLJ, which folds up, can be used for dry suit as well as wet suit divers. Comes complete with new 0.4L-232 BAR, lightweight Aluminium AIR cylinder — Optional AP3 Direct Feed, shown on inflated jacket.

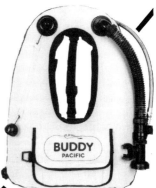

BUDDY DOUBLE GOLD. Chosen by the Royal Navy, for their Search and Rescue Helicopter Divers. This lifejacket has more buoyancy than most ABLJs — Suitable for the larger diver. Comes complete with new, 0.4L-232 BAR, lightweight Aluminium AIR cylinder and AP3 Direct Feed.

BUDDY PACIFIC. This is the most popular ABLJ in Britain — The work-horse for most diving clubs and schools. Comes complete with new 0.4L-232 BAR, lightweight Aluminium AIR cylinder and AP3 Direct Feed.